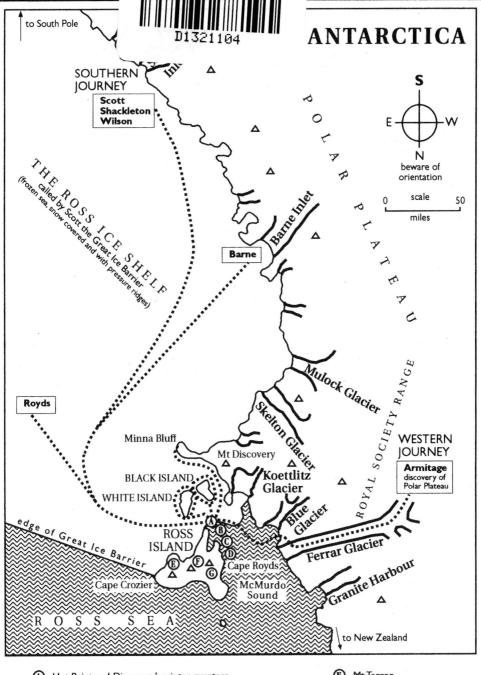

ANTARCTICA

to South Pole

SOUTHERN JOURNEY
Scott
Shackleton
Wilson

S
E — W
N
beware of orientation

scale
0 ————— 50
miles

THE ROSS ICE SHELF
called by Scott the Great Ice Barrier
(frozen sea, snow covered and with pressure ridges)

P O L A R   P L A T E A U

Inl

Barne Inlet

Barne

Mulock Glacier

Skelton Glacier

Royds

ROYAL SOCIETY RANGE

Minna Bluff

Mt Discovery

Koettlitz Glacier

WESTERN JOURNEY
Armitage
discovery of Polar Plateau

BLACK ISLAND

WHITE ISLAND

Blue Glacier

Ⓐ
Ⓑ
Ⓒ
Ⓓ

ROSS ISLAND

Ferrar Glacier

edge of Great Ice Barrier

Ⓔ Ⓕ
Ⓖ
Cape Royds

Cape Crozier

McMurdo Sound

Granite Harbour

R O S S   S E A

to New Zealand

Ⓐ Hut Point and Discovery's winter quarters
Ⓑ Dellbridge Islands
Ⓒ Erebus Glacier Tongue (where coal was stored)
Ⓓ Barne Glacier and approx. position of Terra Nova 5/11/1904
    A to D is 20 miles

Ⓔ Mt Terror
Ⓕ Mt Terra Nova
Ⓖ Mt Erebus
△ peaks
••••••• key sledge journeys

THE RESCUE OF CAPTAIN SCOTT

McKay rescues *Discovery*. From the cartoon that appeared in April 1904 in the *Weekly Press* of Christchurch, New Zealand, by W. Bowring.

THE
RESCUE OF
CAPTAIN SCOTT

Don Aldridge

TUCKWELL PRESS

First published in Great Britain in 1999 by
Tuckwell Press Ltd
The Mill House
Phantassie
East Linton
East Lothian EH40 3DG
Scotland

ISBN 1 86232 070 5

British Library Cataloguing in Publication Data

A catalogue record for this book is available
on request from the British Library

Typeset by Hewer Text Ltd, Edinburgh
Printed and bound by Biddles Ltd, Guildford

For Val and Chris

Contents

PART THREE   *The Legend*

Picture Credits

(numbers refer to plate numbers in the plate section)

Foreword

In the early 1980s the City of Dundee was experiencing a period of industrial change, with job losses in traditional industries and a general loss of confidence within the community. The city and Regional Councils were determined to secure a sound future, and with the Scottish Development Agency, they initiated "The Dundee Project". It was my good fortune to be the SDA. officer who was asked to head the Dundee Project to attempt to give back confidence, pride and belief. I had a feeling from the outset that Dundee's traditions and unique history would form a solid building block in this process. Thus one of the first pieces of work to be commissioned was a comprehensive study to look at Dundee's potential for interpretation. Who better to undertake the work than Don Aldridge, recognised as the person who introduced interpretation planning to the UK, respected for his work with the Countryside Commission for Scotland, and who for over thirty years has lived and worked in Dundee's hinterland.

In 1984 Aldridge proposed three major groups of themes worthy of development:

★ Dundee's extraordinary maritime story including the polar, whaling and Indian links and the famous shipbuilding inventions and skills of Gourlay and Stephen.
★ The story of textile development to answer the question – why jute?
★ The introduction of graphic journalism by D. C. Thomson.

This was no hackneyed Jam, Jute and Journalism report. Aldridge lamented the fact that Dundee had for so long turned its back on the superb river frontage and he stressed the maritime and polar themes. Contacting the Maritime Trust, we learned that the RRS *Discovery* might be available, but only if we acted quickly and Aldridge had given us total justification for bringing *Discovery* back to her home city. One year's hard work raising finance and clearing legal hurdles was rewarded by the sight of *Discovery* sailing up the Tay Estuary, cheered by thousands of people on the shore. This bestowed the title "City of Discovery" on Dundee, a title used for projecting excellence in technology and education and many other positive activities which lay ahead.

Between 1984 and 1993, the waterfront proposals took shape with a dock for *Discovery* and heritage centre alongside. Don Aldridge worked on the research, interpretation and scripting for the designers of Discovery Point, including the script for the spectacular audio-visual programme. His researches unearthed the story of why Scott had to come to Dundee to get the ship built and the incredible fact that had it not been for a Dundee whaling captain, *Discovery* would have been lost in the Antarctic in 1904. At the opening of Discovery Point on 1st July 1993, the Duke of Edinburgh wondered who was responsible for the idea. Few of those crammed into the foyer to hear his opening speech knew the answer!

This book came to be written in response to requests made by the visiting public who had been intrigued to hear the rescue story and who wanted to know more about Harry McKay. Why was there not a statue of him in front of Discovery Point? Why have his exploits been covered up, even in his own city? And who was responsible for covering up the truth and even snubbing the entire ship's company of McKay's *Terra Nova* Rescue Expedition? After more than a decade of painstaking research, mostly in Australian and New Zealand archives, Don Aldridge has vindicated McKay and tells the story of one of the greatest feats in Antarctic history.

Jeff Lonsdale

Introduction

Some of the layers of myth which have surrounded Robert Falcon Scott's picturesque and literary account of his adventures on the Antarctic continent have been stripped away in recent years. The purpose of this book is to right a wrong perpetrated for too long – the cover-up of one of the most extraordinary polar feats: the rescue of Scott's ship *Discovery* when the Admiralty brought the work of the British National Antarctic Expedition of 1901–04 to an abrupt and unexpected end.

The spectacular rescue of the ship in 1904 was the work of two Captains – William Colbeck from the port of Hull and Harry McKay from Dundee in their ships the *Morning* and *Terra Nova*. If they had not gone to the Antarctic, all the evidence indicates that *Discovery* would now be at the bottom of McMurdo Sound. As McKay said to Scott on their first meeting in Antarctica, "She has to come out!"

The narrative of this incredible rescue and how the story was then covered up when the three ships returned to New Zealand is presented here for the first time. It has been made possible with the help of a decade of research into forgotten or unknown records, some from the Colbeck family archives in Dundee and New Zealand (made available by kind permission of the family) together with many from other Scottish and New Zealand sources in Dundee, Christchurch and Wellington. The two captains received little by way of appreciation and McKay was even snubbed and insulted by the gentlemen whose ship he and his colleagues on the *Terra Nova* saved from destruction.

In this research the writer had no particular wish to attack the Keepers of British Myths who for the best part of a century have woven a web of sentimental nonsense around the character of one famous schoolboy hero. Nor was the intention to besmirch heroic images – on the contrary the object was to counter besmirching done to Colbeck and McKay by this quintessential English hero. The establishment view is that the words written by the men of the three ships *Discovery*, *Terra Nova* and *Morning* will reveal the truth and this is so. Indeed this is the basic principle on which this narrative has been founded – quotations straight from the pages of the original, not from the imaginary observations honed into shape in some much admired beautiful prose. Even though the *Discovery* has been returned to its birthplace in the city of Dundee, our remarkable Dundonian McKay and his extraordinary rescue feat are still not properly credited there, or anywhere else in his own country. Few people know just how important a part Dundee ships and captains played in the history of polar exploration and why these two captains, Colbeck and McKay, deserve to be much better known.

Acknowledgements

First I must thank the members of the Colbeck family, Carolyn Irvine, Andrew Colbeck, for permission to quote from the William Colbeck papers (1900-1905) and for their very generous assistance, and Anthony Robinson for his researches of the Colbeck family tree. Their wish to see the extraordinary feat of William Colbeck and Harry McKay recognised has been a great source of encouragement. In similar vein, Joyce and Donald Morrison gave me permission to use the amusing and eye-opening papers of J. D. Morrison. I owe them a debt that can never be repaid for their successful search for his photographic albums. These pictures support my narrative of a forty days and forty nights story which has been covered up for a century. I thank Chris Aldridge for restoring these faded images which tell this story of the amazing feat by the men of the two rescue ships *Morning* and *Terra Nova*, and the prints pay tribute to this and to these two remarkable polar photographers.

My special thanks to A. G. E. Jones for his pioneer discovery that official versions of events require careful checking and for his generosity in putting a lifetime of Antarctic research at my disposal, for giving me copyright permission to quote from it and for his tireless efforts in providing me with encouragement. This book could not have been written without his support. I also wish to thank Roland Huntford for permission to quote from his definitive study *Scott and Amundsen* and for friendly help in depressing times. I thank Philip and Janet Oswald for many kindnesses and support and for making my visits to Cambridge so pleasant. To Jeff Lonsdale, former Director of the Scottish Development Agency in Dundee, I owe a debt of gratitude for supporting my *Discovery* proposal from the very beginning and likewise to John Foster, former Director of the Countryside Commission for Scotland, for his encouragement of my *Discovery* research reports. I also thank Jonathan Bryant, former Chief Executive of Discovery Point, for fighting off evil spirits, and his colleague, Hugh Scott, for help, encouragement and for conserving *Discovery* with such diligence and enthusiasm. I much appreciate the permission to see the Dundee Industrial Heritage Archive, granted me by Gill Poulter who met all my requests with patience and courtesy. My thanks to R. J. Caird of D. C. Thompson, Publishers, for copyright permission to quote from their Dundee newspaper archives, and I also wish to thank Joyce Lorimer for help in locating material in their archives. I must thank David Henderson of McManus Galleries and Dundee Museums (Dundee City Council Arts and Heritage Department) for his researches into the whaling industry and Pat Gibb and the staff of the Dundee University Archive for help with their records. I am indebted to Ian Flett of the Dundee City Archives and I am exceedingly grateful to G. Barrie Kinnes for all his expert help and encouragement and for copyright permission to quote from his firm's Dundee whaling archives. My thanks are also due to the staff of Aberdeen University Library who helped me to locate the Ommanney paper which was the origin of the 1901–04 expedition. For his expert advice I am grateful to Dr R. Cameron, Department of Naval Architecture in the University of Glasgow, and for his analysis of the different capabilities of the three expedition ships.

I should like to thank Mrs Topen of the University of Glasgow Business Records Archive for data on the Stephen Linthouse Collection regarding the Alexander Stephen and Dundee Shipbuilders records. For steering me through the Royal Scottish Geographical Society's library collection I thank the Director, Dr David Munro, and the staff of Strathclyde University's Andersonian Library, and I must also thank staff of the Royal Society for much help. I am indebted to Dr Miles Oglethorpe of the Royal Commission on the Ancient and Historical Monuments of Scotland and owe a special debt of gratitude to John Dolan of the Royal Society of Chemistry, not only for his expert advice in interpreting photographs of explosions and explosive lists but also for directing my historical research into the use of gun cotton and early high explosives. I am grateful to the staff of St Andrews University Library for access to the Valentine photographic collection.

I should like to thank Mrs Christine Kelly, Dr Andrew Tatham and Erik de Brink of the Royal Geographical Society for permission to consult the Society's archives. I am grateful to librarians William Mills, Philippa Smith, Peter Speak and Shirley Sawtell of the Scott Polar Research Institute for permission to work in the Library and to their Archivist, Robert Headland, for what he calls 'gophering'. I am grateful to the staff of the British Museum of Natural History for access to the scientific results of the *Discovery* expedition and to the staff of the British Antarctic Survey in Cambridge for information on early magnetic surveys. I especially wish to thank the staff of the India Office Library for access to historical records concerning the Dundee jute connection and for their patience and support on all my visits. For help with some nautical and whaling questions I must thank the National Scheepvaartmuseum of Antwerp, the Norsk Sjøfartmuseum of Oslo, the Historisch Scheepvaart Museum of Amsterdam and Frans Weitenberg of the Arctic Centre, University of Groningen.

I wish to thank all my friends and colleagues in Australia and New Zealand, not least: Josie Laing, Jo Ann Smith, Baden Norris and Kerry McCarthy of Canterbury Museum, Christchurch. I also thank the Christchurch Museum for giving me permission to quote from the James Paton diary. I thank David Harrowfield for being a one-man museum archive, a walking encyclopaedia, a never-failing source of sound advice, for opening doors and discovering two doors for me that I did not know existed. I also wish to thank Jennifer Barrer for her kindness. My thanks to Rosemary O'Neil and Dawn Macmillan of the Public Library in Christchurch, to Max Broadbent, Jeffrey Palmer and Bronwy Matthews of Macmillan Brown Library, University of Canterbury and for the permission to quote from the Burgess papers. Thanks to Tim Lovell Smith of the Manuscripts and Archives Section of the Alexander Turnbull Library in Wellington, to Graeme Powell, Manuscript Librarian of the National Library in Australia, Ian Pearce, Archivist of the National Library in Tasmania, and to Janet Weaving, Library Manager of the *Mercury* in Hobart for much help with historic records. I have been much impressed by the friendly and encouraging interest shown to me in all these Australian and New Zealand libraries and museums and am grateful to the many donors for placing their archives with them.

My thanks are due to John Parsloe and the New Zealand Antarctic Society for giving me permission to quote A. G. E. Jones' article on McKay and to Anthony Petre of the *Press* in Christchurch for permission to quote from these New Zealand newspaper sources which first drew me into this project. The idea of researching my Discovery Point audio-visual script further to tell the story of Colbeck and McKay with the possibility of a publication began with discussions with Colin Haycraft of Duckworth. I felt his untimely loss keenly and am grateful to him. I am also grateful to Jim Caffin, former editor of the journal *Antarctic* and E. B. Lock, sometime editor of the *Press*, for introducing me to the valuable New Zealand sources. I wish to thank Marc Sagan and the National Georgraphical Magazine Library for tracing sources in Washington D.C.

For permission to quote from George Seaver's *Scott of the Antarctic* I am indebted to John Murray Publishers Ltd, for the use of Walter Marsh's papers I must thank Ann Goodsell and other members of the Marsh family. I thank the British Copyright Council, British Library of National Biography, the Publishers Association, Whitakers, Elsevier Science, and the Scott Polar Research Institute for helping me trace the holders of the following copyrights: Sir Clements Markham's *Threshold to the Unknown Region*, C. Turley's *The Voyages of Captain Scott*, G. Doorly's *The Voyages of the Morning*, R. F. Scott's *The Voyage of the Discovery* Vols. I and II, H. R. Mill's *The Siege of the South Pole* and the diaries of Hartley Ferrar, Charles Royds, Reginald xxii *The Rescue of Captain Scott*

Skelton, and Edward Wilson. I am grateful to the *Illustrated London News* for permission to quote Shackleton's 'Supplement' of June 1903 and the *Sphere* for a quote from the 'Antarctic Supplement' of June 1904. I am grateful to the Trustees of the National Maritime Museum, London and their curator Clive Powell for permission to quote from the diary of A. Jackson of the *Terra Nova*, and Eleanor Heron and D. J. Pearsall for help with material held in the museum archives. I am especially grateful to Patricia Bernacchi and Janet Crawford for permission to quote from the Louis Bernacchi family papers. I thank Ken Wilson of Baton Wicks Publications for the quote from Kenneth Mason's *Abode of Snow* and John Maxtone-Graham for allowing me to quote from his *Safe Return Doubtful*. Angela Mathias, widow of Apsley Cherry-Garrard, kindly gave me permission to quote from her late husband's famous book *The Worst Journey in the World*. Faber and Faber allowed me to quote from Francis Spufford's *I May be Some Time: Ice and the English Imagination*, and the publishers Edward Arnold granted me leave to quote from Albert Armitage's *Two Years in the Antarctic*. I am grateful to Bill Thompson for his cartography. I thank Jocelyn Chamberlain-Mole, formerly Curator of Peterhead Arbuthnott Museum, for valuable criticism and assistance. I thank the Public Record Office for allowing me to quote from the archive in their custody ADM/116/944 in which I finally discovered a rare piece of Harry McKay's prose. The McKay report has gone missing from two other sources in which it was recorded so I have quoted it in full in the Postscript. I am grateful to Dr. Herbert Dartnall for generously using his expertise to identify men in the group photographs of ships' companies and I look forward to his forthcoming *Who was Who?* I am most grateful to Bill Howatson-Heald and his family for allowing me to read the 1904 log and for all their hospitality. The Souter family, spread between Scotland, England, Australia and Canada – Dr Alex Souter and Marlene, Caroline Souter, Dr Evelyn Morgan, Elcy Broadhead and Duncan Ritchie – all contributed to a mammoth search operation which resulted in the finding of Dr William Clark Souter's pictures published here. Had it not been for Dr D. Emslie Smith and Julia Davidson I would not have even started the Souter chase. Finally, I dedicate this book to my wife and son for enduring its dominating presence in the family for so long and also for their help and support which made the whole task possible. If I have omitted to thank anyone who has helped me in the course of my researches, I apologise.

PART ONE

Prelude

CHAPTER ONE

Storing Up Problems for *Discovery*

Sir Clements Markham as a Problem

The National Antarctic Expedition of 1901–4, led by Commander Robert Falcon Scott, sometimes called the *Discovery* Expedition, was the brainchild of Sir Clements Markham, President of the Royal Geographical Society between 1893 and 1905. The conquest of the geographical poles, in particular the South Pole, had been an obsession with him since he had first gained experience of polar travel with the Royal Navy in 1850, serving under Erasmus Ommanney, Captain of HMS *Assistance*, from whom he caught this bug. Ommanney lectured in Aberdeen at the 1885 meeting of the British Association for the Advancement of Science on the subject of over-wintering an expedition ship in the Antarctic. Both he and Markham were convinced that all polar expeditions should be led by naval officers, and Sir Clements was fond of listing what he regarded as the attributes of naval men – they needed to be to be born calm, decisive and quick: Markham did not believe in training for polar expedition work. Learning from others was an admission of weakness. This element runs like a thread through the records of the 1901–4 *Discovery* expedition; it was frequently the case that good equipment was taken to the other side of the globe without being checked to see if it was in working order and without anyone being instructed in its use. This was true for many things from the newly invented primus stoves to skis, ice axes to ropes, even for the *Discovery* herself.

Sir Clements Markham learned his naval Arctic lore on HMS *Assistance* which took part, along with many other ships, in a search for Sir John Franklin's expedition to the Arctic to find the North-West Passage. The tragedy of Franklin represented a loss of over 100 officers and men and two ships, so it was hardly surprising that the Admiralty's enthusiasm for polar expeditions, searches and polar relief ships was waning by the 1860s. Prime Minister Gladstone and the Sea Lords were deaf to entreaties for financial help to send an expedition anywhere. Then, in 1872, the Austrians, Von Payer and Weyprecht, suddenly made a bid for the North Pole and changed the situation, shaming the British government into action, and a highly successful expedition in HMS *Challenger* was sent to study the world's oceans between 1872 and 1876. This was something entirely new, being under the captaincy of George Nares and the scientific leadership of Charles Wyville Thomson, the Edinburgh scientist. This separation of powers did not accord with Markham's idea of how to run an expedition. He paid lip service to science, being far more interested in the glory and the naval tradition, and did not see the naval commander as a mere ferryman. Another *Challenger* scientist, Dr. John Murray, also wanted to see the expedition run on Nares' lines with naval vessels landing scientists to over-winter, as he told the Royal Geographical Society in 1893.

It is difficult to understand the history of twentieth-century Antarctic exploration without some knowledge of Arctic exploration in the century before and we have to flit from Pole to Pole to see why the 1901–04 expedition was planned on an ancient 1850 blueprint.

A Theatrical Cure for an Antarctic Illness

George Nares was on his way back to Britain from the *Challenger* Expedition when the new Prime Minister, Benjamin Disraeli, promised support for a bid to reach the North Pole. Nares was to captain it but Albert Markham, Clements Markham's cousin, was picked to lead the attempt on the Pole. Although Albert did not manage the conquest, he established a new "Furthest North" record but, sadly, four of his men died from scurvy in the attempt.

This terrible affliction had once been eradicated in the Royal Navy by the brilliant work of one of its Scottish surgeons, James Lind, who in 1747 showed that, in effect, it was a deficiency disease and neither an infection nor something caused by tainted food. Cook and Nelson discovered much the same thing independently. By ensuring a plentiful supply of fresh food with meat, vegetables and fruit on their ships they avoided deaths from scurvy. The disease was eradicated in the Navy during the first half of the nineteenth century – but no thanks to the Admiralty who ignored all the evidence and practical advice sent to them. Then came disaster: in 1848 the Admiralty implemented new practices which were to prove fatal, changing from the use of fresh lemons to bottled lime juice (limes had far less of the active ingredient of ascorbic acid or vitamin C than lemons, even before being bottled), and bottled juices froze solid. Worse still, fresh meat, vegetables and fruit were replaced by tinned foods. Scurvy reappeared in the Navy.

Thus it happened that an independent enquiry, set up to investigate the deaths on the Nares expedition, criticised Albert Markham for not taking lemon juice on his sledging parties. Sir Clements Markham disagreed, insisting that his cousin was not at fault.

Indeed, Clements Markham had written a book for the Navy listing the names of officers who were jolly good at entertaining their men when they were all wintering in the Arctic. Plays, charades, talks about plants, or the wind, that sort of thing, jolly songs, all these were the answer. In the long days and nights, when the sun was below the horizon for three dark months at a time, entertainment was the best thing to prevent the disease. As he put it: 'a contented state of mind is the best guard against scurvy.'[1]

Sadly, the 1901 expedition's medical advice derived from Markham and followed the fashionable Dr Coplan's Tainted Food Theory. Fortunately two men in *Discovery* had served on the Jackson Harmsworth polar expedition to Franz Josef Land of 1894 and they could tell their leader about their proven experience, if only he would listen.

Over-wintering of Discovery in the Ice

The Markham cousins had a fund of nineteenth-century Arctic lore to pass on to polar expeditions in the twentieth century, undeterred by having had no experience of the Antarctic themselves. In his 1885 Conference paper, Captain Ommanney observed that:

> No man has ever wintered in the Antarctic Zone. The great desideratum now before us requires that an expedition should pass a winter there, in order to compare the conditions and phenomena with our Arctic knowledge.[2]

So, Markham was convinced by his captain that *Discovery* must winter in the ice despite the considerable risk of being crushed to pieces, as had happened to so many whaling ships in the Arctic in the age of sail. The danger was reduced with the coming of steam though it was certainly not eliminated. It happened that Ommanney's idea of over-wintering also gave maximum opportunity for Pole-bagging, and in his Aberdeen lecture he made reference to A. E. Nordenskjöld's techniques of sledging. But the conquest of the South Pole was not Markham's priority, though it soon became obvious that it was precisely what the expedition Commander, Robert Falcon Scott, wanted.

In theory, over-wintering a ship in the Arctic ocean made good sense if an expedition was aiming to reach the North Pole, for the party might gain a head start the following summer when the ship was found to have drifted in the ice nearer to the goal. It was not such a clever idea for an Antarctic expedition in a ship which had no hope whatsoever of sailing one centi-

---

1. Clements Markham, *The Threshold of the Unknown Region* (1875), page 278.
2. Erasmus Ommanney, *Over-Wintering in the Antarctic*, British Association of Science, Aberdeen 1885.

metre nearer to the South Pole across the continental land mass. Furthermore, there was no convincing scientific reason for wanting to reach the Pole. By the end of the nineteenth century enough was known to put in question the wisdom of wintering ships in the Antarctic where icebergs the size of office blocks drift around the coast. When Sir Clements chaired the Sixth International Geographical Congress in London in 1895, a decade after Ommanney's Aberdeen lecture, on his favourite theme of reviving interest in exploration of the Antarctic, he was unaware that a lieutenant in the Belgian Navy was planning just such a venture for 1898. Adrien de Gerlache's ship *Belgica* was trapped in ice seven feet thick and drifted through the frozen Bellingshausen Sea for over a year. Two men died and two went mad. It was a warning but by no means the first in Antarctic history. Sixty years before, the French explorers Dumont d'Urville and Charles Hector Jacquinot were trapped when a channel in the ice closed behind them. Four years later, James Clark Ross and Francis Rawdon Moira Crozier, after ploughing through the pack-ice and discovering the sea and island which were named after Ross, sailed into a nightmare of fog, gales and huge icebergs and their two ships collided. They were fortunate to escape. The worrying thing about *Belgica* was that she was an auxiliary steam whale ship designed to avoid being nipped in the ice. So, one might imagine that Markham's *Discovery* would not be founded entirely on the old man's Arctic experience gained so many years before, but it was.

The Problems of Very Heavy Loads

Another piece of naval lore applied to what was, until recently, still basic to much overland polar travel – man-hauled sledging. The exploration work of the 1901–04 expedition was mostly done by hauling heavily loaded sledges without skis for long distances at as fast a speed as could be sustained given the condition of the snow and ice, the topography of its surface, the state of the wind and weather, the visibility, the temperature and the health of the men. This was, after all, what geography was all about. At today's Royal Tournaments the Royal Navy shows off with pride how easy it is to dismantle field guns and carry them overland to relieve some stricken outpost. In 1899, when the Royal Navy was not expected to play an inland role in the South African War, the bluejackets triumphantly secured the relief of Ladysmith. This was truly superhuman hauling! But Markham thought that to employ skis to assist the progress of a man-hauled polar sledge was at best cheating and at worst impossible, and furthermore it was not British. Nobody jibbed at using a sledge design devised by a Norwegian but skis were a different matter.

Much the same was true of using dogs to assist in pulling sledges: it was cruel. When done efficiently, it puts some of the dogs' lives at risk. The 1901–04 expedition proved that when it was done inefficiently it was even more cruel: it put all the dogs' lives at risk, and none returned. There was more sentiment than logic in the anti-dog argument, for man-hauling was also cruel: it put the lives of men at risk. Albert Markham proved to his own satisfaction that everything depended on brute strength and ignorance, and all that was needed, according to the most famous man-hauler of them all, author of the naval sledging manual, Admiral Sir Leopold McClintock, was a 'useful compound of stubbornness and endurance which is so eminently British'.[3]

Sir Clements Markham measured a man's worth as a polar explorer not by what he had discovered in real terms but by the length and speed of his sledge journeys. The old Arctic Admirals found their way into the committees of the Royal Geograpical Society according to a sort of sledging scale which they had clocked up in the searches for Sir John Franklin in the 1850s – Sir Leopold McClintock 1200 miles at 11 miles per day, Sir Vesey Hamilton 1000 miles at 14, Sherard Osborn 935 miles at 10, Sir George Nares 665 miles at 10, with the addition of Sir Clements himself whose total was a mere 140 miles at some unrecorded speed.

The problem is how to travel safely away from base by determining the optimum size of a party, relating loads to energy needs, placing supply depots and employing support parties to cope with the unforeseen. Bees are quite good at it but even they sometimes make mistakes.

Blueprints for Survival?

John Rae, an Orcadian in the employ of the Hudson Bay Company, was perhaps the most remarkable of a band of famous Scottish Arctic explorers. In 1854 Rae successfully solved the riddle of the missing Sir John Franklin Expedition but in doing so he made mention of cannibalism amongst its members. Lady Jane Franklin did not believe that it could happen on a Royal Navy expedition, least of all one led by her husband. So she sponsored a private expedition commanded by the Navy's Sir Leopold McClintock but the Navy learned little from this, or from Franklin's mistakes, despite a decade's searching. Everyone knows that we should not blame intrepid explorers for bravely venturing into the unknown. Even today after a polar or mountain accident we say 'these things will happen if people go to these dangerous places'. We

3. Quoted in John Maxtone-Graham's *Safe Return Doubtful* (1988), page 72.

never ask ourselves if some of those who have accidents are just dangerous people.

Rae was one of the few Europeans who understood this. He had learned how to travel safely in polar areas from the greatest of all experts – the Esquimaux or Inuit peoples. His clothing and especially his footwear was efficient; his sledges were lightweight and strong; and his technique of building rock or snow shelters made him a great survivor. For him the key to safety was to live off the country and travel fast and light and with the minimum number of companions. Few, if any, polar areas had the resources to support a grand naval expedition of over one hundred men. Rae had travelled an incredible 23,000 miles in the Arctic, some by kayak, most on foot, much of it in winter on snow shoes, on ski, some with dog teams and all with a variety of sledges appropriate to the type of terrain. He made journeys of 1500 miles in winter darkness as a matter of course.

McClintock learned something from Rae's example but he failed to take the point about the size of parties and survival techniques. When the Admiralty published his manual on sledging it set the pattern of future expeditions. Their ideal was an over-large naval party which would have to haul overweight sledges and because of their numbers they invitably had to rely on canned food. Scott's oversized 1901–04 party of well over 50 was without a doubt in the Franklin mould. However, an earlier three-year Arctic expedition from 1894 to 1896 was led by Frederick Jackson, who had lived with Samoyeds in Arctic Russia, and he passed on his Siberian knowledge of sledges, diet and survival techniques to Albert Armitage and Reginald Koettlitz who were to join Scott's expedition.

Some of Scott's men questioned the wisdom of a scientific party trying to reach the South Pole because going south took them away from matters of scientific interest which they were competent to explore and away from the wildlife which would enable them to live off the country and so avoid starvation and scurvy.

Need for a Relief Ship

The Markhams' experience was to stock a ship with three years' or more supply of food and fuel, then get it iced-in for the winter, having first littered the polar wilderness with a number of messages placed in little tin canisters within rock cairns built to protect them from the elements. These messages gave information to the men of a relief ship about the location of the expedition, and as the canisters had to be easy to find they were usually located on prominent headlands.

It was, therefore, known from the earliest planning stages that the

Discovery would be iced-in and would need a relief ship. Thus, Scott had 'secret orders' to over-winter in Antarctica, secret in the sense that they were contrary to the wishes of the Joint Committee of the Royal Geographical Society and Royal Society set up to oversee matters. The relief ship would need a captain capable of finding Scott's expedition in the Antarctic summer of December 1903.

A relief ship was not usually intended to supply food or fuel but to bring mail, deliver reprimands from superiors and take off invalids and insubordinates. Relief ships were not expected to rescue an expedition; they were more a kind of insurance policy in the most unlikely event of a Markham theory being invalidated. It was not an entirely foolproof plan, for relief ships could not always land a party on the headlands when the coast was heavily iced or when the weather was blowing at hurricane force. Even when a successful landing was made, hours were often spent by the relief parties searching for canisters.

In 1899 Sir Clements Markham's plan was to raise enough money to build the new purpose-built expedition ship *Discovery* which could withstand conditions that were expected to be even more severe than any Arctic winter and also to purchase a relief ship. So he was fully aware from the start that a government grant would be essential.

To obtain this he worked tirelessly to recruit influential high-ranking supporters whose knowledge of the Arctic would be respected. Initially this meant winning over the old Arctic Admirals and naval scientists, and the two most relevant places to start were the club of geographers (the Royal Geographical Society (RGS) established in 1830), and the more senior club of scientists (the Royal Society (RS) established in 1662). As it happened, Sir Clements had already gained some experience of this task a quarter of a century before as a member of an earlier Joint Committee of the Royal Society and Royal Geographical Society set up to plan the Nares expedition of his cousin Albert. Indeed, there were still four of the members of this old committee in the two societies who could be persuaded to form the nucleus of the new body, and although they were somewhat older now, they were more useful to Markham, having matured into generals and admirals in the intervening years.

The Problem of Old-Style Geographical Discovery

Geographical exploration by the Royal Navy meant discovering other people's lands for them and placing Union Jacks here and there or, as Admiral Sherard Osborn put it so succinctly:

The navy needs some action to wake it up from the sloth of routine and to save it from the canker of prolonged peace.[4]

Clements Markham, referring to the proposed conquest of the North Pole in 1875, had put it rather differently:

England will watch and applaud the efforts of this vanguard of her chivalry while, in the face of obstacles which Britons love to encounter and to overcome, our naval explorers are gallantly forcing their way across the threshold of the unknown region. God speed their noble exertions![5]

By the middle of the nineteenth century the British Navy appreciated the need for men to travel safely in Arctic waters and overland in high latitudes. After the Napoleonic Wars there were large numbers of surplus naval officers and the Admiralty felt that a spell on ice would wake them up. During the Crimean War there were even plans to make naval attacks on Russia from the north. Sherard Osborn's peace was shattered when war broke out in South Africa. Much nearer home Germany was beginning to threaten Britain's naval supremacy. However much the ice was good for them, sending naval officers Pole-bagging at such a time did not appeal to the Admirals. In particular sending sailors to the South Pole where they might be incommunicado for a year at a time was a problem, for in 1901 radio communication and air transport still lay some years ahead. In 1895 Antarctica was virtually an unknown and untrodden continent. Then the Norwegian, Carsten Borchgrevink, went back in 1899 with an expedition financed by the British newspaper proprietor Sir George Newnes who, despite the preponderance of Norwegians, insisted that the party be called the British Antarctic Expedition. Landing at Cape Adare, ten men wintered there in 1899 in huts bedecked with Union Jacks. Surely this qualified as a British crossing of the threshold of the unknown region? Unfortunately for the President of the RGS, the old style of geographical discovery and what had always been the traditional naval sciences of magnetism, meteorology, astronomy and surveying, together with a little rock-collecting, were no longer a sufficient prospectus to attract the scale of finance that Sir Clements Markham was seeking. The old order of heroic travel was coming to an end and new initiatives were about to be triggered by new sciences, such as oceanography and glaciology.

4. Clements Markham, *The Threshold of the Unknown Region* (1875), page 273.
5. Clements Markham, *The Threshold of the Unknown Region*, page 326.

A Problem of New-Style Scientific Discovery

There was a contrast between old-style descriptive geographical surveys and new *Challenger*-style expeditions which brought back important scientific results written up in fifty volumes. Although the contrasts were there in 1872, it was another twenty-three years before the last of the *Challenger* scientific reports finally appeared and brought the question sharply into focus. Sir Clements Markham's Joint Committee of the Royal Society and Royal Geographical Society implied a joint venture, a jointly financed expedition and a joint appeal to the government.

It was this decision of the two societies to work together which more than anything else set *Discovery* on a disaster course for there could be no compromise between the Royal Geographical Society and the Royal Society. What the two societies required were really two quite different expeditions, old style versus new. The immediate result was a ridiculous attempt to plan the expedition by means of a huge committee.

Matters came to a head with a debate on whether Scott was to be the overall expedition leader, as Markham insisted, or whether he was a ferryman appointed to get a landing party of scientists on the Continent for a summer season and take them off again to winter in Australia, as the Royal Society wanted. Markham had appointed Scott with a haughty disregard for the views of the Royal Society scientists whom he described as 'dreaming professors and pedants'.

The eminent geologist Professor Gregory, who had made the first crossing of Spitzbergen (Svalbard) with Conway in 1896, was appointed Scientific Director of the expedition and, not unreasonably, he expected to direct. It was after all an expedition which claimed to have modern scientific aims. Gregory also thought that he should decide what work was done both overall and on a day-to-day basis. Another famous Scottish scientist, Sir Archibald Geikie, who became Director of the British Geological Survey, supported Gregory in the Joint Committee. Markham saw at once that Gregory wanted the power to decide the duration of the landing party's stay and he engineered Gregory's resignation, but the dispute did not auto-matically go away. It turned into a conflict about whether Scott should be permitted to over-winter in the ice in *Discovery* or whether the whole party should winter in New Zealand or Australia.

The Admiralty had at this stage already agreed that two naval officers, Scott and Royds, should join the expedition and was just about to agree that many more naval personnel could go for an unknown period of time. Consequently their Lordships and the scientists had a very real interest in what Markham had described as a 'pedantic debate'.

Royal Society versus Royal Geographical Society

What appeared to be a debate between the two learned societies on operational matters was in reality a disagreement about the aims of an expedition. Superficially it seemed reasonable for Markham to argue that Scott should be given the powers to make decisions which would affect the safety of the ship's company but in reality it was the scientists who had more concern for safety.

The issue underlying the squabbles that followed was whether the aims of the expedition were scientific (particularly in the fields of geomagnetism and geology but to a lesser degree in descriptive marine biology and ornithology), or whether the expedition's aim was the conquest of the South Pole. The Royal Society gained the impression that the balance was heavily weighted towards the epic rather than the scientific. Why, on what was ostensibly being described as a modern scientific expedition, did scientists make up only ten per cent of the company? In the absence of a firm expedition plan, instructions to Scott were messed about in true British fashion by committees of experts and non-experts, drafted and re-drafted, resolved and then contradicted until Markham excelled himself by setting up a further committee to ensure that Scott did what Markham wanted him to do. So it was not surprising that the Royal Society remained unconvinced by Scott and Markham, who saw the achievement of the expedition in terms of numbers of long sledge journeys, the furthest south being the most important. In the event only two scientists were allowed to lead sledge journeys and, with the exception of one of Wilson's journeys to the Cape Crozier penguin rookeries, these were all of very short duration. The majority of the expedition's thirty journeys made between 1902 and 1903 were not planned to assist scientific work at all. The expedition's frustrated geologist, Ferrar, was rarely invited along on these trips which were all claimed to be of geological value. Scott was Scientific Director of the expedition in name only; indeed Thomas Vere Hodgson, the marine biologist on the expedition, disgusted at the lack of support he was given, was in no doubt that the Navy should not be encouraged to run scientific expeditions and wrote a comprehensive list of all the shortcomings of the organisation.

The Joint Committee voted against wintering in the ice but the RGS Secretary, Major Leonard Darwin, inserted the clause 'if it can be avoided' in the minutes, thus making a nonsense of the instruction. Markham refused to sign the joint agreement, thus storing up problems which would boomerang back on the expedition, annoying in particular three very influential scientists: Sir Michael Foster who succeeded T. H. Huxley at Cambridge as Professor of Physiology and was General Secretary of the Royal Society, Sir Edward Poulton, the geologist and author of a great work on natural selection, and Sir William Wharton, Royal Navy Hydrographer, author of the standard work on the subject and also author of the Royal Geographical Society's *Hints for Travellers*. Up to that time Wharton had been a supporter of the expedition, but unlike many people, Wharton knew that Scott had no real experience of sail.

Into the Unknown

The enormous scale of the Antarctic landscape can be as daunting to the present-day explorer as it was to the first men to set foot on the Continent in what has been called the 'heroic period'. The 1901–04 British National Antarctic Expedition was a polar expedition that belonged to this heroic age and it was the first really extensive exploration of the continental interior. However, not all members of the expedition were ignorant of this so-called 'completely unknown' Continent.

One man on *Discovery*, Louis Bernacchi, had wintered in the *Southern Cross* Expedition's hut at Cape Adare in 1899. William Colbeck, who would be picked to captain the relief ship *Morning* sent in 1902 to find *Discovery*, had also been in the hut. In addition two men, Albert Armitage and Reginald Koettlitz, who had wintered in remote Arctic Franz Josef Land on the Jackson-Harmsworth Expedition, were selected to join the *Discovery* party of 1901. All four brought with them considerable knowledge of the problems of over-wintering, though they were not allowed to make use of this experience.

The bold route from New Zealand to the Antarctic through the pack ice that girdles the Continent was not new: it had been discovered over sixty years before by James Clark Ross, who in turn followed Captain Harvey who made probes nine years earlier, according to the researches of A. G. E. Jones.[6] The site chosen as *Discovery*'s winter quarters under the shadow of the active volcano Mount Erebus was not new either: it was chosen for Scott in a secret exchange of letters between Markham, Colbeck and Bernacchi and was suggested on the basis of work done by the *Southern Cross* expedition. So some men knew that they would find winter quarters under mountains as high (12,448 ft.) as the volcano of Erebus that dominated McMurdo Sound and that the coast and great ice-capped plateau were, in all probability, underlain by granitic and possibly sedimentary rocks in the manner of Greenland. They knew that valley glaciers radiated out from a

6. A.G.E.Jones, *Polar Portraits* (1992), pp. 130–133.

polar plateau ice cap and that they descended steeply to the coast. Indeed, the fact that ice ringed the Continent had been known from the time of Cook, and the Great Ice Barrier had been described some sixty years before Borchgrevink gained access to it in 1900. Furthermore, William Colbeck had mapped the Great Ice Barrier two years before Scott reached it and he had calculated how far it had retreated since the time of Ross.

Members of the party with polar experience knew they were about to explore a mountainous continent, yet not one was chosen for the skills of alpinism. Markham's most famous mountaineering colleague in the Royal Geographical Society was William Martin Conway and, whilst one can understand why Markham did not offer the leadership to Martin Conway, it is odd that he did not introduce his novice expedition leader to this great Victorian explorer, or suggest that the unholy alliance of Royal Society and Royal Geographical Society might be joined by the Alpine Club which was almost next door.

Mountaineers Need Not Apply

When the expedition was all set to go, the RGS's great interest in mountain exploration was quite absent and their President seemed quite unaware of the seriousness of this. His intense dislike of Borchgrevink, and foreigners in general, blinded him to the consequences of sending men there led by such an inexperienced leader, but in his usual devious way he learned what he wanted from the expedition without Borchgrevink's knowledge. Since the second half of the nineteenth century British climbers had been teaching the world how to travel safely over the highest mountains and traverse the world's greatest glaciers. Martin Conway was more interested in traversing mountain ranges than in the first ascents of particular peaks, as his *The Alps from End to End*, written in 1894, demonstrates so spectacularly. Before the members of the *Discovery* expedition had even unpacked their crampons in 1902, Edward Whymper (of Matterhorn fame) had made great discoveries in the Andes and Conway had also spent three years up to 1901 exploring these great mountains.

Markham may not have known it, but this was the Golden Age of Exploration of the world of snow and ice. The great mountain ranges were about to be mapped and their more accessible peaks attempted. In 1892 Conway had led the first British Himalayan Expedition and explored the great glaciers of the Hispar-Biafo in the Karakoram. Support for this expedition came from none other than the joint committee of the Royal Society and the Royal Geographical Society. Exploration was about high latitude and high altitude records; Conway was to establish a 23,000 feet altitude record, then in 1895 he turned his attention to the exploration of polar areas and made the first traverse across Svalbard with Gregory (a non-person in Markham's book which may partly explain the President's aversion to climbers). In 1890 A. F. Mummery explored the Caucasus, followed by Douglas Freshfield, but Mummery lost his life in an avalanche on Nanga Parbat in the Punjab Himalaya in 1895. In the 1880s the New Zealand Alps were first explored by W. Spotswood Green, and in 1894 Tom Fyfe's party made a successful ascent of Mount Cook, followed by explorations by Edward Fitzgerald and Mattius Zurbriggen.

The problem was that Markham's experience was limited to frozen sea water, not the crossing of glaciers and ice caps. He was not interested in recruiting a Conway, still less in getting involved with those Himalayan climbers who served in the Indian Army and hob-nobbed with Gurkhas in order to get all their equipment carried for them. General Charles Bruce, one of the most famous of their number, had observed how strange their behaviour would have seemed if they had tried it in Switzerland and 'ordered a whole village to send every available man with an unknown Englishman to stay for a fortnight above the snow-line'.[7]

More Great Explorers

Markham knew that the show must be run by the Navy and there was no need to ascend a 3000-metre ice plateau; they had never found it necessary to do that sort of thing. He had met famous mountaineers, Douglas Freshfield (who in 1899 had reconnoitred Kangchenjunga) and Francis Younghusband (the Everest explorer), both of whom became Royal Geographical Society Presidents. There was even a high-ranking expert mountaineer who was also a young naval officer, Luigi Amadeo, His Highness Louis of Savoy, Duke of the Abruzzi, a famous alpinist. He had climbed in Svalbard the year after Conway and Gregory and made a bid for the North Pole from Franz Josef Land in 1899 and over-wintered. His Captain, Cagni, made an epic sledge journey almost to the Pole, setting up a new furthest north record. Markham was impressed, but how tragic that all the members of this expedition were foreigners! In the first decade of the new century Abruzzi and De Filippi reconnoitred K2, accompanied by Alpine guides and the greatest of all mountain photographers, Vittorio Sella. They traversed these most powerful of glaciers, fifty miles long. There were young Britons equally experienced at high altitudes and high latitudes who could have raised Markham's expedition's standards of competence in 1902.

7. Kenneth Mason, *Abode of Snow* (1987, reprint), page 132.

Indeed the son of the National Expedition's principal benefactor, young Tom Longstaff, was one such. He was the sort of man who could look at a high col from afar and tell from the reflections on the clouds whether the other side of the col was rock or ice. His father tried to buy him a place on the Scott expedition. Markham would not hear of it and this snub led Longstaff Senior to refuse further financial support in 1903 when a relief expedition was being mounted.

When Clements Markham's cousin Albert was preparing to join George Nares in 1875 on their bid for the conquest of the North Pole, the Royal Geographical Society was coming to terms with some new facts about the all-male sport of polar exploration. The Royal Geographical Society's Manual for that year drew attention to the existence in Greenland of Inuit people who appeared to be a survival from the ice age, like mammoths only smaller, a sort of caveless cavemen, though it was discovered that they weren't all men. It appeared that women were better at resisting hypothermia than men and eventually it turned out that hundreds of these foreign women had been surviving in the Arctic for longer than the men of the Royal Navy, for thousands of years in fact. Clements Markham acted quickly. The Royal Geographical Society wanted to know more about them and so he personally encouraged closer study. But this did not lead to invitations to women to become members of expeditions, or even Presidents of the Royal Geographical Socirty, though mountaineering was not an exclusively male preserve at this time. Peaks of up to 7000 metres had been climbed successfully in the Karakoram, and the Hispar-Biafo glacier traverse had been made by the American explorer, Mrs Fanny Bullock Workman, in the course of seven years of Himalayan climbing. Not long into the twentieth century Freda du Faur became the first woman to make the ascent of that hair-raising peak, Mount Cook.

CHAPTER TWO

Dundee Discoveries

The Dundee Dimension

In March 1900 the keel of Scott's ship *Discovery* was laid in the Panmure Yard of the Dundee Shipbuilders. One year later, in March 1901, she was launched and began her trials on the Tay. In March 1902 she was frozen solid into the sea ice of McMurdo Sound. In March 1903 an attempt made by Captain Colbeck's Relief Expedition ship *Morning* to free her had to be abandoned. By March 1904 the Admiralty had commissioned a Dundee whaling captain, Harry McKay, to sail in another Dundee built ship, the *Terra Nova*, to extract *Discovery* from the ice. But this chain of events does nothing to explain *why* Dundee played such a central part in this Antarctic story. It is a narrative that spans five hundred years of history and, although a considerable diversion from this expedition story, sheds a great deal of light on it, and without the Scottish dimension there would simply be no *Discovery* today. Indeed, the contribution made by Scots to polar exploration has been very little appreciated.

In the Middle Ages, Dundee grew from a small fishing settlement into a key commercial port. It served religious houses – the Tironensian Abbeys of Arbroath and Lindores on either side of the Tay Estuary and, more important, the Cistercian Abbey of Coupar Angus. All three establishments encouraged the lay brethren to till the soil and become skilled in useful crafts. They produced high-quality fine wool which attracted continental buyers from wool-manufacturing towns of the Low Countries, in particular the area south of Holland in Flanders and in Zeeland.

The port of Dundee 'faced' the North Sea. Its merchant ships sailed to two outports of Antwerp, both in Zeeland – Veere (originally called Campvere) and Middelburg (near Vlissingen or Flushing). Dundonians could reach these ports in less time than it took them to reach the English ports of London or Bristol. In addition, Scots wool could reach Veere by sea more quickly than Scots overland transport could reach England's wool markets.

By the sixteenth century Dundee and Veere experienced a common problem which brought them closer together: the English Navigation Acts forbade Dundee trade with England's Far Eastern and American colonies;

under the Spanish occupation of the Netherlands the merchants of Veere were similarly restricted as regards trade with the Spanish colonies. The effect was to encourage Scottish Royal Burghs to make trading deals and seek the privileges of a wool staple in Zeeland. Veere and Middelburg were equally keen to obtain that monopoly of Scotch wool and the competition between the two ports was fierce. Today, Veere has many architectural features that record the presence of the Scots staple.

Polar Maritime

Dundee ships carried corn, barrelled pork, salmon, furs and animal skins – the fur of Scottish pine martens being particularly prized. The ships returned with wines and salt, flax and exotic textile dyestuffs – initially European woad but later tropical indigo and madder dye obtained indirectly through the great supermarket of Antwerp which was a centre of world trade.

Another aspect of this link across the North Sea was nurtured by Calvinist resistance to the Catholic counter-revolution. Dundee had offered support to Flemish weavers long before the sixteenth century when the persecution of the French Huguenots began. In the late sixteenth and early seventeenth centuries other religious refugees from Leyden, escaping from persecution in the Spanish Netherlands, settled in Dundee and in the process encouraged the town's infant textile-manufacturing industries. Soon a religious and civil war waged not only in the Low Countries but in Scotland too. The Scots Covenanters' army, aided by their continental allies, helped Cromwell in his early campaigns against Charles I, capturing the King at Newark. Their ships slipped past royalist blockades of ports to bring guns and ammunition from the Continent. Then, in 1651, Dundee's Covenanters were strangely rewarded by Cromwell when he sent General Monck to destroy their port and sixty ships berthed there. By 1688 the Scottish staple at Veere was declining and with the Act of Union in 1707 Scotland virtually became an English colony in economic terms and was to remain so for some time to come.

Arising out of the restrictions on navigation and all the political and religious turmoil, Dutch and Scottish merchants looked in the only direction that was left to them – to the North. What had begun as an attempt to find a North West Passage round Canada to the Far East turned into a cod fishery, a fur trade and then the whale fishery of Spitzbergen and, when this was exhausted, the whaling industry moved to the Greenland coast and Davis Straits. At first in the seventeenth century, Dundee, in common with other east-coast Scottish ports as far north as Shetland supplied both crewmen and fresh water to the Dutchmen as they made their way northwards. In the eighteenth century Dundee established its own Whale and Fish Company and then started to build whale ships and by 1786 was able to send four ships to the Greenland fisheries.

The Dundee whaling fleet gradually grew in importance in the nineteenth century, despite a series of disasters and tragic losses of men and ships in the 1830s. Dundee entrepreneurs hung on grimly and eventually prospered whilst many other fleets were forced to give up. The picture is complicated by changes in the use of whale oil and bone but the outcome was that Dundee was able to become Britain's premier Arctic whaling port well before *Discovery*'s keel was laid.

Tropical Blues

At the end of the sixteenth century Dundee imported more dyestuffs than all the other Scottish Burghs put together. The favourite dye colour was blue and at that time plaids used woad grown in Flanders. In the seventeenth century the much more economic blue dye of indigo from Asia was imported by the Vereenigde Oost-Indische Compagnie (the Dutch East India Company or VOC) into the Netherlands, and the Book of Customs and Valuation of Merchandises in Scotland of 1612 records the direct import of indigo by the VOC into Zeeland at the time that the Scots staple was operating there.

When Clive took Bengal in 1757 the English East India Company's first plantation crop was indigo. Many Scots worked in Bengal managing the Company's indigo production. Some Scots planters owned as much as twenty thousand acres of indigo plantation land and employed ten thousand native workers. The best known of the Dundee families with indigo interests were two Carmichael families – the famous engineer James Carmichael's daughter Margaret married Peter Carmichael, the son of a successful flax spinner, and they were closely linked with the business of the Drummonds and Munros, two Scottish indigo plantation families.

In the late eighteenth century one Director of the English East India Company was George Dempster, the best known of Forfar merchants and entrepreneurs with many Dundee connections, and he was succeeded as Director by the Dundonian, Hugh Lindsay. It was Lindsay who encouraged indigo planting at a time when production stood at only twenty-five thousand pounds per annum, and thirty years later he had achieved a three hundred fold increase to over seven and half million pounds. This was a measure of the popularity of the colour blue after the victory of Waterloo. Soon after Victoria came to the throne, uniforms were already becoming indigo – nurses, postmen, railway porters, soldiers and sailors – the demand soared phenomenally and over-production was about to trigger a series of catastrophes as the price of indigo plummeted and the Bengal supplies dried up.

There was one possible way out. The English East India Company's Scottish doctors were trained in botany in Edinburgh where the two disciplines were one in this period and they were asked by the company to note any local crops having economic potential which might benefit the company. It happened that when North East Bengal's indigo production crashed so spectacularly there was one other crop with identical growing conditions found in exactly the same areas. This was the coarse textile fibre called jute and the doctors suggested to the company that it might fill the gap in the Bengal economy. Jute, which thrives in Bengal's hot and humid rainy season climate, did indeed save the day at a time when the situation was extremely urgent, for by the first quarter of the nineteenth century millions of Ryat peoples were in danger of starvation.

Juteopolis

In 1796 there had been some experiments conducted on jute fibres when the English East India Company (EIC) sent parcels from Bengal to London, Hamburg and America but the material was intractable and no further action was taken. Then when the first indigo crash came in the 1820s a parcel was sent to Thomas Neish in Dundee at Balfour and Melville's Chapelside Works. The first bales were of mixed fibres and were a disappointment but in 1832 Neish obtained a better sample and succeeded in processing it. At this same time an EIC employee in London, A. B. Anderson, received some jute which he sent to his brother William who was a Dundee linen manufacturer. Linen was by then the major textile industry of Dundee and these skills played a key role in the jute story. Anderson joined forces with William Taylor of Ruthvenmill, near Perth, in experiments to soften jute fibre by the technique known in linen processing as 'batching', which they hoped would make it possible to spin and weave the fibre by machinery. They hit upon a brilliant solution very peculiar to Dundee – the answer was to batch or soften the jute with a mixture of water and whale oil.

The effect of this discovery was quite extraordinary. Dundee's Douglas Foundry made the world's first jute machinery almost immediately in the 1830s. There was at the time a slump in whale oil prices following Murdoch's invention of gas lighting and the introduction of domestic appliances and gas supplies, when suddenly this entirely new demand for whale oil burst upon the port of Dundee. There followed the building of fast and powerful whale ships in the 1850s powered by steam and introduced by the shipbuilder Alexander Stephen and his shipowner brother-in-law William Clark, who just happened to be a friend of William Taylor of

Ruthvenmill. Such was the close-knit community of Dundee, a port destined to continue in the whaling business longer than any other in Britain. When the Crimean War cut off supplies of flax from Russia in 1854 and the American Civil War cut off supplies of cotton in 1861, Dundee's jute industry prospered. Jute proved itself to be an all-purpose and inexpensive textile with many wartime uses from sandbags to horses' nosebags, from webbing to gun covers. After the wars Dundee jute sacks circled the entire world of commerce.

The opening of the Suez Canal in 1869 and the building in Dundee of the world record-breaking sailing clippers plying between the Far East, Australasia and Dundee were about to turn Dundee into a Juteopolis in the last quarter of the nineteenth century. So, at a time when most British shipbuilding yards no longer had the expertise to build strong wooden ships suitable for polar voyages, Dundee became the one exception, building wooden whalers to replace the losses of her whaling fleet. As *Discovery* was to be designed on the lines of a whale ship it was not surprising that Dundee should win the bid to build her.

The Ladies Go A-Whaling

The hunt for the whale developed from a demand for its oil for domestic and street lighting, lubrication of machinery and the manufacture of soap. In addition, whalebone, a unique, lightweight and flexible material, anticipating our age of plastics, became a key raw material of the European fashion industry for almost three centuries.

Dutch sailors began fishing for the whale in the first decade of the seventeenth century, that period in the Netherlands which we associate with the age of classical portrait painting. The sitters were the high risk-taking successful merchant capitalists and their wives, wearing their enormous white collars. Here was a new all-white Protestant fashion creating a demand for soap and for strait-laced corsets. One cannot believe that the portraits of Rembrandt, Frans Hals, or the domestic interior groups of Pieter de Hooch would have been possible in that century without its abundance of soap.

The use of whalebone, or baleen, on the Continent began when men and women came to be enslaved by fashion. It determined their outline, for new underclothes compressed the rib cage of the fine lady and army officer alike. From the mid-seventeenth century to the early eighteenth a baroque style of figure required ladies to wear a corset to push the waist down and give uplift to the bust, resulting in a demand for whalebone and its uplift from this new Dutch industry. The English Navigation Acts of 1651 played their part in this for the Acts did not apply to the Dutch export of whale oil to Britain and this trade across the North Sea even entered the main whaling centres in Britain at this time. In the Netherlands

> notarial records in 1654 for the first time mention whalebone as a commodity of some value. It became a more and more viable compensation for falls in prices for oil.[8]

Then by the end of the eighteenth century ladies of fashion were fired with a revolutionary zeal for freedom and liberty, rather than uplift and constriction. A change in taste, made possible by an industrial revolution able to mass-produce fine muslin at an affordable price, had occurred. Underclothing and corsetry lost out to a new classical look brought from Pompeii by Sir William Hamilton and modelled by Lady Hamilton herself posing in the new see-through muslin shifts which caused distress to elderly moralists. In the words of one doctor: 'how often have I not seen distracted friends and relations escort sweet and gentle maidens to an early grave!' One assumes he was referring to pneumonia.

A further swing in the 1850s brought the Victorians a welcome return to modesty and to great layers of underwear, to hooped skirts and crinolines, to cages and half cages, to tightly laced corsets and to non-existent waists. From 1850 to 1890 mineral oils gradually replaced whale oil for lubrication and lighting though they had not yet ousted coal as fuel for shipping. So demand for whalebone to produce crinoline hoops kept Dundee's Arctic hunters in business and the price of bone increased tenfold during this period.

The Ice Horse

When Dundee whalers were forced to seek new hunting grounds, they scarcely changed their hunting methods. They had close contact with the crews of Norwegian ships and so had long been aware of the experimental harpoon guns, but Dundee had always clung to traditional industrial methods. There can have been few occupations at this time which were more traditional than hunting the great Leviathan in the Arctic Ocean, for it has long been amongst the most primitive of the extractive industries practised by civilised peoples in Europe, and even in the 1880s the Dundee whaling technique was to contine throwing their harpoons at the Bowhead or Right Whales.

In the 1880s, William Crondace, a neighbour and contemporary of the

8. J.R.Bruijn, 'From Minor to Major Concern: Entrepreneurs in 17th Century Dutch Whaling', in A.G.F.van Holk (ed) *Early European Exploitation of the North Atlantic*, page 49.

whaling captain Harry McKay from Broughty Ferry, went to the Davis Straits and he has left us one of the most graphic descriptions of the life of the whaling men in the last quarter of the century.

Leaving Dundee in early March on a whale ship provisioned for ten months and carrying 300 tons of coal, they first called at Lerwick to make up the ship's company to fifty men. At that time the Shetland economy depended heavily on hundreds of men being offered this work by the Peterhead and Dundee whaling companies, though their earnings were pitifully small and the whale ships often returned 'clean' – with no catch – and with the men no better off.

Moving up past the southern tip of Greenland into the Davis Straits, Crondace described how 'things got serious' as the ice was abundant and the captain followed the ice edge south to Disco Island:

> Progress is slow as the narrow passage is obstructed by accumulations of blocks of loose ice which roll and crush in every imaginable way, amongst which the ship dashes and plunges in such a manner as would make you believe she would be swallowed up from time to time, for the ice is often as high as the forecastle but thanks to her strong construction and the skill with which the Captain handles her she clears a road, always advancing like a horse, surmounting all obstacles, clears a channel and arrives in the neighbourhood of the island of Disco.[9]

On reaching the whaling grounds they began work at once:

> the crew is divided into three watches of which one always remains on deck to work the ship and watch for prey. The Captain and officers relieve each other in turn every four hours on the watch in the crow's nest, for being perched at this giddy height, it is well known that the view is much further than from the deck and in consequence it is generally from this position that the whale is first seen throwing her water spout, or sporting in the water.[10]

The Great Silence

Crondace then described the silent ritual which had been practised since the Dundonians first learned it from the Dutch whalers in the eighteenth century:

---

9. William Crondace, *Journey to the Davis Straits* (1884).
10. William Crondace, *Journey to the Davis Straits*.

As soon as she appears the officer of the watch calls out 'a fish!' Immediately the word is repeated from mouth to mouth and in no time the crew leave their quarters and rush off pell mell into the boats in their underclothing, whilst the boats are lowered in the water. The men have their other clothes in bundles but they take to their oars and dress themselves as best they can. The ship follows them under sail and in this manner the boats and ship advance stealthily towards their prey, making the least possible noise.[11]

One can now see the reason why Dundee captains continued in their traditional old-fashioned but successful ways and why they still launched the small rowing boats or whalers from the parent whale ship with muffled oars, for the noise of any engine would frighten off their prey. Whilst the introduction of steam-powered ships had solved the problem of not being able to reverse the ship, it had introduced the problem of the sound of the engines being heard by the whales. In January 1881 the Davis Straits captains had called a special meeting in Dundee to restrict the movement of ships which were under steam in the fishing areas that season, particularly between June and July. The whale captains made a voluntary agreement to navigate and fish under sail when they were north of 74 degrees N. In calm water ships were to keep six miles apart and it was agreed that the masters should consult each other if in doubt about using their engines.

Crondace then described the slaughter with no hint of sentiment, for him there was no romance of whaling, which is so much a feature of many of the other first-hand accounts:

As soon as the fish is within firing distance the Harpooner takes his best aim and shoots off his harpoon and if he does not miss the harpoon plunges into the back of the animal which starts off at its greatest speed for refuge amongst the ice, drawing the lines out of the boat so rapidly as to set them smoking from friction on the billet head round which they are passed to retard their progress. At the same time they put up the boat's flag which announces to the ship that the fish is fastened, then they hoist a flag on ship to show the other neighbouring whalers to which ship it belongs. If the whale is not mortally wounded she will run as many as ten lines on end from the fast boat. Then the boats chase her furiously and ply her with lances every time she comes to the surface so that, exhausted at last by violent swimming and her vast efforts to get free, she rises for the last time, thrashes the water with her immense tail, throws out from her respiracles vast jets of air and water mixed with blood until she is completely exhausted and in her death agony she turns on her back and expires. . . to the hearty cheers of the crew.[12]

11. William Crondace, *Journey to the Davis Straits*.
12. William Crondace, *Journey to the Davis Straits*.

The Flensing

As soon as the monster is dead the boats tow her alongside the ship and without loss of time they begin flensing. Each harpooner is provided with long knives and small sharp spades. They range themselves along the upper part of the animal which is turned over in the process of flensing, and cut off the blubber in long strips and hoist these on deck where they are cut into small pieces to go in the hold to be afterwards put into the tanks which can store 200 tons of blubber. This work usually occupies seven or eight hours although all hands are employed in the work. The weight of the blubber is about twenty tons and the bone about seventeen hundredweight. The carcass being of no value is allowed to sink to the bottom.[13]

Crondace's ship followed the whales in the vicinity of Disco until the end of May when the ice covering Baffin Bay to the north of the Davis Straits began to break up. The Dundee fleet in the 1880s consisted of between ten and fifteen whale ships. These vessels varied considerably in age from newly launched whale ships like *Resolute* and *Chieftain*, which were over 400 tons, to the old *Active* which was over thirty years old and only half the tonnage of the new ships. The average age of the ships in the fleet was twenty years. They also varied considerably in their power consequently the most powerful of the new Dundee ships took the lead and opened a channel to the north as Crondace describes:

small channels close to the land wind about amongst the ice on the one side, and grounded icebergs on the other, in a fantastical and dangerous way through which the whalers collected in this position strive to make headway to the north. Melville Bay is by far the most dangerous part of the whole and it is absolutely necessary to surmount so as to reach Lancaster Sound and Admiralty Inlet, two places frequented by whales in the months of June and July. Having fished in these parts the ships return to Baffin Bay about the commencement of August for it would be dangerous to remain there longer for fear of being inextricably beset in the ice which encumbers these regions in the beginning of autumn. Besides, for days together at this season nothing can be seen because of fog. The month of August is passed coasting along the south-west shore waiting the return of whales towards Hudson Straits.

For unknown reasons there never is a single whale seen during this month. They re-appear before the commencement of September but at this period all the arms of the sea and the north part of Baffin Bay have already re-frozen

13. William Crondace, *Journey to the Davis Straits*.

which forces the whales, by instinct for their own preservation to go further south. It is then that whalers waylay them for the last time and intercept them in the passage after which the season being terminated the ships make sail and quit these inhospitable regions in all haste and arrive safely home about the middle of the month of October.[14]

The Risk and Uncertainty

Dundee whaling went through so many vicissitudes that it is difficult to judge whether it was the entrepreneurs or the whalers who took the greater risks. It helps to divide the fortunes of the city's whaling fleet into three thirty-year periods: 1800-1830; 1831–64; and 1865-95. In the first period English whaling fleets outnumbered Scotland's fifty whale ships but this lead came abruptly to an end in the second period when a series of disasters decimated English fleets. Yet the Dundee fleet lost only six vessels in the first period and actually benefited from disasters because 1830 was a boom year with the price of whale oil reaching a record £60 per tun.

The second thirty-year period saw the rise of the port of Peterhead. Initially the Greenland whale fishing produced record catches and ten ships in the Dundee fleet still caught over a hundred whales a year with a record catch in 1832 of 240, and Captain Davidson on the *Dorothy* brought back 35 of them. The typical oil yield was almost two thousand tuns, but even though prices plummeted to a mere £20 per tun, the oil still brought in a vast annual fortune of £38,000 and the whalebone yielded another £16,000, at £8 per hundredweight. These were the happy days of Dundee whaling, and though it cost £2000 to send each of the nine ships in the fleet out to Greenland, the companies were feeling buoyant.

Then overfishing began to take its toll. The Greenland stocks of Right or Bowhead Whales could not possibly sustain such a huge slaughter and whale captains began to fish the Davis Straits in addition to trying their luck in the old grounds. Soon financial returns in every sector declined to a fraction of their former sum. The size of the fleet was halved with the knock-on effect of a reduced catch and a downward spiral: as receipts were not sufficient to pay for the replacement of ships lost there was further decline. Between 1857 and 1864 seven Dundee ships were lost but a slow recovery began and these losses were replaced in this period. Prices had begun to rise in wartime and oil and bone prices doubled, triggering a recovery.

In the third thirty-year period in the time of William Crondace's trip,

14. William Crondace, *Journey to the Davis Straits*.

Dundee became Britain's premier whale port and, with another boom, oil prices rose to £70 per tun and bone prices rose steeply. Dundee's fleet increased to a record sixteen ships and, as competition from other Scottish fleets declined, so, despite the overfishing of Davis Straits and Greenland stocks, the impending crash was not obvious. Warnings about sustainable resources make little difference: one only knows that a stock isn't sustainable when it is too late to sustain it and it has virtually collapsed. Perhaps one day we will learn from Dundee's bitter experience.

Sail versus Steam and Screw versus Paddle

Of the fifty-seven whale ships which entered the Dundee fleet in the course of the nineteenth century, only seventeen survived long enough to reach a breaker's yard. In the first half of the century all whaling was done by sailing ships which found themselves completely at the mercy of the elements. They could be 'nipped' in the ice as the wind-driven and current-propelled icebergs and floes bore down on them, for they had no means of reversing and in one season there were as many as a thousand men on the Arctic ice all fighting for survival.[15]

However, in the first half of the nineteenth century Dundee had also established a reputation for marine engineering. The local engineer, James Carmichael, produced a steam-powered marine engine as early as 1821 and he also invented a reversing gear for steam-powered ships. The Dundee, Perth and London Shipping Company, utilising the Carmichael inventions, introduced the first paddle steamer on the River Tay in 1834. Then, in 1845, the Admiralty arranged a tug-of-war between the paddle steamer *Alecto* and the screw-propelled ship *Rattler*, and propellers won the day. Orders for propeller-driven ships flooded in and the shipbuilder Henry Gourlay set up in Dundee in 1853.

Gourlay's engines were in the forefront of steam age technology, the shipbuilder Alexander Stephen moved from the Moray coast south to Dundee with his brother-in-law William Clark, and they began to build auxiliary steam whale ships. The first of these began life as the sailing ship *Tay* but in 1857 she was converted to steam by Gourlay. In 1859 Stephen and Gourlay produced the first purpose-built auxiliary steam ship, the *Narwhal*.

Although both Gourlay and Stephen were great innovators, when it came to building for the Arctic ice they appeared to be solidly traditional and favoured building wooden ships. On her maiden voyage the *Narwhal* went

15. University of Dundee Archives: Dundee Whaling Fleet.

to the assistance of the *Empress of India* – a steel whale ship which sank. Peterhead experimented with two whale ships built of steel but disaster overtook both of them. Wood was favoured because of its insulating properties and because of its relative flexibility which made it possible for whale ships to ram or butt ice floes, an essential technique in the polar regions. By 1860 all Dundee's leading whale ship and sealer yards were building in wood – Thomas Adamson, Peter Borrie, John Brown, David Calman, and Alexander Stephen. Iron and steel were for fast clippers and Dundee became famous for these too. In the second half of the nineteenth century Stephen's Yard designed and built twenty of the most famous whale ships of all time. The *Discovery*, built on the lines of a Stephen's whale ship for Commander Robert Falcon Scott by Dundee Shipbuilders, was the last in a line and is the last to survive.

Two Dundee-Built Discoveries

Alexander Stephen's Panmure Yard was taken over by Dundee Shipbuilders in 1894. In 1900 Scott's ship *Discovery* was built there by Mr R. Paterson, an ex-Stephen's manager with a workforce of Stephen men. Their relevant experience was second to none. It was the experience that had created the successful innovations in design in all their nineteenth-century Arctic ships, in collaboration with Gourlay who perfected the powerful triple expansion engines. It was the experience that invented the steam auxiliary whale ship and had built twenty of them since. It was the experience that had supplied the Arctic not only with ships for whaling but with ships for Royal Naval Arctic exploration and relief expeditions. But typically, despite his professional expertise, Paterson was messed about by committees of amateurs who altered specifications, vacillated, changed their minds, assumed that however many changes they made there would be no extra charge and refused to see Paterson when he came to London expressly for the purpose of correcting the mistakes that they had made.

Ten years before Scott's expedition, the Dundee firm of Robert Kinnes had sent four of their famous whaling captains (Robertson, Adams, Davidson and Fairweather) with a team of scientists (W. Speirs Bruce, Campbell and Donald) on a Scottish expedition to the Antarctic in four ships from Dundee's whaling fleet: *Balaena* built in Drammen (1872), *Active* in Peterhead (1852) and two Dundee ships: *Polar Star* (1861) and *Diana* (1871). Bruce and Robertson returned to plan a National (Scottish) Antarctic Expedition for 1902. Markham was not pleased and described Speirs Bruce's plan as *mischievous*. However, at the launch of *Discovery* the shipyard manager Paterson and foreman John Smith were praised as men who knew more about building wooden ships than any men in Scotland. Seven famous whaling captains, including Harry McKay, came to the launch but were only mentioned in speeches by one guest – H. R. Mill, Secretary of the 1895 International Geographical Congress which had pioneered the renewal of interest in the Antarctic. He said (pointedly) that W. Speirs Bruce

> knew more about both Polar regions than any other man, except perhaps some of those splendid Dundee skippers.

Bruce in reply referred to his plans and with Markham's gibe in mind said that despite the lack of any official financial British support his expedition would

> go in the spirit of co-operation, feeling the necessity of earnest scientific research rather than of sensational pole-hunting.[16]

There was no need for further comment.

Purpose-Built in England for Science?

Sir Clements Markham had set his heart on a new purpose-built ship designed for Scott from the very beginning. Naturally, the first essential was to appoint a committee of Admirals who, according to Sir Clements, had all the necessary expertise, though he did go to Norway to look for a ship and consult with experts whose advice he did not take. Scott's book *The Voyage of the Discovery* has a whole chapter about the building of 'his' ship and he summed up the situation in his masterly prose:

> In deciding to build a vessel for the purposes of the expedition the Ship Committee made a new departure, for the *Discovery* was the first vessel ever built in England for scientific exploration.[17]

Clearly he knew that Scotland had been an English colony since 1707. Just to emphasise the insult he added that his ship 'was built on good and well-tried English lines'.[18] What Scott meant by this was that an English naval architect would draw up a design closely following those well-known English lines exemplified by a ship which was renamed *Discovery* in 1875 (*Bloodhound*, built in Dundee by Stephen's Yard). George Nares and Albert

16. H.R.Mill and William Speirs Bruce, Speeches at the launch of the *Discovery*, Dundee Advertiser 22 March 1901.
17. Robert Falcon Scott, *The Voyage of the Discovery* (1905) Vol.I Ch.II pages 43 & 47.
18. Robert Falcon Scott, *The Voyage of the Discovery*, Vol.I Ch.II pages 43 & 47.

Markham, the two Admirals who had led the 1875 Polar expedition in the old *Discovery*, were members of Markham's Ship Committee. Of course, there was nobody on this Committee from Dundee Shipbuilders who had been commissioned to build this ship and Paterson was exasperated at the discourteous way in which he was treated. Yet those on the Ship Committee whose expertise was relevant, rather than irrelevant to the task in hand, regarded the old *Discovery* (alias *Bloodhound*) as the best ice ship ever to be employed in the Royal Navy's Arctic service. They recalled that in 1875 the Dundee-built ship was sent ahead to clear a passage through the ice for all the other expedition ships. So whilst Mr W. Smith, the Royal Naval Architect in London, was re-designing the late Mr. Stephen's *Bloodhound* for him, the Committee were asking another of their Royal Navy contacts, a Commander Marrack, to design the triple expansion engine, which must have come as something of a shock to the Scottish inventor Henry Gourlay. However, Gourlay offered constructive criticisms but these were ignored. After the launch Markham criticised Dundee Shipbuilders in a public lecture and this drew an infuriated reply from Paterson in February 1902 – he retorted that the so-called 'Dundee leak' was caused by putting *Discovery* into dry dock fully laden! His remarks were dismissed out of hand. The most accurate account of the ship controversy is by A. G. E. Jones, whose comprehensive assessment concluded:

> It is not surprising that there were major faults in the *Discovery*. In his letters and reports home, Scott wrote in praise or criticism, according to the impression he wanted to give.[19]

Dundee workmanship saved the lives of the expedition members in 1904 when, according to some authorities, the wind ran her aground, but according to Bernacchi, the commander ran her aground on a reef of which he had been aware for many months.

---

19. A.G.E.Jones, 'The Steam Yacht Discovery', in *Polar Portraits,* pages 127-9.

CHAPTER THREE

The Polar Scots

From the Clearances to the Fur Trade

British and Canadian Arctic exploration in the nineteenth century was orchestrated by the Admiralty and by Canadian fur trading companies for quite different reasons. The Hudson Bay Company developed into a fur trading empire covering three million square miles, almost one twelfth of the earth's land surface. The Hudson Bay Company and the North West Company competed for dominion over this trade and it was a struggle personified by two rival Scots, Simon McTavish and the explorer Alexander Mackenzie. Thanks to the Clearances they were able to recruit evicted families from the Highlands of Scotland to settle in Upper Canada. Further Scottish connections came with emigrating lairds, like the 5th Earl of Selkirk, an 'improver' with a difference who saw a future for the crofters evicted from their land and homes with the coming of extensive sheep farming to the Scottish glens. Selkirk came to own vast areas of Canada and dominated the fur trading companies. In 1844 the Hudson Bay Company sent the Orcadian, Dr John Rae, to survey its northern shores; English and Scottish techniques of Arctic exploration were about to clash.

Second Secretary of the Admiralty, John Barrow, fostered the idea of employing surplus naval officers in the peace which resulted from the Congress of Vienna of 1815. Exploration by John Franklin, William Edward Parry, John Ross and James Clark Ross added to the fund of knowledge of the Arctic in the first half of the nineteenth century. Then, in 1845, Franklin's largest expedition of 129 men went missing. The navy sent forty search parties into Arctic Canada with interesting results. The naval officers included Erasmus Ommanney, George Nares, Horatio Austin, Edward Belcher, Sherard Osborn and Clements Markham. They searched Beechey Island and two hundred men spent the summer of 1851 sledging eleven thousand miles. They used the Dundee whaling ships *Resolute* and *Assistance* for four years. Richard Collinson, with Robert McClure, made important contributions but it was Leopold McClintock who won the prize of solving the mystery. However, the real prize for most of these officers was fame and promotion to Admiral later in their careers.

The searches brought together the Royal Navy and the Hudson Bay

Company in a strange and short-lived alliance. They produced two solutions: the first, from Rae, provided the truth, which was unacceptable to Lady Franklin and polite English society; the second, from McClintock, were the findings which ended the long searches of 1847-1859 and reinforced the navy's belief in its own expedition techniques. Scottish techniques, derived from Rae's journeys, and the Inuit were ignored by the English but found a place in American expeditions.

The Polar Conquest Theories and Scottish Interests

Interest in the search for a North West Passage to the Orient, which had triggered so much of nineteenth-century Arctic exploration, began to wane. Technically Franklin had discovered the way and, although he didn't live to realise it, he had shown that it was a commercially useless route. Barrow's job creation efforts were superseded by a renewed interest in the conquest of the Poles, encouraged by the update of an old theory that they might not be permanently frozen. It was thought that they were just encircled by a ring of ice which could be broken through. It was an age of mad theories and August Petermann was a mad German geographer of the first order with no first-hand experience.

Looking down at the North Pole of his globe, Petermann saw four possible routes for a conquest of the Pole. The first was from the Bering Straits between Alaska and Siberia and then via the New Siberian Islands. The second (and according to Petermann the least hopeful of the four) was between Canada and West Greenland. The Americans favoured this route precisely because it provided the firmest ice on which to sledge. The third possible route was between East Greenland and Svalbard and, lastly, the fourth was between Svalbard and Novaya Zemlya.

Petermann thought that the three routes he recommended received warm ocean currents feeding into an ice-free Arctic Basin. Although the theory was attractive, it was soon proved to be wrong, as most experienced whaling men could have told him. The Austrians Julius Von Payer and Karl Weyprecht took up the challenge, set off from Novaya Zemlya and discovered Franz Josef Land, thereby making Petermann's fourth route much more attractive.

There was a great increase in the output of expedition lore distilled from the journeys encouraged by Barrow; from the twelve long years of the Franklin searches; from the disasters brought about by the Petermann Theory; and not least, from the experience of the polar Scots including the Scottish whaling captains equipped with new steam whale ships after 1859. This was a period when Scots were recruited to serve all over the globe for English causes. However, having lost their nationhood in 1707, few Scots took much interest in the polar flag-waving conquests that motivated naval explorers from 1875 to 1900. Those Scots who had such desires, like the Edinburgh scientist William Speirs Bruce, waved a different coloured flag, much to Markham's annoyance.

The three most vital Scottish contributions to polar exploration were the ships built in Scotland for work in the polar ice, the Scottish scientists, and the Scottish ice captains who played a key part in the rescue of adventurers and foreign scientists.

Testing Theories in Remote Places

Petermann's theory encouraged the American Navy to send Commander George Washington De Long to take the expedition ship *Jeanette* through the Bering Straits to the New Siberian Islands in 1879 for a polar bid. There she met disaster, crushed in the ice. The expedition succeeded in one respect: disproving Petermann's theory of an ice-free polar sea warmed by the North Atlantic Drift. Some identifiable wreckage from the *Jeanette* turned up in South-West Greenland three years later. This gave Nansen the idea of the *Fram*, a ship designed to ride on the frozen surface as the ice rotated round the top of the world (assuming the north is the top). All Nansen had to do was to get off at the right stop, or so he thought.

The Americans were then plunged into another tragedy, this time on their favourite polar route between Greenland and Ellesmere Island. It was here that Albert Markham and George Nares explored in Dundee's Stephen-built ship *Discovery* in 1875–6, making the polar bid with which Albert Markham sledged into history. The U. S. Navy failed in 1879 and now the U. S. Army, represented by Lieutenant Adolphus Greely, were being given a chance but ostensibly this was not an American polar bid. In fact, quite the contrary, for Karl Weyprecht had proposed an end to national pole bagging expeditions with a plan for an International Polar Year in 1882 and this was America's contribution. But these good intentions gave way to nationalism and a new "Furthest North" record bid.

Greely established the most northerly base at Lady Franklin Bay, sailing there in the Dundee whale ship *Proteus* in 1881. 1882 was quite different, heavy ice prevented Dundee's *Neptune* from reaching Greely and she took most of her supplies back to Newfoundland, over two thousand miles away. In 1883 *Proteus* made another bid and was crushed with the loss of all her supplies at the entrance to Smith Sound, near Cape Sabine. The Dundee whaling men escaped and rowed seven hundred miles to Upernavik and safety. Then Greely had orders to leave his base where the men had managed to live off musk ox. He headed south for Cape Sabine – a horrendous journey for soldiers with no whaling men in sight, and they faced unimaginable hardships and starvation. It was decided that the U. S. Navy should rescue the U. S. Army. Eight more Dundee ships were brought into the fray to attempt to reach Cape Sabine but the navy failed to command them effectively in the severe ice conditions. Dundee's *Thetis* and *Bear* were met at Disco by Captain Fairweather in *Aurora. Arctic, Esquimaux, Narwhal, Resolute*, and *Wolf* followed in their wake until *Bear* struck a rock. Fairweather lent a hand plugging her leak with handfuls of hemp produced from nowhere to the amazement of the relief expedition's American commander, Winfield Schley, who was on the *Thetis*. Greely was found alive but seventeen of his twenty-two men had starved to death.

Reporters on Thin Ice

In the last quarter of the nineteenth century exploration caught the attention of newspaper magnates seeking to build up mass circulation papers. They shifted the emphasis from scholarly accounts of discoveries to popular stories, spiced with ripping adventures. The new emphasis played up bids for the Poles and stories were built around personalities. The American newspaper editor who started the trend was James Gordon Bennett of the *New York Herald*. He found that expedition material lacked news value and needed more events. He dreamed up the idea of sending Stanley on an expedition to Darkest Africa to find Livingstone, which became a true American venture. When it came to polar bids he put his money on Lieutenant De Long and found himself embroiled in the aftermath of a ghastly tragedy. It increased circulation no end. But when Nansen followed up the discoveries made unwittingly by De Long, as wreckage from his ship *Jeanette* reached Greenland, James Gordon Bennett missed a trick.

The Austrian discovery of Franz Josef Land inspired a Scottish expedition led by Benjamin Leigh Smith and Captain Lofley with a crew of Dundonians in the Peterhead whale ship *Eira* in 1880-2. They forced a way through the ice to Cape Flora where they built a hut well sited for polar bids, as was proved not long after when Frederick Jackson approached the London newspaper owner Alfred Harmsworth (later Lord Northcliffe) of the *Evening News, Daily Mail* and *Daily Mirror* seeking financial backing for an expedition to Franz Josef Land in 1894. Buying the Dundee whale ship *Windward* for Jackson to continue Leigh Smith's work seemed an ideal investment to Harmsworth. Meanwhile, unknown to them, two men were about to cross a thousand miles of sea ice from the Pole to Cape Flora. Fridtjof Nansen and Hjalmer Johansen had stepped off the *Fram* but were unable to reach the North Pole despite being near and they turned south with their kayaks in the hope of finding relief at Cape Flora! They received British hospitality and a trip to Tromsø on Harmsworth's relief ship *Windward* which was just about to arrive from Dundee. At Tromsø they were re-united with *Fram* and her Captain Sverdrup in an incredible piece of timing.

Another American newspaper man, Walter Wellman, chose the Svalbard way in 1894 then sought Franz Josef Land's imaginary land bridge to the Pole in 1898 with support from the American National Geographical Society. He did not bag the Pole but mapped new land and produced good newspaper copy. In 1898, newspaper proprietor Sir George Newnes, who was responsible for *Tit Bits* and the *Strand Magazine*, financed Carsten Borchgrevink's Antarctic expedition. Here was a team of Norwegians all set to go South apart from the little matter of £35,000. In return for this sum they had to pretend to be British, wave Union Jacks and take William Colbeck and Louis Bernacchi with them. A bargain price.

CHAPTER FOUR

The Dundee Rescuers

A Professional Polar Rescuer

Harry McKay, who is a central character of this narrative, was born in Dundee in 1857 and was destined to become one of that port's band of famous whaling captains who sailed the polar seas.

He rose to prominence at a time when whaling was undergoing catastrophic changes. In the first half of the nineteenth century some ten ships of the Dundee whaling fleet sailed to the west coast of Greenland every year where they were greatly outnumbered by over a hundred other British ships and in that fifty-year period the Dundee fleet caught two thousand whales.

At the start of the second half of the nineteenth century there were only four ships in the Dundee whaling fleet. The Greenland whale stocks had been devastated and the search was extended to the Davis Straits (between Eastern Greenland and the north-east coast of Arctic Canada). By the 1860s many captains began to fish for seals rather than whales. Although, overall, as many whales were caught by the Dundee ships in the second half of the nineteenth century as in the first half, it required many more ships to catch two thousand whales than had been the case in the first half of the century.

Thus it came about that although the Dundee whalers after 1859 were powered by steam and able to reduce the risks of being crushed in the ice, the number of ships lost was actually greater than in the previous half century, when ships were entirely under sail – in fact the losses were three times greater!

This increase was partly due to the larger size of the Dundee fleet – it had in fact doubled. It was also partly due to the increase in the number of trips made to the whaling grounds by the ships of the fleet, which had also doubled in frequency. But more important, in order to achieve their targets after 1860, the men of the Dundee fleet had to spend longer at sea and had to cover a much greater sea area than ever before. As the whales retreated to more inaccessible areas, the whaling men took many more risks in the ice and the fog-bound fiords of the high Arctic, working at the very limits of maritime navigation in that period. It was partly for these reasons that the Dundee whale fisheries gained their reputation as a school for ice masters and

Arctic rescuers of whaling crews, scientists and many unfortunates from a variety of navies.

McKay was described as modest, professional and much liked by all those who worked with him in the Arctic. His name is now associated with two Antarctic expedition ships but in 1892 when a chance came to go South he had only just become the youngest-ever master of a whaling ship, the *Aurora* (famous for Mawson's 1911 Antarctic expedition). Understandably, McKay had no burning desire to go on Dundee's very own Antarctic Expedition (1892–93). So that famous quartet of Dundee ice masters – Adams, Fair-weather, Robertson and Davidson – took park in the early venture without McKay, even though it was sponsored by McKay's own firm Robert Kinnes.

Rescue by Convoy

In 1878 Harry McKay was twenty-one and he was just being initiated into the whaling business when the Dundee whale ship *Camperdown* got herself into great trouble as she approached the notorious Melville Bay on the coast of West Greenland. Gravill, her captain, had ten years' experience in the Dundee fleet. Furthermore, he was in the company of three of the most famous ice masters that had ever served in the Dundee whaling fleet – the legendary Captain Adams (Senior), Captain Fairweather (Senior) and Captain Yule. Their ships were mostly newly built in the Dundee Panmure Yard by Alexander Stephen. There was *Aurora* (1876), *Arctic* (1875), *Maud* (1865), and *Esquimaux* (1865). Even *Polynia* (1861) and *Camperdown* (1860) could hardly be called old by the standards of the day. Here were six whale ships which were in fact the pride of the city, and many hundreds of Dundonians would turn out to see them leave or enter port on their return from months in the Arctic.

Despite Gravill's experience *Camperdown* was twice 'nipped' by ice as she nosed her way into these, the more dangerous of Arctic waters. His crew were relieved to see at least one of the Dundee fleet in sight and Captain Yule responding to Gravill's distress signal. Ice had badly damaged *Camperdown* but Gravill continued to fish until he ran into 'a formidable piece of ice' when his ship was found to be leaking fast. The pumps simply could not cope and Gravill called his crew together and, doubtless to their amazement, proposed that they should continue to fish for whales! Such was the effect of poor wages and tempting bonus rates. To his surprise, the men refused to continue fishing until the ship had been examined. It was then found that the iceberg had carried away twelve feet of their keel and that *Camperdown* was making thirty-seven inches of water an hour. Time for discussions with the experts. Three of the senior masters made a survey and declared that his ship

> was not in a fit condition to continue the prosecution of fishing and could not be repaired.[20]

In effect, what had evolved that year, though it had its origins earlier in the 1830s, was a Convoy System in which the fleet kept close together on arrival at the fishing grounds in order to effect a rescue of the crews if any ship was crushed in the ice. The advantage of this system was that not only were the famous whaling captains from other ships on hand to lend their expert advice but because, in the majority of cases, they were senior partners of the Dundee whaling firms they could therefore support the taking of the most difficult decisions – like the conclusion that the *Camperdown* was beyond repair and should be abandoned. This experience clearly had a considerable influence on the young Harry McKay who was serving with this extra-ordinary cohort of Dundee ice masters. He was destined to become the most famous of them all.

Saving the Ship: The Iceman Cometh!

Harry McKay was made First Officer of the new whale ship *Resolute* in 1882, serving under Captain Kilgour. They sailed from Dundee very early that February. There was an unusual quantity of ice on the coast of Labrador and within sixteen days they were frozen into the ice near St John's, Newfoundland. Ultimately they got free after being jammed solid for twenty-four days. Freeing one's own ship was always a more difficult task than butting the ice to get close enough to rescue the crew of another ship. McKay learned the techniques – using ice saws to keep open a channel around the ship, butting or ramming the ice front to break it up, sallying or rolling the ship from side to side to propel her forward through ice floes and (in the last resort because it was the most expensive of all the ice master's techniques) blasting with explosives. McKay entered the whaling scene at the time when Dundee captains were changing over from the use of black powder (gunpowder) for blasting to the newly invented high explosives (initially guncotton) and he was quick to learn the new techniques.

Captain Kilgour was an elderly man with over ten years' experience in the Dundee fleet and was just about to retire and, not surprisingly, he was very careful in his use of explosives. Nevertheless when Harry McKay suggested to him that they should use much larger charges of guncotton this was done

---

20. John Ingram Shipping Notebooks, Dundee University Archive.

and they got free. The crew reckoned that but for McKay's explosive techniques they would not have escaped from the ice that season. So from about this time McKay began to make a name for himself in employing special techniques.

On reaching Conception Bay the *Resolute* had arrived back in the Atlantic and ran into yet more solid pack ice. Another big charge of guncotton was used at McKay's suggestion, which, together with further butting of the ice, resulted in her getting clear once more.

When they finished whaling they were in the quarter where Sir John Franklin's expedition had wintered and gone missing. Kilgour came upon a large pack of walrus and in the course of chasing them the *Resolute* went aground. It was not an unusual occurrence on that coast for whalers to come to grief when in pursuit of walrus. The Captain was in a terrible state and he went below. Quite naturally the crew thought that he had gone to brace his nerves with a bottle. They were surprised to find then that he was actually praying for their safety. After this Captain Kilgour left in a boat with some of the crew to get help from another whale ship. He was away for three or four hours and to his surprise when he returned he discovered that *Resolute* was afloat. McKay, realising that they were on a sandbank, got out all the stores from the ship and succeeded in refloating her.

Losing the Ship but Saving the Crew

In October 1891 Captain Guy in the famous Dundee whale ship *Polynia* was homeward bound from Lancaster Sound when she was caught in the stern by a movement of ice floes on both her flanks. Guy estimated that each ice mass was two miles in circumference and able to exert huge pressure. Sure enough, the rudder was soon crushed and in Guy's words: 'ice masses creaked and cracked and the wind howled dismally among the shrouds'.[21]

Despite pumping the water gained rapidly and when it drowned all the fires in the engine room they had to give up – thirty-seven men, a sinking ship, no help in sight and land twelve miles off. But although four boats set off at once for the land they could not get over the ice by boat or on foot. Later that afternoon Captain Milne in the *Maud* and Captain McKay in the *Aurora* appeared on the scene some ten miles off. McKay succeeded in powering his way through the ice to within three miles of the *Polynia* and took the men aboard. Crossing those three miles on foot over the ice to reach the *Aurora* took them seven hours.

Next year it was the turn of the *Maud*. Usually the last of the fleet to sail

21. Whaling Newspaper Cuttings 1891, University of Dundee Archive.

from Dundee, Captain Milne had not left until the end of March. It was early October before he made his way back from Lancaster Sound and arrived at Coutts Inlet, still some four hundred miles north of the Arctic Circle. A whale was sighted and as there was no ice at all in the Inlet the boats set off in pursuit and secured it about ten miles off. The wind then rose steadily and reached hurricane force and it came on to snow heavily. During the night there was a sudden change and the Inlet began to fill with great fields of ice, swept south by the gale. In the morning the *Maud* was beset. The clear water of the Inlet had been completely replaced by heavy sheets of ice. Milne tried to move the *Maud* using chains and ice anchors or kedges to swing the ship free but to no avail.

At this point Jackman in the *Eagle* and McKay in the *Aurora* came to Milne's assistance and attempted to tow the *Maud* but the pressure of the ice was breaking her up. They gave up the attempt to rescue the ship but McKay took the crew of the stricken vessel back to Dundee in the *Aurora*. At that time Jackman was regarded as the most daring of ice masters. He thought nothing of ramming his way through miles of ice and in 1886 he actually butted through a hundred miles of young ice which was rapidly closing behind him. Harry McKay had served with Jackman before becoming master of his own ships *Aurora* and *Terra Nova* and he learned many of his ice techniques from the wild man of the *Eagle*.

Lost!

The *Chieftain* left Dundee at the beginning of March 1884 under the command of Captain Gellatly for the Greenland seal fishing but none of the Dundee fleet could reach the seals as the ice was too thick that year. The captain gave up trying and boldly decided to try fishing for the Bottlenose Whale instead but unwisely he left the Dundee convoy. He thought he was fortunate on 26th May when a school of whales came in sight but Gellatly was a novice in his first season with the Fleet and it proved to be his last. Unaccountably, he left his ship and took four boats in pursuit of the whales, harpooned two 'fish' and, leaving three boats to follow him, he returned to the *Chieftain* with one whale, early on the morning of 27th May. Thick fog then blew up which he was not expecting, and when the boats did not return he again went to their relief, leaving an inexperienced officer in command of his ship.

The captain found the lost boats that afternoon and when the fog lifted briefly they saw the *Chieftain* only six miles away. So all four boats set off, taking the second whale with them. But the fog came down again suddenly. Meanwhile, the *Chieftain* sounded a fog horn madly and fired a harpoon gun every few minutes. The four whalers rowed about vainly all night and the men suffered from frostbite, exposure, hunger but most of all from thirst. In desperation they abandoned the whale and never saw it again as it was taken by Norwegian whalers. Bewildered and exhausted, the Dundee men rowed for two more days and nights hearing and seeing nothing, blowing their own portable foghorn. A storm came on but still the fog did not clear.

On 29th May a ship sailed right past them without seeing or hearing them. Then out of the fog came several boats in pursuit of a Bottlenose Whale; they were Norwegians from the schooner *Schrieder*. However, only one of Gellatly's boats was found – some said it was found by a whale because the Norwegians had been on the point of making for home when they had seen this one last Bottlenose and gave chase. The rescuers gave up their own bunks to nurse the unfortunate Dundonians back to life.

Meanwhile Gellatly with the other three boats was still lost and they decided to row the 200 miles to the north coast of Iceland. Older and more experienced hands could have told them that many men before them had attempted this in an open boat and had perished. Almost at once crewman David Buchan was knocked overboard as a wave struck his oar and he was drowned. Some think he was lucky for they then ran out of food. Gellatly and two boats reached Brimness but as they were picked up by the smack *Jemima* another man died. The third boat drifted on for two weeks; all died except for one who lost both his legs.

Searching for Scientists

It was just as well that McKay left the *Resolute* at the start of the 1886 season. He joined Captain Fairweather on Dundee's latest and most powerful Stephen's whaler the *Terra Nova*. In that fateful year the wild man of Newfoundland, Captain Arthur Jackman, came to Dundee to command the *Resolute* on what was to be her last voyage. *Resolute* was beset by ice and with a vengeance; she was held in the vice-like grip of a floe when suddenly shore ice was thrust in a contrary direction beneath the surface of the floe. The two halves of the ship parted company and she was sliced in two along her waterline. Jackman, typically, had on board the crews of other ships that he had rescued that year. He got 260 men to safety and they all went off to St John's, Newfoundland, arriving just in time for his own memorial service which, he was pleased to note, was well attended.

When in 1893 McKay captained his ship *Aurora*, he was asked to go in search of two lost Swedish naturalists, Bjorling and Kalstennius, who had disappeared when working in Baffin Bay. The Swedes had chartered the schooner *Ripple* from her owner but she was quite unsuitable for working that far north and it is believed that the owner thought that they were intending to go south, not north. The scientists were unlucky at the outset for they found no ice at all and so were enticed up the west Greenland coast as far north as 77 degrees. It was a fatal attraction.

McKay searched the inlets of the fiord coast, found the wreck in the Carey Islands at the mouth of Smith Sound and discovered the fate of the scientists and three crewmen. The *Ripple* had been badly holed and clearly was not capable of repair. McKay was able to recover Bjorling's scientific papers and the searchers found the body of one crewman and a note which showed that the scientists had attempted an overland escape route but for some inexplicable reason had walked towards the Pole. They had returned and left a second note to say that they were heading for Cape Faraday, a lifeless area of Ellesmere Island, devoid of both wildlife and Inuit settlers. There was nobody there who could have saved them, but Harry McKay then turned towards Ellesmere Island and searched. That year the ice was too thick and the risks of venturing that far north were too great and he was forced to give up.

On his return, McKay was awarded a medal by the Swedish Geographical and Anthropological Society for his rescue bid, retrieving the scientific papers and providing information. The Royal Geographical Society contented itself with a severe reprimand of this party of foolish, inexperienced and ill-equipped Scandinavian scientists who had ventured into British polar regions. The passage in the *Geographical Journal* can only have been written by Clements Markham.[22]

Matters of Life and Death

In 1846, a substance was discovered which later proved to be of great value to the Dundee whaling masters: it was the first high explosive. The 1840s were a period in which there was intense interest in organic chemistry – the synthesising of substances from an organic base. These were studies and discoveries capable of shedding light on the very basis of life and, at the same time, creating the deadliest of weapons.

The German chemist, Christian Friedrich Schönbein (1799-1868) steeped cotton in nitric and sulphuric acids and in the process he discovered guncotton. Unlike gunpowder, which is a chemical *mixture* of charcoal, potassium nitrate and sulphur, guncotton or nitro-cellulose is a chemical *compound*. Its German inventor, Professor of Chemistry at Basel University, announced his discovery on 11th March 1846 at a scientific meeting of the

22. *Geographical Journal* Vol.3. No.1. 1893, pages 63-64.

Naturforschende Gesellschaft. In this same year nitro-glycerine was discovered; thus 1846 saw the discovery of the two families of high explosives. There are nine members of the nitro-cellulose chemical family; each varies in its percentage of nitrogen, and only the most highly nitrated form is the explosive we call guncotton (known as Dodeka Nitro-cellulose by those who speak the language).

News of Schonbein's announcement soon reached the ears of British mining engineers and Schonbein was invited to give two demonstrations of guncotton in Cornwall which proved to be successful. Following these demonstrations, the gunpowder manufacturing firm, John Hall of Faversham in Kent, was granted sole rights to manufacture guncotton in England but until 14th July 1847 its power was not fully appreciated. On that day an explosion at Faversham's Marsh Works killed twenty-one people and completely demolished John Hall's factory. Production was then stopped for almost twenty years whilst chemists looked for ways of making it safe to handle.

In Austria, Baron Lenk realised that removing impurities by boiling was an effective method of stabilising the explosive and from 26th January 1864 guncotton was at last in commercial production. In that year Alfred Nobel, known for his nitro-glycerine explosives, of which Dynamite (1866) and Blasting Gelatine (1875) are probably the best known, had invented the Mercury Fulminate Blasting Cap or detonator which proved to be the safest way of initiating his explosions. He established his factory in Scotland at Ardeer on the Ayrshire coast in 1871 at a time when the whaling industry was beginning to take an interest in these new products. By the end of the century guncotton was rapidly being replaced by Nobel's high explosives, but there were exceptions.

Cold Blasts

In 1856 the Dundee whaler *Princess Charlotte*, which had returned safely from the Greenland fisheries every year since 1820, was suddenly crushed between two powerful ice floes in the Davis Straits. She went down in fifteen minutes, so quickly in fact that the men scarcely had time to escape with their lives on to the ice. They were then able to blast their way back into the ship to retrieve their clothes and provisions by the use of gunpowder. Black powder or gunpowder undoubtedly saved many lives on this occasion as it had done earlier that century, but the invention of high explosives and safe detonators would soon lead to its replacement.

The American Naval Expedition of 1879 led by Lieutenant De Long in the *Jeanette* was one of the first to take guncotton and electrical leads with which to detonate it on the ice, on what was to be an unsuccessful attempt to reach the North Pole. Beset in the ice almost before they had started, they attempted to blast the ship's rudder free of ice but failed owing to an electrical fault in their detonation equipment.

In the early 1880s the Dundee whaling captain Lofley, master of the *Eira* expedition with a crew of Dundonians, made use of guncotton. Leaving Dundee, they made their way via Svalbard and sailed north-east with the intention of penetrating the ice to land on the shores of Franz Josef Land. There, their private scientific expedition, under the leadership of Mr Leigh Smith, was hoping to find a land bridge to the North Pole. After several abortive attempts to find a lead of clear water the Dundonians eventually blasted their way through heavy pack ice and succeeded in reaching land. Later the *Eira*, a Peterhead whale ship, was crushed with most of the stores entombed in her hold. The men tried to blow a hole in the deck, just as De Long had done, but like him they could not get their detonators to work. Harry McKay had worked with Lofley out of Dundee in the Davis Straits but it is clear that Lofley did not have McKay's expert knowledge of the use of guncotton.

Fifteen years later, in 1895, Frederick Jackson's Arctic expedition reached Leigh Smith's base and, with his second-in-command Albert Armitage, he successfully experimented with guncotton in a temperature of minus 54 degrees Fahrenheit. He then spent several days on a blasting operation using small charges of two pounds to link up channels that they had cut with their ice saws and so freed their ship *Windward*. It is clear that the Dundee whaling captains came to use guncotton rather than black powder because of its waterproof and low temperature qualities. A low-freeze waterproof variety had been widely available since 1880 and, as these last examples show, it was proving to be effective for use under water as an explosive ideal for breaking ice.

A Scottish Boom

By the last quarter of the nineteenth century not only was nitro-cellulose taking over from black powder but Nobel's nitro-glycerine explosives were then taking over from nitro-cellulose (guncotton). Understandably perhaps, the term 'guncotton' began to be used loosely at this time to describe any of the new high explosives. From descriptions of the McKay blasting technique, which he evolved in the Arctic and employed later in the Antarctic, there is reliable evidence that he was using guncotton *sensu stricto* for breaking up the ice because the high explosive not only had greater power than black powder, it also had special properties with which he had become familiar. It is clear to an explosives expert that McKay had a considerable knowledge of the techniques of blasting ice and had discovered a proven method of his own.

The technique was to use either 16 or 35-pound explosive charges in sealed canisters and place these in a triangular pattern of three. They were wired in series and fired simultaneously with an electrical exploder. Whenever possible the canisters were placed in holes drilled right through the ice and so fired in the water underneath the ice, which had the effect of fracturing the surface by lifting up the whole mass. When the men of the blasting parties encountered the thicker ice they placed their charges in a hole which was made half way down to the waterlevel and the shothole was carefully stemmed. This had the effect of producing fractures radiating out from the hole. McKay used both techniques to achieve different effects and then he followed this up by butting the fractured areas with his ship to open up the cracks. He also fired three englacial charges in one pattern and three submerged charges in a different pattern, which mystified his onlookers.

By the time that Sir Clements Markham was thinking about sending an expedition to the South Polar regions, Captain Harry McKay had already earned his reputation for the spectacular use of guncotton. The whaling captain's baptism of fire had begun by freeing the *Resolute*. He then took part in the ill-organised American rescue of the 1881–84 Greely Expedition along with other Dundee ships. In their first rescue bid in 1883 the main relief ship *Proteus* was lost with all her stores. The other whalers were beset but eventually managed to blast themselves free. On 22nd June, the Dundee whalers *Bear* and *Thesis* rescued the six survivors of the U. S. Arctic outpost. The Greely Expedition had established a new furthest north record but at a cost of nearly twenty lives. One of the rescued died on the way home. Such feats and tragedies as these were just a part of the everyday life of a Dundee whaling captain and his crew.

But Nobel and McKay had more in common than a knowledge of high explosives: they were peace-loving, practical men who disliked publicity.

CHAPTER FIVE

Discovery's Officers and Gentlemen

Commander Robert Falcon Scott

Scott was born in Devonshire in 1868 and was projected from a sheltered Victorian childhood into the Royal Naval College at the tender age of thirteen. There he proved to be a good student and soon climbed the promotion ladder to the rank of lieutenant. His future prospects then began to look less bright. He was an unobtrusive yet very ambitious officer, a difficult combination which induced him to try specialising, first in torpedoes (introduced to the world by the Russian navy when Scott was just two years old) and then in the time-honoured peace-time road to promotion of polar exploration. Polar travel was then a naval specialism, equivalent to abseiling today which, as everyone who has ever been on a proper management course knows, is an absolutely infallible test of a young person's character and has the great advantage that what it teaches can be transferred immediately from the outward bound training course to the relevance of the director's desk, or any other real-life situation.

It was characteristic of the cult of amateurism of the early Edwardian age that Commander Robert Falcon Scott, on his own admission, had no knowledge of, or interest in, techniques of polar exploration or mountaineering nor, initially, did the majority of the officers and men of the Royal Navy who were selected to serve with him on the National Antarctic Expedition of 1901–04. When one realises that this was not just an oversight but was fundamental to Sir Clements Markham's entire selection policy it is truly amazing that there were as many as three men in Scott's team who did possess some relevant experience of travelling safely and survival techniques in snow and ice conditions.

Scott's sole motive for wanting to lead the 1901–04 expedition despite the nuisance of this complete lack of relevant experience for the job, was the furtherance of his own naval career. This partly explains why, had he been left to his own devices, he would have picked only men of the Royal Navy, men who would understand completely what was at stake and what was required of them. Scott shared with Markham a worry that if someone like Professor Gregory was given control, civilian scientists would completely take over and run the show once the expedition was on terra firma. They had quickly to establish the fact that a naval hierarchy of rank would determine who went where and with whom, without having to decide on anything as complicated and inflexible as a work programme. Nowhere was this more obvious than during the expedition's first winter when, instead of making up for their lack of relevant polar skills, the main outdoor pursuit for everyone, with the exception of a few dedicated scientists, was football on ice.

An objective observer might be forgiven for thinking that the greatest mystery of the expedition was why Robert Falcon Scott was ever allowed to lead it. Even Scott's most sycophantic biographers list a chapter of his greatest shortcomings – his physical weakness, his indolent and lethargic ways, his volcanic temper, his capriciousness and violent mood changes. The evidence for these traits comes principally from members of his family but his biographers deftly sweep them all away at a stroke by explaining that by attending Royal Naval College he was knocked into shape. He became an administrative genius with a brilliant talent for organisation, developed a God-fearing love of justice, an affection for his subordinates, and a concern for their welfare that was positively saintly. In adulthood any lingering faults, we are told, were not his real self or, if they were, they were the result of indigestion. Apparently he met disaster with a smile, though how his biographers know this is quite difficult to explain.

Discovery was built in Dundee and was launched in 1901 on March 21st but she did not leave England until 23 weeks later, for one had to be seen at Cowes. When the ship eventually reached McMurdo Sound, *Discovery* followed the route of Sir James Clark Ross, although, being steam powered, *Discovery* was able to approach much more closely to the continent's ice cliffs than Ross's ships *Erebus* and *Terror* had done. On January 31st 1902 Scott turned back to spend the summer searching for the place where Markham had told him to winter. This was a serious drawback of over-wintering that had not really been thought through. The journeys of exploration would have to wait until next season, beginning in the spring of September 1902. Wintering the ship would produce other problems but on March 28th she was finally secured and *Discovery* was at last nicely iced-in. Before the sun disappeared on 23rd April new mountain peaks had been sighted, and by the end of the 1903 season 200 peaks had been named with much diplomacy. This was a considerable achievement.

Scott hinted that he only intended to stay for the following year (the season from September 1902 to January 1903) and some officers felt sure that he was planning to return to Lyttelton in New Zealand sometime between February and March 1903 and was bound to make his plans known to them. If this was the case the plan was soon altered by two unexpected events, first that *Discovery* would not budge from the ice and second, that the South Pole was not so easy to 'conquer' as he first thought and would require some further attempts. Thus it happened that Scott came to plan with his closest confidant, Edward Wilson, to return to Lyttelton in March 1905 at the earliest, but not to let others into his secret yet. The official line was that he was only going to spend one winter in the South before returning via New Zealand, and this was the message that was allowed to reach the outside world when the relief ship *Morning* came in 1903 to bring news and take news away.

Lieutenant Albert Armitage

One of the few members on the *Discovery* expedition with relevant polar experience had been on the 1894-7 Jackson-Harmsworth Polar Expedition to Franz Josef Land, a desperately remote area that features prominently in polar history. He was Lieutenant Albert Armitage. In addition to spending one thousand days in the Arctic, during which he proved his considerable leadership qualities, he had considerable navigation experience with the P & O Line.

Although Armitage was not a Royal Navy officer, he figured somewhere in the middle echelons of the Edwardian caste system – he would certainly have been rather less acceptable had he come from any other lower sector of the Merchant Navy. As recently as World War II the Merchant Navy was not always appreciated and its members were often considered to be social outcasts by 'the senior service', so it is not surprising to find in 1902 a conflict between expedition members who were Royal Navy and those who were Merchant Navy, and Scott, lacking leadership skills, was the first to admit that he preferred naval personnel so that he could pull rank in order to maintain discipline and respect for gold braid.

Armitage was second-in-command, a fine navigator on land and sea. He clearly revelled in the challenge of charting a passage for *Discovery* and was an ideal choice to trace the extent of the shelf ice, continuing the work of Ross. *Discovery* began working along that 'impregnable coastline' of high sheer ice cliffs (which Borchgrevink had succeeded in finding a way through). For a brief period they were nearly locked in the ice going round in circles, after which they retraced their route. It was a strange way to start and, tragically, Armitage's experience was seldom called upon.

Armitage was interested in finding a way into the Antarctic interior as a possible route to the South Geomagnetic Pole, since science was a major objective of the expedition. So he was allowed to make a great sledge journey in December 1902 and January 1903 which proved to be the most competent of all the journeys made by the expedition: he discovered the western route to the Polar Plateau, but his reward was the threat of being sent home early with Shackleton and all the other Merchant Navy men when the relief ship *Morning* located *Discovery* in January 1903. However, Armitage refused to leave, was saved by his contract, and stayed on. For thwarting this great Royal Navy plan he was punished by being confined to duties around the ship, though on one occasion he was allowed to go on what Scott described as an 'excellent little journey' made while his Commander went off in November 1903 to 'discover' Armitage's route to the Polar Plateau, properly this time. This tragic lack of appreciation of his abilities left Armitage embittered for the rest of his life.

Dr. Reginald Koettlitz and Louis Bernacchi

The second man with polar and ski-ing experience was the civilian, Dr Reginald Koettlitz. He had good medical advice to offer about the avoidance of scurvy, since he was responsible for keeping the Jackson-Harmsworth Polar Expedition fit for four years through the long periods of winter darkness. Koettlitz was nevertheless ordered by Scott to open every tin of food to see if it was 'tainted'. Because he found nothing wrong with the tinned food (other than the fact that it *was* tinned food) one writer has accused him, with the mad logic of Lewis Carroll's White Knight, of being responsible for the scurvy outbreaks on the Southern Journey. His must have been a tiresome duty in view of his knowledge and experience, for it was Koettlitz and Armitage who cured the outbreak in October 1902, and they even grew cress on the ship.

The third expedition member to have had polar experience was Louis Bernacchi. He was one of that select band of ten men who were the first to winter in the Antarctic in huts in 1899. The leading member of the scientific staff studying magnetism and gravity, he supervised the erection of pre-fabricated huts designed in Australia for housing instruments, but in attempting to keep a constant temperature in the huts, he used much fuel oil, which was frowned upon. Significantly it was Bernacchi and Armitage who with four crew members made the first of the expedition's sorties from the ship into the interior of the continent on 3rd February 1902. Bernacchi made other important journeys east and south-east of the ship.

The Learning Curve

Despite this polar expertise in the ship's company in March 1902, the expedition's 'first' sledge journey was not exactly a display of mountain craft. In the words of Scott 'our ignorance was deplorable'.[23]

Four men who were competent on skis went with nine who had no skis. Two men in the second team didn't have boots suitable for walking in snow, let alone on ice cliffs. Five days out from the ship, the weaker team was sent back with the least experienced leader, with neither ropes, ice axes, crampons, nor compass. They had tents but could not melt snow and prepare hot food, or quench their thirst – all for the want of a primus pricker, that half an inch of wire necessary to keep the stove's jet clean. Prime candidates for hypothermia, they got lost on an ice cliff as blizzard conditions descended. Tragically, Able Seaman Vince fell to his death into the sea and the youngest, Clarence Hare, disappeared from sight to reappear, ghost-like, thirty-six hours later when everyone had given him up for lost. His companions were not equipped in any sense to mount even a relatively simple mountain search party. This was the legacy of Clements Markham's staff selection policy.

Hartley Ferrar and Thomas Vere Hodgson

The other four missing men were found by one of the most competent explorers on the *Discovery* expedition, a man sent out from the ship by Armitage who recognised his worth early on in the expedition. This was the young Cambridge geologist, Hartley Ferrar. Although this was Ferrar's first polar expedition, he proved himself to be an experienced mountain man. He knew more about the glacial terrain in which *Discovery* was trapped and about the nature of snow, ice and glaciers than most of his fellows. Scott was amazed that one so young could know so much more than his Commander about the place in which they now both found themselves:

> It is a curious fact that I rarely meet Ferrar in my walks and yet cannot speak of any feature of the numerous hill-slopes without finding out that he knows it well.[24]

This is one of the oddest passages in Scott's writings, for it reveals that our strict disciplinarian of a Commander frequently seemed to have no idea where his men were during the ship's stay in McMurdo Sound, and even in winter darkness men went off on skis for hours at a time without reporting where they intended to go, or when they might be thinking of coming back.

Armitage realised that a knowledge of geology and glaciology was not

---

23. Robert Falcon Scott, *The Voyage of the Discovery* (1905), Vol.I,Ch.VI, p. 229.
24. Robert Falcon Scott, *The Voyage of the Discovery* (1905), Vol.I,Ch.VIII, p. 314.

simply an academic pursuit but had great practical value when it came to travelling safely on glaciers and through glaciated mountains. He picked Ferrar and Skelton to help him find the way to the high altitude Polar Plateau. It was guarded by a wall of very impressive mountains, with the only breaches in the wall's defences made by valley glaciers debouching steeply from the 9000-feet high plateau down to sea level in less than fifty miles. Naturally they found the glacier heavily crevassed. On their return, in appreciation of Ferrar's work, the glacier which they had successfully ascended was named after him.

The expedition biologist, Thomas Vere Hodgson, came from the Marine Biological Association's laboratories in Plymouth where he was a research worker. Later he became curator of Plymouth Museum. On the voyage he attempted to trawl the oceans but complained that the officers of the Royal Navy made his work impossible; consequently his main contribution was not to oceanography. He had an exhausting time for the duration of the expedition. Wintering at McMurdo Sound, he was delighted to find that he could trawl beneath the sea ice in what was arguably one of the most unpleasant of all the scientific tasks. So intent on his work was Hodgson that when fishing for invertebrate specimens down holes in the ice floes he had been observed to float out to sea – too engrossed in his fishing hole to notice what was happening to him until he was retrieved. But he was not the only one who needed rescuing.

Dr. Edward Wilson and Lieutenant Ernest Shackleton

Dr Edward Wilson was a vertebrate zoologist and water-colour artist responsible for a series of beautiful paintings of animals, landscapes and aurora phenomena in the Antarctic executed under conditions which were hardly conducive to painting in water-colour. Wilson was picked by Scott to accompany him and Shackleton on the Southern Journey, the first polar attempt made between November 1902 and February 1903. Wilson also played an important social role which today we should call psychological counselling, a function much valued by his colleagues on the 1901–1904 expedition.

Sub-Lieutenant Ernest Shackleton was another Merchant Navy officer but, unlike Armitage, he was not the quietly efficient discoverer of routes up glaciers but more the dashing type of leader who inspires absolute confidence in his men, as he showed so brilliantly on his own Antarctic expeditions in later years. The epic of Shackleton's 1914-16 *Endurance* expedition is a classic in the annals of Antarctic history. When his ship was crushed in the ice, he led his men to safety across 800 miles of ocean in a flimsy whaler and traversed the formidable mountains of South Georgia to get help. This was the man that Scott sent home with most of the Merchant navy men and civilians when Colbeck brought the relief ship *Morning* in 1903 (scientists could not be sent home, it was against the rules). Scott said that he could only work with men of the Royal Navy for he wanted to exercise tight disciplinary control, and even though it was a private and not an official naval expedition he nevertheless decided to live, 'exactly as though the ship and all on board had been under the Naval Discipline Act'.[25] The fact that the career of everyone on the expedition was to some extent dependent on a good testimonial helped to ensure obedience. On the mess deck punishments, mad chores and inane routines were imposed on the men. Over-ambitious officers, however, presented a more formidable problem and had to be 'invalided' home.

The excuse for sending Shackleton back was that he had suffered from scurvy returning from the Southern Journey when Scott, Wilson and Shackleton made their unsuccessful bid for the Pole. But all three men on this journey suffered from scurvy. Indeed almost all of the men on *Discovery* suffered from scurvy at some time. Furthermore, Scott had just claimed that the disease had been eliminated and everyone was now fit. Dr Coplan's Tainted Food Theory had been forgotten whilst Scott was away and Armitage and Koettlitz were able to effect their Franz Josef Land Expedition cure of fresh meat. Sending just one invalid home gave the impression that this was the act of a Commander who showed more concern for his officers and men than for the conquest of the Pole. It also just happened to imply that the 'invalid' had held them up and explained why they had not reached the Pole. But Ernest Shackleton was no more an invalid than his companions.

Lieutenants Michael Barne and Charles Royds

Little has been recorded about Lieutenant Michael Barne. He was a family friend of Sir Clements Markham and had served under Scott on HMS *Majestic*. He assisted Bernacchi with the magnetic observations both in the field and the huts and he carried out a scheme for measuring sea temperatures at various depths. He received no encouragement from his scientific director who, writing of the temperature study, observed:

it is doubtful if it even possesses the advantage of being useful.[26]

25. Robert Falcon Scott, *The Voyage of the Discovery* (1905), Vol.I,Ch.VII, p. 76.
26. Robert Falcon Scott, *The Voyage of the Discovery* (1905) Vol.I,Ch.VIII, p. 314.

Barne's best work was in helping Mulock make a topographical survey in the summer of 1903 on a journey through the pressure ridges south-west of the ship which lasted over two months and encountered a period of very low temperatures which made such work very difficult.

Lieutenant Charles Royds was an experienced young naval officer. He proved himself to be an important link-man on the expedition, liaising between officers and men. This was a role which Shackleton had performed extremely well until early 1903 when the relief ship took him away. Royds filled the gap in the second winter . He was allowed to lead several sledge journeys and, with Skelton, made important discoveries of Adélie and Emperor Penguin rookeries at Cape Crozier. But his finest effort was his thirty-day journey in the summer of 1903 south-east from the ship over the Ice Barrier which he proved was an unbroken shelf. He was also responsible for setting up the 'record post' on Cape Crozier which was found by Captain Colbeck in the relief ship *Morning* and confirmed the whereabouts of the *Discovery* in January 1903.

Royds was the only naval officer on the expedition to be put in charge of a major section of the scientific work, namely the meteor-ology. This required regular two-hourly readings between 10 am and 8 pm. It was a strain on him as his other duties frequently put him under considerable pressure, and in these conflicting loyalties he found himself writing letters to Scott asking to be released from mundane chores and given some time to work on his scientific results. In the event it was the meteorology which suffered, through no fault of his. Amongst his other pursuits Royds played the piano well, which he did each evening before dinner, smoothing over 'many a ruffle'. Later he was responsible for the Royal Navy's main contribution to freeing *Discovery* from the grip of ice. Royds displayed common sense in everything he tackled. Conscious of the folly of an order to take the boats off the *Discovery* and put them onto the ice (whereupon they sank under the weight of the winter snowfall), it was Royds who saw the importance of digging them out quickly.

Lieutenants Reginald Skelton and George Mulock

Like Barne, Lieutenant Reginald Skelton had served with Scott on HMS *Majestic* where he was senior engineer. Scott secured his services as Chief Engineer on *Discovery* and praised his work on the machinery. He was also very capable with a half plate camera and, as expedition photographer, produced some very fine pictures which deserve to be better known. Skelton was competent on snow and ice and a good skier but as a mere engineer he did not enjoy sufficient status in the navy to be honoured to lead one of the sledge journeys. His duties were those of a general dogsbody amongst officers. In the words of his superior officer:

> every officer in every department has had need sooner or later to solicit his services . . . the work varies from the roughest to the most delicate task; without [his] mechanical skill we should have been hopelessly at sea, and it is not too much to say that the majority of our scientific observations would have been brought to a standstill.[27]

His finest and happiest achievement was the journey with Armitage to the west seeking a route to the Plateau. When the journey was repeated by Scott in the next season it was Skelton and not Armitage who was invited to come along to guide Scott on the route up the glacier and take over the second sledge party. Skelton's team understandably 'broke down' (a condition which ought to have been diagnosed as altitude sickness resulting from their not having been on as many journeys to acclimatise as had Scott's team). For failing to keep up with the Commander's sledge, disciplinary action was taken and they were, of course, sent back to the ship but fortunately they were still in the care of Skelton.

George Mulock was the 21-year-old Royal Navy sub-lieutenant who replaced Shackleton in 1903. As a qualified surveyor serving under Colbeck on the relief ship *Morning* he volunteered to transfer to *Discovery* for the coming winter. He was immediately pressed into service making charts for the expedition survey data. It was maps rather than Pole-bagging that Markham wanted and, knowing this, Scott approved of his work and said he could now see

> much more clearly what we ought to try to do during our next sledging season.[28]

Mulock went on two sledge journeys. The first was south-east of the ship to White Island in extremely cold conditions with temperatures down to minus 70 Fahrenheit. The second was to Barne Inlet where he experienced gales but succeeded in measuring the rate of movement of the ice shelf, a considerable achievement.

27. Robert Falcon Scott, *The Voyage of the Discovery* (1905), Vol.I,Ch.VIII, p. 315; and Vol.I,Ch.XVI, p. 193.
28. Robert Falcon Scott, *The Voyage of the Discovery* (1905), Vol.I,Ch.VIII, p. 315; and Vol.I,Ch.XVI, p. 193.

All the Others

Depending on how you do the sums, between forty-nine and eighty served on the *Discovery* expedition. The smaller figure represents those who feature in Scott's book; it includes the seven officers and five scientists and the two men who died (Bonner and Vince). The other figure comes from the researches of A. G. E. Jones and it includes men who were sent back at varying stages, including six naval ratings: Baker, Macfarlane, Page, Peters, Reid and Waterman; and thirteen Merchant Navy officers and men and civilians: Brett, Duncan, Dowsett, Hare, Hubert, Mills, Miller, Masterdon, Mardon, Roper, Shackleton, Walker, and Sinclair who jumped ship, plus two Chief Scientists: Professor J. Gregory (who resigned) and George Murray (who was discharged in 1901). By April 1903 only two Merchant Navy men remained (Armitage and Weller). Two civilians (Buckridge and Job Clark) had been sent off and another cook (Charles Clarke) clung on. All of which makes interesting percentages for those with a statistical bent, whichever of these figures is taken as correct.[29]

Scott, following the caste system of the Edwardian Age, in his published account of the expedition, *The Voyage of the Discovery*, described the officers and scientists in his ship's company in detail. Then followed a brief mention of all the Warrant Officers (Thomas Feather the Boatswain was adept at working on sails and sledges, James Dellbridge, Second Engineer, was praised for his work on the engines, Fred Dailey, a carpenter, had worked on the construction of the ship in Dundee, and steward Charles Ford kept track of all the stores on board with his excellent book keeping). Scott mentioned four of the six Petty Officers who were chosen from his Channel Squadron colleagues, two men who had served with him on HMS *Majestic* (Edgar Evans and David Allan) and men who were recommended to him by officers who had sailed with him in that squadron (Jacob Cross and William Smythe). Petty Officer Thomas Kennar gets scant mention. Amongst the six stokers he singled out two: William Lashly, who made their footwear safer, and Arthur Quartley, who had also sailed with Scott before, but stokers Frank Plumley and Thomas Whitfield are mentioned for their ability to smoke a pipe or improvise a biscuit tin oven at very low temperatures.

From the sixteen ordinary seamen he picked four for honours (Thomas Crean, Ernest Joyce, Frank Wild and William Heald). The first three became famous because of their association with Shackleton. Heald was the unsung hero of *Discovery*, appearing at critical moments, picked by Armitage to go on his longest journeys, and later proving himself a key man in the 1904

29. Correspondence with A.G.E.Jones 1997.

rescue. Scott's book also names Arthur Blissett, George Croucher, James Dell, Jesse Handsley, Arthur Pilbream, Gilbert Scott and, last but not least, Thomas Williamson, a seaman who kept a diary which was critical of his leader but who found the pay good and despite everything volunteered for another Scott expedition in 1910.

CHAPTER SIX

Discovery's Expedition Achievements

The Conquest of the Pole Begins

It is not easy to understand the two years of sledge journeys undertaken by the expedition, some thirty in number. If one assumes that the objective of the 1901–04 expedition was to conquer the South Pole, then the great Southern Journey made by Scott, Shackleton and Wilson was the first attempt ever made to reach the South Geographical Pole. Although the true objective of the expedition was clearly to find a route south, the official object was supposed be scientific. In this case one would expect the sledge journeys to be planned radiating out from the base in all directions, and initially one would not expect to find any particular direction being more favoured than any other unless it had some scientific value.

Most of us have never made journeys remotely like any of those made by the men of this expedition and few of us have ever wanted to, but none would dispute that what they all did was certainly epic. The Southern Journey across the coastal shelf ice confirmed the fact that the great mountain barrier ran south towards the Pole with glaciers which appeared to offer the experienced mountaineers a safe way onto the high plateau of the interior. But their journey did not ascend a glacier to that plateau on which the Pole is situated and it faced few of the hazards that Scott had to contend with on his second expedition of 1910/13 when he successfully reached the Pole by ascending the Beardmore Glacier.

Two other long sea ice journeys were made which are not so well known. Barne sledged to the mountain front where he saw a major glacier, and he journeyed there and back in two months. Royds made the last of these three traverses on the shelf-ice in one month, and by striking out in a south-east direction he confirmed the nature of the Great Barrier.

There was a second quite different type of sledge journey, the sort of high mountain exploration that Martin Conway and the Duke of Abruzzi had perfected in the glaciers of the Karakoram and the Arctic. Armitage, Koettlitz, Skelton, Ferrar, Allan and Macfarlane pooled practical knowledge of glaciers and glaciological theory to find a route from McMurdo Sound and they discovered the high Polar Plateau by ascending the Ferrar Glacier. It was a splendid piece of mountaineering sledging over highly crevassed glaciers in just fifty days – it may not have been breakneck speed but they were not trying to break necks. Theirs was a feat which deserved a place in the annals of Antarctic exploration but it didn't get one because the following year when Scott repeated Armitage's route to the Polar Plateau, taking Skelton and Ferrar with him to lead him up the Ferrar Glacier, he claimed the route as his finest achievement. The leaders of both these journeys fell into crevasses: Armitage's account is an honest description of a mountaineering event, Scott's narrative of his escape from a crevasse is pure "Boy's Own Paper".

The Other Journeys

The third type of sledge journey had nothing to do with conquest, with epic deeds, pitting macho strength against the elements or steep gradients, and nothing to do with having adventures or character-building. It was the relatively short sledge journey from the ship to explore the nature of McMurdo Sound: its frozen shoreline and tidal ice forms, its fascinating volcanic landscapes of cones and vents, the life of the rookeries of Emperor and Adélie Penguins, marine mammal species and its invertebrate marine fauna – teeming life that populated this apparently dead land. All around them was a mountain backdrop of geological fascination. The duration of their journeys was mostly one week out and one week back but, as most parties were accompanied by scientists who on arrival at a destination were not keen simply to retrace their steps immediately, they often lasted an additional week. They were, with one exception, very much less hazardous than the long epic journeys because they were never far from the coastal habitats where the Weddell Seals provided fresh meat and so scurvy was not a problem. Nevertheless, they required just as much sledging skill as the long journeys, sometimes more.

Sadly, the first of these shorter trips was taken by an inexperienced leader: the March 1902 journey to Cape Crozier which led to the death of Vince and to Hare's very close shave. After this things improved greatly. Royds and Skelton, sometimes with and sometimes without Dr. Wilson, made Cape Crozier their speciality. Ferrar built up his expert knowledge of the surrounding islands and never missed an opportunity to commission the men of other parties to bring him geological specimens. Koettlitz explored the far side of Minna Bluff, then walked round White, Black and Brown Islands and probably knew the McMurdo winter quarters coast as well as Ferrar, though they could not explore in the winter. Armitage went off with Wilson and Heald to the Koettlitz and Blue Glaciers and explored New Harbour Glacier.

These relatively short journeys were seen by some as reconnaissance for the important long journeys but they were regarded by the scientists as the more important journeys of discovery and would certainly have been viewed as such by Clements Markham. To underline the point, Dr Wilson, on being honoured by an invitation to join Scott and Shackleton on their great Southern Journey, asked why he was being taken further away each day from his main areas of interest, expertise, and indeed of discovery. He openly expressed the view that the expedition's aim should not have been to reach the South Pole, which makes it all the more odd that he allowed himself to be taken polewards in 1902 and that he volunteered to join Scott's second expedition of 1910-13 to the Pole from which neither of them returned.

Louis Bernacchi's Magnetism Studies

Ever since the earliest use of lodestone, the study of magnetism has been associated with navigation. In 1600 William Gilbert published a book on the subject, *De Magnete*, in which he claimed that the whole earth was a magnet, a prediction which was some four hundred years ahead of his time. The geomagnetic poles 'wander' from place to place and ships have been wrecked as a result of miscalculations, so the British navy was concerned to determine the exact position of the magnetic poles.

The whole subject was elevated to a new mathematical plane in 1839 by the German physicist Gauss. He made the Dip Needle which measured the strength of a magnetic field. Sir James Clark Ross who, with his uncle Sir John Ross, had already reached the North Geomagnetic Pole in 1831, began at once to prepare an expedition to the South Geomagnetic Pole (it was anticipated by the Frenchman D'Urville and the American Wilkes in 1840 but the Pole wasn't reached until 1909 by Douglas Mawson's party). Oddly, Scott showed no interest in this particular Pole, even though it was the 1840 discoveries of Ross and his deputy Crozier that led to Markham's interest in McMurdo Sound as the base for Scott. Indeed, the Geomagnetic Pole was nearer to the *Discovery*'s winter quarters than the Geographical Pole. Markham colluded with William Colbeck, who was a magnetic observer in Borchgrevink's expedition, in order to confirm the suitability of the winter quarters.

Armitage's discovery of the Polar Plateau was related to his interest and experience in magnetism and navigation but he was not equipped to press on to the Magnetic Pole. Stranger still, Markham's choice of the expedition's winter quarters was partly because the admirals of the Royal Geographical Society and the scientists of the Royal Society had at last agreed on one thing – the importance of magnetic studies.

Bernacchi, who joined *Discovery* as physicist at Lyttelton, knew that the earth's magnetic field was produced by the planet's rotation similar to that of a dynamo generating an electric field with north and south poles. He knew the aurora was an electrical phenomenon but didn't know that it is caused by the magnetic attraction of particles from space which enter our ionosphere's gases 100 to 200 miles up and cause them to glow in the way that neon light tubes do. Oxygen produces green and red, nitrogen produces violet, aurora. Since Bernacchi's work with the Barrow Dip Compass the instruments used to study magnetism have become more sophisticated and his work is now only of historical interest. The International Geophysical Year of 1957-58 led to the discovery of belts where solar particles are concentrated. Antarctic research then looked at ozone levels and in 1981 the 'hole' in the ionosphere was discovered. An area of *Discovery* had an all-wood and non-ferrous metal specification to accommodate a magnetism laboratory but Bernacchi also had his prefabricated building from Australia.

Ferrar and Geological Science

Ferrar was the father of Antarctic geology. He was a newly graduated Cambridge geologist. His discoveries were remarkable, having a relevance that extended beyond the Antarctic to encompass aspects of what has become known as the global theory of plate tectonics. This is the concept that our planet is made up of continental 'plates' which have drifted towards each other (folding the intervening ocean sediments into great mountain ranges), slid under each other (resulting in parts of the crust melting at depth and giving rise to fringes of volcanoes), or have drifted apart (producing volcanic outpourings in the middle of the oceans in the shape of oceanic island ridges). Ferrar recognised the importance of the different geological ingredients of the Transantarctic Mountains. First, an ancient basement (grey gneiss, metamorphic limestone and schist, intrusions of pink and grey granite); second, resting on this core, sedimentary rocks that he named the Beacon Sandstones (sandstones and arkose); third, these rocks injected by contemporary intrusions of liquid rock (dolerite) which we now associate with the first stage of break-up of a Southern Super Continent (meaning that South America, South Africa, Australia, New Zealand, Eastern and Western Antarctica were all the one great continent of Gondwanaland 180 million years ago).

Twenty years after Ferrar's work Alfred Wegener suggested that the continents 'fitted together' and showed geological similarities on either side of the fit. Later, Alexander du Toit's book *Our Wandering Continents* showed how Ferrar's Beacon Sandstone matched South Africa's Karroo Beds.

Professor Gregory shed light on these processes, working in the African Rift Valley. In 1950 Arthur Holmes explained the mechanism of earth movement, and Bruce Heezen's work on the geology of the ocean floors contributed further proof, but it took another decade before the sequence of plate tectonic movement was properly understood.

Ferrar is known for his discovery of plant fossils in the Beacon Sandstone. What he found represented a warmer climate. The study of fossils was his specialism but his contribution to volcanic geology was also important. He recognised lavas which had reached the surface when it was covered by ice, resulting in the strange tuff palagonite. He knew exactly where all the active vents were situated and was the only member of the expedition to climb on Mount Erebus with a true appreciation of the volcano's scale. In early November 1903, accompanying Scott to the Plateau to help with yet another epic journey, he was unexpectedly released with Weller and Kennar and he could scarcely conceal his enthusiasm:

> I found I had a month in which to examine 600 square miles of new country and get back to the ship by December 12th![30]

The Biological Studies of Thomas Vere Hodgson

Hodgson's biological work in McMurdo Sound was carried out in all seasons by trawling under the ice, drawing a net between two adjacent holes to collect specimens of invertebrates of a sea teeming with life which was invisible to most members of the expedition until he revealed it. It was a chore which he preferred to carry out alone, and in the Antarctic winter he must have been amongst the most dedicated of all the scientists. The sheer amount of work Hodgson achieved was incredible. Of the ten published volumes of the *Discovery* Expedition's Scientific Reports, Hodgson's extensive biological collections were written up in five books by no fewer than thirty-two scientists, though much of his work was later lost in London. The comprehensiveness can be appreciated from his invertebrate reports:

SPONGES, JELLYFISH, CORALS, SEA URCHINS, SEA LILIES, STARFISH, PARASITIC WORMS, SPIDER CRABS, AMPHIPODS, CRUSTACEA, PLANKTON, POLYCHAETE WORMS AND SEA SQUIRTS.

In addition to invertebrates Hodgson also collected fish specimens but his specialism was spider crabs. He published nine papers on them and became

30. Hartley Ferrar Antarctic Diary, entry for 12 October 1903.

the recognised authority. What had begun with the oceanographic work of the voyage of the *Challenger* which surveyed the marine life of the oceans of the world between 1872 and 1874 was continued by Hanson and Evans on the *Southern Cross* 1898 British Antarctic Expedition of which Louis Bernacchi was a member. The work culminated in the researches of William Speirs Bruce's Scottish Antarctic Expedition of 1902-04 on the *Scotia*.

Bernacchi and Armitage had gone to great lengths to co-operate with scientists in South Africa, Australia, New Zealand and Germany to ensure that their magnetic results were compatible and Hodgson was also much aware of the value of international co-operation. On his return he compared his work with the findings of Borchgrevink's zoologists, Nicolai Hanson and Hugh Evans, and with William Speirs Bruce. However, Hodgson's work was frustrated by what he called 'naval hands' and the inconvenience of siting his laboratory within thirty feet of the magnetic observatory. He could not use enamelled apparatus and had to take glassware, much of which was broken on the voyage. His oceanography always conflicted with magnetic work as trawling required an iron gallows. He found that siting the lab on the upper deck rendered it useless for nine months of the year. However, his studies of animal plankton were an early investigation of the food web of these surprisingly rich waters and since the ecological sciences were in their infancy this makes his work particularly interesting. The modern ecological work of the British Antarctic Survey now concentrates on studies of the plankton in the Southern Ocean ecosystem and how organisms adapt metabolically to life at low temperatures.

Dr. Edward Wilson and Vertebrate Zoology

Dr Edward Wilson listed six species of whales and dolphins in the Ross Sea area, the Orca or Killer Whale, Dusky and what he called the Hour Glass Dolphin, the Blue Whale or Rorqual, Finner and Beaked. He observed four seal species – Crab Eater, Ross, Weddell, Sea Leopard. He recorded the accidental occurrence of a Sea Elephant, a seal species which he had seen in its native Macquarrie Islands. Wilson's bird list included the Giant, Snow and Wilson's Stormy Petrels, the Southern and Antarctic Fulmar, McCormick's Skua, the Black-browed Albatross, Blue-grey Whale Bird, and lastly (but for Wilson the most important birds) the Adélie and Emperor Penguins. It was Skelton and Marine Blissett who discovered the Emperor Penguin rookery on Cape Crozier in October 1902, and Wilson and Royds then paid further visits. The most famous visit of all to this rookery took place in Scott's final expedition when Wilson, Bowers and Cherry-Garrard sledged through winter darkness to observe the Emperor Penguins incubating eggs. Apsley

Cherry-Garrard's book about this appalling sledge journey of 1911, entitled *The Worst Journey in the World*, is a fitting epitaph to the scientific zeal of Wilson.

Wilson's vertebrate zoology research stood the test of time, and his work on whales, seals and penguins is still cited in population studies. He also pioneered animal behaviour studies, though his descriptions are often anthropomorphic. For example, he wrote that seals

> use language unfit for publication, flash their eyes in anger, gaze upwards in perfect rhapsody!

Notwithstanding all this, his accurate observation and his meticulously detailed water-colour paintings won Wilson the position of one of the last great nineteenth century-style natural historians. He would have been at home voyaging with Cook, collecting and painting specimens with Hooker, writing with Darwin and sketching landscapes with Darwin's illustrator Martens. What is also true is that Wilson's work won him a place as one of the first modern observers of the biological sciences. In a curious way the sheer excellence of Wilson's water-colours has created the impression that his work belongs to the old descriptive style of a previous century and lacks the precision of modern science, which is not the case.

William Speirs Bruce's discoveries on *Scotia*, the National (Scottish) Antarctic Expedition of 1902-04, overshadowed both Hodgson's and Wilson's findings yet they cost the taxpayer nothing, for his expedition was funded by the textile firm of Coats, a fact which did not go unnoticed in the corridors of the Admiralty. Markham did his best to play down the achievements of the *Scotia*.

Scientific Successes

In the decade between 1892 and 1902 there was a spate of Antarctic expeditions all with some scientific aspirations or at least paying lip-service to science. There had been a partly successful 1892/93 Dundee Whaling Ship Expedition with William Speirs Bruce and other scientists, although Bruce was disappointed that he did not do more science; there was the unfortunate 1898/99 *Belgica* of de Gerlache which was locked in the ice for a year; there was the highly successful 'British' expedition on *Southern Cross* which had achieved some modest scientific aims between 1898 and 1900 and which paved the way for all later expeditions of this time; there was the disappointing 1902/03 German expedition of Von Drygalski on the *Gauss* which had been trapped in the ice; and there was the tragic loss of the ship *Antarctica* crushed in ice with dire consequences for the 1901/04 Swedish party of Nordenskjold which somehow managed to carry out a scientific programme against quite incredible odds. Then, just on the horizon, was William Speirs Bruce's own Scottish Antarctic Expedition on the *Scotia* which, when its ambitious scientific programme was finally written up, proved to be the most successful by far; however, nobody knew that when Scott was due to return to New Zealand, in 1904. And Markham in London could boast about his own expedition, making this extraordinary claim:

> it is conceded on all sides that the expedition has been most satisfactory and also has the honour to be the only Antarctic expedition to attain its objective.[31]

As scientific director, Scott did not seem to be very familiar with the work of his scientists, and with the single exception of Wilson, the Commander made disparaging remarks about them all. Dr. Hodgson had collected a large number of marine invertebrate species which Scott suggested were not likely to be of much interest, Scott thought that Ferrar was lazy and said that his geological work was a disappointment, Bernacchi he considered to be an idler and he said his work could not be expected to reveal anything new. Nor did their scientific director present their findings well. He preferred to say that Antarctica was so destitute of life forms that it would be wrong to expect too much from the scientists.

Later, Scott had to defend the expedition from attacks by the Physical Society of London and the press on the shortcomings of the meteorological work. It was noted that weather recording was the one subject which was not the responsibility of a qualified scientist. Scott had to give way but this fracas cast doubt on the other scientific work. Even today the view prevails that the expedition's results were poor, a conclusion unfair to Bernacchi, Ferrar, Hodgson and Wilson. It was not Hodgson's fault that his and Koettlitz's collections were lost by the national authorities in the remote wastes of London.

31. Success of the Expedition. Article in the *Press*, New Zealand, 2 April 1904.

CHAPTER SEVEN

A Fatal Mistake

Markham Buys a Bad Relief Ship and a Good Captain

Soon after the launch of *Discovery* Markham, with astonishing energy and perseverance, went immediately in search of a relief vessel for her. With typical obduracy and perversity he again turned his back on Dundee, rejecting a most generous offer from Robert Kinnes (the Dundee whaling firm) of the modern whaler *Diana* which already had a proven Antarctic record on the 1892/93 Dundee Expedition. Markham went to Wales on the advice of an old naval crony and then on to Norway.

Scott and Markham were unaware of Dundee's polar expertise. This had been evident from the way that they had gone about managing the building of Scott's ship. Markham went to Norway not to seek the skills of Colin Archer, designer of Nansen's *Fram*, but to buy one of the least functional whale ships ever to sail into Antarctic waters, the sealer *Morgenen*. The Glaswegian appointed to be her Chief Engineer fortunately had a richer sense of humour than any of his or Scott's shipmates, which was just as well. He said of the little ship:

> I cannot imagine what it would be like working through ice without engines because we can hardly get along with them and when they are stopped we are quite helpless.[32]

Markham persuaded the Royal Geograaphical Society to purchase *Morgenen* with the fruits of his appeal fund. She was indeed as wooden as any Stephen whale ship but as far as horse power was concerned she proved to be an embarrassment to the man who was appointed to sail her through the ice floes of the southern ocean, William Colbeck. At one point he said of her:

> Oh! Why won't this beastly ship go faster![33]

However, the choice of Colbeck was inspired. He was a first class seaman, albeit of the merchant classes but, like Armitage, he came from a reputable line and was no whaling captain. He was, however, a native of the whaling

---

32. J.D.Morrison Antarctic Diary, 12 Jan 1903.
33. William Colbeck Letter to Edith Robinson 30 Sept 1904.

port of Hull. He had gone to sea at the tender age of fifteen. He had been taught navigation by Headmaster Z. C. Skeaping of the Trinity House School in his home town and he began his career in 1885 in the Clipper *Loch Torridon* on the Calcutta run. He obtained all his certificates, including his Extra Masters Certificate, with speed and efficiency by 1896 at the age of 27 and by then had unrivalled experience on the oceans of the world, all of it gained under sail. So, still not thirty years of age, it is not surprising that Markham jumped at the opportunity.

Relief by the Morning

It was, ironically, his introduction to steam with the Wilson Line that completely changed Colbeck's life and introduced him to the ice of the Antarctic. The year was 1897 and Colbeck had never heard of Markham, Scott or their *Discovery* plans. But whilst serving on his first Wilson liner, on the run between Hull and Christiania (Oslo), Colbeck met the Norwegian explorer, Carsten Borchgrevink, who was a frequent passenger on Colbeck's ship the *Montebello*. Borchgrevink was in the throes of planning his *Southern Cross* Antarctic Expedition and he intended to land at Cape Adare and to be the first to winter on the continent. With extraordinary foresight he invited Colbeck to join his expedition as the navigating officer and magnetic observer. And so it came about that after only one year's service with his new employers, Wilson Ltd, Colbeck was given leave to join the *Southern Cross* British Antarctic Expedition of 1898-1900. Colbeck became one of ten men, including Borchgrevink and the physicist Louis Bernacchi, to winter intentionally on the White Continent.

By way of preparation Colbeck was sent on a course in magnetism at Kew Observatory under the direction of Dr Charles Chree and, judging by the meteorological and magnetic records of his work on the *Southern Cross* expedition, Colbeck was a better scientist than most. Indeed it was that same Dr Chree of Kew, President of the Physical Society of London, who would be the first to draw attention to the errors in Scott's scientific results in 1904. So, at long last, Markham had found an experienced seaman, a splendid navigator of Armitage's calibre, a fine leader, a scientist of considerable stature and a man far more deeply interested in polar exploration and far better versed in its ways than ever Scott was. But sadly it was two years too late.

In London Colbeck worked with Markham on the preparations for Scott's expedition before *Discovery* had departed, for Markham was quick to realise that on the *Southern Cross* expedition Colbeck had made a map of the Great Barrier and had suggested McMurdo Sound as possible winter quarters for an expedition. Colbeck and Bernacchi were able to brief the expedition about where to leave messages in canisters on six islands or promontories where Colbeck would then be able to find them and thus locate *Discovery*.

Morgenen was renamed *Morning* and Colbeck's relief ship set off on 9th July 1902, reaching Lyttelton on 16th November. On 6th December she sailed south to look for the expedition and experienced heavy floes and large icebergs. Without power in *Morning*'s engines to force a way forward, Colbeck had a rather rough time.

Searching the Tin Cans

Morning's company consisted of William Colbeck (Captain), R. G. England (Chief Officer), Lieutenant E. R. G. R. Evans RN (2nd Officer), Gerald Doorly (3rd Officer – another Merchant Navy man from the P & O Line), G. F. A. Mulock R. N. (4th Officer), G. A. Davidson (Surgeon), J. D. Morrison (Chief Engineer) and twenty (mostly anonymous) able seamen to stoke the boilers and mend the sails.

On 8th January 1903 they landed at Cape Adare, redolent of memories for Colbeck of the *Southern Cross*. This was the first agreed landing point where they found a message from *Discovery* but not one with information that fixed Scott's position. That message was found at the sixth locality, Cape Crozier, a week later where Royds had left it. So the Expedition's whereabouts in McMurdo Sound were located with amazing speed. Unfortunately *Morning* was then beset and took another week to round Ross Island. On 23rd January they sighted *Discovery* firmly iced-in by ten miles of sea ice. This great solid expanse wasted, but only very slowly.

Concerned at having found the *Discovery* beset by ice, Colbeck was more worried to learn that Scott was away sledging. In the Commander's absence he tried to persuade Armitage to start blasting the ice but all *Discovery*'s men had been convinced by Scott that the ice would go out of its own accord. Colbeck realised that this was a fatal mistake but it was obvious that everyone was under orders and it was clearly Scott's view that Armitage was voicing. Colbeck gave up and returned to his ship. The following week Scott returned to base and Colbeck again tried to

get some scheme afoot for releasing the Discovery[34]

– but Scott was too busy to see him. Another week went by and Colbeck again made the twenty-mile round trip over to *Discovery* on the same thankless errand, but this time it was now altogether too late and he

34. William Colbeck, letter to Edith Robinson, 11 March 1903.

approached the problem from a different angle – *Morning* could not afford to be iced in too! He could not rely on Scott's hunch that the ice would suddenly drift away and asked him for help in transferring stores without delay. Scott accepted the argument and Colbeck wryly observed:

> this is the best I could do as they all firmly believed that the ice would break away and were betting ten to one that they'd get to New Zealand before us.[35]

Colbeck had to depart without knowing where Scott would be if he did not make it back to New Zealand quickly and he had visions of having to perform another 'paper chase', as he called it, next season. It was typically inconsiderate, verging on the unprofessional.

What the Morning *Brings and Takes Away*

In forcing Colbeck to abandon his instructions from the Royal Geographical Society (which were to help free *Discovery* in 1903) Scott had shifted a heavy burden of responsibility onto the shoulders of the captain of the relief ship but had not thought through the consequences of his actions. What would their masters in London think when Colbeck came to send his report from Lyttelton? What would be the outcome of his decision to send a large party of men home on the *Morning*, as he now proposed? The most serious effect of his attempt to rid the expedition of all but the Royal Navy men was on the two officers concerned. Armitage simply refused to be sent home[36] and was a changed man from this time onwards, Armitage carried out orders to saw the ice with an almost zombie-like lack of interest. More problematical was the effect of dropping Shackleton, and this was certainly not thought through. Scott knew that Shackleton did not want to leave and that health was not a convincing excuse. There was a risk that the full story of Scott's shortcomings as a leader would reach their Lordships' ears in the Admiralty and at the Royal Geographical Society before Scott could give his own explanation. Shackleton was bound to be asked to account for his early return and would be quizzed about the full extent of the outbreak of scurvy. It was a most risky plan.

The arrival of the relief ship had brought welcome letters and fresh food. A depressed Armitage, now weary of his companions, consoled himself by going to see Colbeck and enjoyed 'a glorious spread of beef, mutton and potatoes!' It was there that he learned about something quite unexpected –

35. William Colbeck, letter to Edith Robinson, 11 March 1903.
36. Roland.Huntford *Scott and Amundsen*, p. 180.

Markham's orders to Colbeck. Armitage now realised that Scott and Markham had always intended to winter the ship in the ice of McMurdo Sound, notwithstanding the smokescreen to disguise the fact and that Markham had also embroiled Colbeck in his Presidential secret plan. Shackleton, writing in the *Illustrated London News* on his return home, admitted that Scott was reluctant to send the *Morning* away on 2nd March 1903, and (covering up as best he could for Scott) he added the odd comment:

> the thermometer showed minus 23 Fahrenheit at this time and it could not have been foreseen when the ship went into winter quarters that this would occur.[37]

Then, in a further attempt to placate Admiralty criticism, Shackleton followed the illustrious example of his Commander and wove yet another fictional story:

> every effort was made to extricate the ship from her position, but time would not allow of it, so she still remains down there.[38]

Their Lordships were not so easily deceived.

Why Discovery Was Not Freed in 1903

During the *Morning's* five-week stay the wasting of ice reduced the distance between the ships from ten to five miles. The men of *Discovery* might have reached New Zealand before Colbeck had they listened to him. Blasting five miles of ice in six weeks would have been perfectly feasible if they had learned how to do it. There was just one drawback: they had no incentive to free themselves. The scientists were content to collect data for another year or two, and more time was needed by the Pole conquerors. It would have been unwise to send Colbeck back to New Zealand with the message that they were all in perfect health, were having an enjoyable time and had no intention of freeing the ship. In January that year Scott had planned to stay two more winters, returning in 1905:

> Provisions for three years included 42, 000 lbs. flour, 10, 000 lbs. sugar, 3000 lbs. roast beef, 800 gallons of rum and 45 live sheep.[39]

37. Ernest Shackleton, second article in the 'Furthest South' Supplement of the *Illustrated London News* (1903).
38. Ernest Shackleton, second article in the 'Furthest South' Supplement of the *Illustrated London News* (1903).
39. David Harrowfield, *Icy Heritage* (1995), page 34.

Scott waited a year before he even shared his thoughts with Wilson. He told Colbeck a rather different story: that he was ready to leave now (a remark intended for Markham's ears). Burgess' diary records that no serious attempt was made to free *Discovery* in 1903 and, contrary to Scott's claim, Burgess found the morale of the men at this time was low:

> Discovery men were all downhearted at being left behind.[40]

So, before Colbeck was sent north, a charade had to be performed for his benefit. On 20th February they went through the motions of blasting. Choosing a site on the edge of the sea near to the *Morning* but well away from *Discovery*, they dug a hole in which a small charge of guncotton was detonated, with no useful results. The 'experiment' was repeated once more that day and on the day following before Scott decided that it was a waste of time and explosive because it was too late. He was right on both counts – it was too late, and it was a waste of guncotton because, as Colbeck's engineer observed, it was the wrong way to use explosive and the wrong way to extricate a ship from the ice:

> the charges should have been exploded at the same time. They have given up hope of getting their ship out this season and are a little downhearted in consequence. The prospect of another winter in the same place is not too enticing.[41]

However, getting rid of the men that Scott called the 'undesirables' was a bonus – fewer mouths to feed, more New Zealand lamb and potatoes for those who were left behind and altogether a better class of ship's company remaining: that was surely a great improvement! But, as Colbeck pointed out in his cable to Markham when he reached Lyttelton, far from being a cost-saving exercise, fares to England had to be paid, and with insufficient hands he might now also have to pay for skilled labour to caulk his ship (in the event, through the generosity of the New Zealanders, he did not have to pay).

A Commander Beyond Recall?

A letter from the Presidents of the Royal Geographical Society and the Royal Society to Scott was delivered by Colbeck in 1903 ordering him to return with the *Morning* in April 1903, or:

40. Len Burgess, Antarctic Diary, 23 January to 2 March 1903.
41. J.D.Morrison, Antarctic Diary, 20, 21 February 1903.

if you find it impossible to return to Lyttelton a ship will be sent to take you back. A third season is not feasible from a financial point of view.[42]

The decision to ignore this request from the two Presidents was Scott's alone. Armitage and Colbeck knew what was in store but Scott, choosing to ignore everyone, was now living in a dream. The passages concerning the visit of the relief ship that Scott wrote, with hindsight, on his return to London are amongst the most revealing in his book *The Voyage of the Discovery*. He weaves a moral tale, stating categorically that the *Morning* had brought nothing but good news and solemnly preaching to those sending relieving expeditions a sermon that implied that *Discovery* could not be freed from the ice because the *Morning* had arrived too late. This was Shackleton's explanation (time would not allow) and it was now elaborated by Scott:

> where an expedition is sent forth to the Polar Regions it is evident that when it has passed beyond the limits of communication, the authorities who despatched it must bear some burden of anxiety for its safety. If the expedition has departed without any definite plan, or has passed into regions which would be hopeless to search, those at home can do nothing. If on the other hand it has planned to pass by known but unvisited places then it is obvious that its footsteps can be traced. In this last case the proper action of the authorities is clear: they must endeavour to take no risk of arriving too late.[43]

Far from being too busy to see Colbeck on 3rd February, he relates how he had the pleasure of welcoming him on board personally, and then he turns Colbeck's request to begin freeing the ship into his own caring suggestion made to ensure that Colbeck would not also be caught in the ice. He adds an illuminating remark about the *Morning* that 'it is to be remembered that she has little power to push through the young ice'[44] – this comment is particularly interesting because the remark was soon forgotten, as we shall see.

Halfway through describing how the stores were unloaded from the *Morning*, it dawned on him that this action weakened his oft-made claim that he needed help from nobody and it might even have implied that he needed to be rescued. So he quickly explained that he could live off seal meat and

42. Letter (DH 1033 Dundee Industrial Heritage Trust Archive) sent with Colbeck Nov.1902.
43. Robert Falcon Scott, *The Voyage of the Discovery* (1905), Vol.2, Ch.XV, pages 153–154 and Ch.XVI, pages 166–167, 169.
44. Robert Falcon Scott, *The Voyage of the Discovery* (1905), Vol.2, Ch.XV, pages 153–154 and Ch.XVI, pages 166–167, 169.

that the ship still had three years' supply of everything, and he then recited a list of items that 'supplied minor deficiencies'[45] (like vegetables, sauces, herbs, tinned soups and socks) which it would have been a pity to send back on the *Morning*.

45. Robert Falcon Scott, *The Voyage of the Discovery* (1905), Vol.2, Ch.XV, pages 153–154 and Ch.XVI, pages 166–167, 169.

CHAPTER EIGHT

Comic Relief or Rescue?

A Cable to London

Colbeck's cable from Lyttelton in New Zealand to Markham in London contained the unwelcome news that another £20, 000 would be needed urgently for a second relief expedition. Markham and Huggins of the Royal Society approached the Treasury for £12,000. But Markham, assuming that the government's response would be a negative one, did not wait for a reply and went into the attack immediately. This brought the wrath of Prime Minister Balfour down on his head. It had already been decided that the *Morning* should winter in New Zealand and not return to England, so that a second relief expedition could be mounted quickly and easily to arrive in McMurdo Sound in January 1904 and so save the expense of sailing all the way from Britain. However, the Admirals noted that the *Morning* had failed to free *Discovery* in 1903 and they wanted to know why.

When Shackleton arrived back in England he wrote two popular articles in the *Illustrated London News* in the summer of 1903 with a definite prescription:

> next year when the relief ship reaches them the Discovery will then be able to get out; for the blasting of the ice will be done on a larger scale than our limited time then allowed, and sawing through the ice will recommence directly the sunlight returns.[46]

Shackleton's articles were illustrated with impressions drawn by a staff artist, A. Forestier, based on descriptions and photographs supplied by the Lieutenant. The artist obligingly added a drawing of an Arctic polar bear for good measure where he had some space to spare, but apart from this error there was an impressive authenticity about it all. Both articles and pictures created as spectacular an impression of the expedition's situation as the 1969 pictures of the Armstrong and Aldrin moon landing gave to a more modern public. Doubtless they struck terror in some quarters for *Discovery* was shown frozen into five miles of solid ice with snowdrifts all but obliterating the ship.

46. Ernest Shackleton, 'second article in the 'Furthest South', Supplement of the *Illustrated London News* (1903).

There was a picture of the ice cliffs where Vince had lost his life, and an imaginative sketch showed how Armitage, having contrived to fall all the way down from the 9000-foot polar ice plateau into a crevasse, was then supposed to be dangling over a 2500-foot precipice with a rope tied tightly round his chest, and yet somehow he was still alive. This was the new sensational journalism and readers were not to know that crevasses do not exceed 100 feet in depth and that men do not survive such constrictions. A new discovery had been made – pictures are worth a thousand words and these pictures struck home.

A Rapid Reaction

The reaction to this news was described by Markham as panic on the part of the Admiralty. Actually the reaction was very sane and amazingly swift. Their Lordships drew the obvious conclusions from their enquiries. The *Morning* had not freed *Discovery* though this was no fault of Colbeck who had achieved wonders. A glance at the specification of the ship and a little insight into the true nature of *Discovery*'s commander was all that was necessary to see the problem that had faced the *Morning*. It was, as one Dundee whaling man remarked, a miracle that *Morning* ever got to the Antarctic.

Further proof that *Morning* could not help the situation had been demonstrated when she had arrived at McMurdo Sound and could not even forge her way through the wet slush at the ice edge, with the result that men from the *Discovery* went up to their waists in their attempts to reach her. So what was needed was a powerful ice ship, an experienced ice master, a tough and unsentimental man with an uncouth crew who knew about such conditions and who had lived in the Arctic for many seasons. In short a Dundee whale ship complete with experienced master and crew.

The boomerang effect was now about to take place. Markham had offended people who were about to be called upon to help. His protestations were irrelevant. When the Markham camp suggested that all that was required was £12,000 to equip the *Morning* in Lyttelton for another season, this was seen as another of his ploys to keep *Discovery* in the South for yet another year. The Admiralty had firmly set its face against this. Markham knew that *Discovery* had to come home in 1904 but he could see no way of achieving this within his limited time scale and financial resources, other than sending Colbeck back in the *Morning*. He had done his best, he had spelled out the urgency of the situation to Scott but apparently to no effect. Markham now became a liability.

The Presidents of the Royal Society and Royal Geographical Society wrote to the government explaining in plain language that *Discovery* needed rescuing (though plain language was the last thing that either Society used much). More plainly, Markham had no money left in what he regarded as his relief fund. Not surprisingly the Admiralty, in this case Admiral Pelham Aldrich and the Royal Navy Hydrographer, Admiral Sir William Wharton, saw things slightly differently from Sir Clements Markham.

If a ship was going to be sent from Dundee, it would have to leave by August 1903, although to speed matters she could be towed by a relay of warships through Suez to the Indian Ocean and sail to Hobart where Colbeck could meet her. The government was prepared to buy a ship but only on certain draconian conditions, drafted by the Treasury.

Markham Loses His Relief Ship

Inevitably Shackleton was summoned by Sir William Wharton to make a report on his experiences in the Antarctic and was then invited to join the Admiralty's miniature Antarctic Relief Committee. With only three admirals – Aldrich, Boyes and Wharton – plus the expedition's Secretary, Longhurst, and Markham nowhere in sight, it was a record achievement. Shackleton joined forces with them in Dundee to oversee the fitting out of a second relief ship – the whaler *Terra Nova*, built in 1884 by Stephen's Panmure Yard. Shackleton was also invited to lead the rescue expedition and understandably he declined the opportunity to turn this so-called fiasco into a Gilbertian farce. Colbeck, recalled to England by Markham to support his cause, was also invited to Dundee and he had a frosty interview with Wharton but somewhat to his surprise he was reappointed to lead the rescue. The climax came in the House of Commons when Prime Minister Balfour was asked if a grant from the Exchequer would be made for the 1904 rescue bid. Selecting his words with more than a hint of malice, he replied:

> the government are prepared to contribute to the relief of the officers and men aboard Discovery which is now ice-bound in the Antarctic seas, but that the course taken by the two societies by which the expedition was controlled in respect of money (the government already having contributed £45,000 and men of the Royal Navy) was greatly to be regretted. I have always leaned towards the principle of extending the very limited aid which the British government have been accustomed to give towards the furtherance of purely scientific research. But such action can only be justified so long as the government are able to feel absolute confidence that the scientific bodies approaching them have placed before them all the information in their possession as to the estimated cost of their proposed action and the limits

within which they intend to confine it. That confidence in the present case has been rudely shaken.[47]

This speech sent shock waves through the corridors of the Royal Society to the committees of scientists who, not for the first time in matters relating to *Discovery*, distanced themselves from the Royal Geographical Society and succeeded in winning back Balfour's confidence. Balfour was very interested in science – he was in fact a fellow of the Royal Society. The Royal Society had considerably more to lose than the Royal Geographical Society from this contretemps. Markham fulminated and claimed that he had always supplied accurate estimates, but he did not realise that he was now reaping a whirlwind that he had created, for there were some civil servants, Admirals and scientists who could scarcely contain their glee at his discomfort, not least Jack Sanders, a private secretary to the Prime Minister, who had been misled by Markham about the cost estimates. So despite protests from their President, the ownership of 'his' ship passed from the Royal Geographical Society to the Admiralty.

The Admirals Take Over

After such an unprecedented public outburst it was not surprising that the rescue expedition financed by the Treasury was organised by the Admiralty. Markham began a personal vendetta, claiming that the arrangements were expensive and incompetent, and Markhamites all around the globe joined in the chorus and were the first to distort the accounts of what was actually a remarkable rescue.

C. T. Bowring, who owned the *Terra Nova*, sold her on 6th July 1903. She was quickly brought from Newfoundland and fitted out to effect the rescue. Three hundred Dundee men worked through the trade holidays to do the job in a fortnight. *Terra Nova* would have a Dundee whaling captain and an experienced crew of 38, mostly whalemen from Dundee.

The *Terra Nova's* orders were to meet Colbeck at Hobart, in Tasmania, avoiding Lyttelton on the way out to save time (much to the annoyance of Colbeck and the New Zealand farmers who had very generously donated 14 sheep and five beasts for the men of the *Discovery*). Once in McMurdo Sound, the two ships under Colbeck's command were to free *Discovery* from the ice, accompany her to Lyttelton and then proceed via Cape Horn to

---

47. Louis Bernacchi, *The Saga of Discovery*, (1938), quoting Balfour's reply to Clements Markham from Hansard 1903.

England, or failing that, bring back the *Discovery's* company and scientific effects.

There was one other little known caveat – the work of a Treasury draftsman, perhaps a civil servant seeking to please his masters, an infuriated scientist perchance, a snubbed Admiral, or even a disgruntled Prime Minister? The gist of this caveat was that if *Discovery* were to be freed from the ice

> she should not continue with her programme of scientific work, apart from her magnetic work on the ship.[48]

Nobody knew what the scientific programme was but the Royal Society knew from bitter experience that a vague Markham programme was simply a device to enable Scott to winter in the ice. Markham had seriously described the scientific objectives of the expedition as 'to go from the known to the unknown', which impressed nobody.[49] The scientific instructions were orchestrated by no less than three muddling committees, drafting and re-drafting, scoring and re-scoring, with a high level descant over the top provided by the President of the Royal Geographical Society and the conductor's baton and score handed over in mid-peformance to Commander Scott who was instructed to make haste to finish. The 'NO MORE DISCOVERY VOYAGES!' clause played an important role in what followed. It had implications for coal consumption and therefore for safety, matters of importance to all three ships involved in the 1904 rescue bid.

Choosing the Captain

Admiral Pelham Aldrich saw twenty-four other ships before selecting *Terra Nova*, and he took the choice of a Dundee whaling captain equally seriously. He rejected completely the Captain who had brought *Terra Nova* from Newfoundland to Dundee that July, explaining to the Royal Navy Hydrographer, Admiral Wharton, how the daring Captain Jackman (famous for his exploits on the whale ship *Eagle*)

> expectorated continually. I could not entertain him in any way![50]

---

48. 'Hobart Complaint', article in the *Press*, New Zealand, 2 April 1904.
49. Speech at the *Discovery* launch by Clements Markham, *Dundee Advertiser* 22 March 1901.
50. A.G.E.Jones, 'Harry McKay, Master of the Terra Nova', in *Antarctic* Vol.6, No.9 (1973).

Aldrich passed on the enthusiastic testimonials for McKay which he received from all sides. Both Admirals had their sights set on a Dundee whaling man like Captain Adams and 'knew instinctively' that McKay was just such a man:

> We could not hear of any other likely master, a whaling captain of large experience.[51]

In 1903 the Dundonian Harry McKay was in his mid-40s, the youngest of masters. After Adam's death in 1889 McKay was widely known as the most experienced ice expert in the Arctic, notwithstanding Jackman's daring exploits in the *Eagle*. Well thought of by his fellow captains, McKay was also popular with his crews – an essential quality since there was no system of artificial discipline on board a whale ship to prop up a weak captain. In the far South, Scott and his officers were to discover the pleasure of McKay's company and experience the sane atmosphere of both his and Colbeck's ship. Everyone soon came to regard the *Terra Nova* and *Morning* as relief ships in more senses than one. Even Scott availed himself of the therapy when he reached his nadir during the first two months of 1904 and said that he found Harry McKay good company. Certainly Captain McKay's twenty-year record in the polar ice was impressive, as they were all soon to discover:

1878 Joined the Dundee fleet. Gained his master's ticket in 1882.
First Officer of the *Resolute* in which he sailed 1879/1885.
1886 Served on *Terra Nova* [Stephen-built in Dundee 1884].
1889 Master of *Aurora* [Stephen-built 1876], Davis Straits 1890, –91, –92. [*Polynia* and *Maud* rescues].
1893 Whaling and the Swedish scientific expedition rescue bid.
1894-97 Captain of *Terra Nova* in the Dundee fleet to Davis Straits.
1897 Master of the *Esquimaux* [Stephen-built 1865], Davis Straits.
1898 Piloted the first Ziegler Baldwin Expedition to Novaya Zemlya[52] & Svalbard with Evelyn Briggs Expedition and then joined
1898-99 American Arctic Expedition with Walter Wellman.[53]
1900 Master of the *Esquimaux* to Newfoundland and Davis Straits.
1901–02 Arctic cruises of the iron screw yacht *Caterina*.

51. A.G.E.Jones, 'Harry McKay, Master of the Terra Nova', in Antarctic Vol.6, No.9 (1973).
52. E.Briggs Baldwin, The Baldwin-Ziegler Polar Expedition.
53. *National Geographic Magazine* Vol 10 pp481–503 1899 The Wellman Expedition.

Three Ships A-Sailing

The three ships *Discovery*, *Terra Nova* and *Morning* look similar in the distant photographic views taken as they came together in McMurdo Sound in 1904. They have many points in common for they are all derived from the tradition of building for working in ice, but they were by no means identical. In terms of length, *Discovery* was 40 feet longer than McKay's ship and almost 90 feet longer than Colbeck's, but there was only a slight difference in the beam (c. 30 ft.), though in construction Scott's ship was without doubt the strongest. The *Terra Nova* was the most powerful whale ship ever built in Stephen's Yard and she could perfectly well keep pace with Scott's ship. *Discovery* was built sixteen years later when Gourlays were still supplying the same type of triple expansion engines, and on her trials on the Tay she exceeded the engine specification with an output of 500 indicated horse power. By way of contrast the *Morgenen*, Svend Foyn's 30-year-old Tonsberg ship, had compound engines of older design with an indicated horse power of only 85, a fact which caused alternately crude amusement and fuming frustration amongst the Dundonians who were expected to accompany her south. Both Dundee-built ships had a speed of 8 knots – twice the speed of the *Morning*. The pairing of Colbeck's and McKay's ships was a bizarre order that can only be explained in terms of 'belt and braces' tactics, plus the thought that for Scott to be rescued by a whaling captain would have been ignominious indeed. This consideration was never far below the surface in the weeks which followed.

All three ships had a coal problem. Firstly, the *Discovery* consumed more coal than was expected and Scott developed a great thirst for coal from the other two ships. Secondly, *Discovery* had problems in storing coal, 240 tons in the bunkers with another 50 tons elsewhere. On the outward journey 'elsewhere' meant on the deck. *Terra Nova* was normally able to store more coal than *Discovery*, 400 tons in fact. But when she met up with the *Morning* in Hobart, Colbeck was not even able to stow the stores and coal that he had been allocated. So, not only did McKay have to find room for what should have been taken in the *Morning*, he also had to accommodate it very rapidly. He would have preferred to sort out the problem of storage properly. Instead he sailed with the coal badly stowed, and the problem was made worse on the return journey as he had to carry much of the expedition's gear. If the Admiralty had sent McKay to Lyttelton instead of Hobart, the coal problem would have been avoided, but they reasoned that whilst McKay was travelling halfway round the world, Colbeck could at least come some of the way from New Zealand to meet him. Morrison, an engineer with a ready wit, had a theory that the Admiralty in London were still living in the nineteenth century and so they still associated the Antarctic with that port,

because Ross sailed from Hobart in 1840.[54]

A Fast Ship To Hobart

When the Chief Officer of the *Terra Nova*, A. P. Jackson, first saw his ship in Dundee harbour on 18th August 1903, he wanted to turn round and take the next train home, despite the promise of a reasonable salary of £220 a year.

A dirty little barque with a coffee mill for an engine[55]

is how he described Alexander Stephen's masterpiece. He met Captain Harry McKay, 'a very nice man', and he was impressed by all the officers and members of the crew: 2nd officer, Arthur Elms; 3rd officer, R. W. Day; Chief Engineer, Alexander Sharp; Second Engineer, William Smith; Third Engineer, Colin McGregor; Stewards, Mr. R. H. Morgan and Thomas Shearer; Boatswain, Alex Aitken; Carpenter, Mr. A. Smith; Sailmaker, Edward Morrison; the Cooks – John Grant and William Clark; Surgeon, Dr. William Clark Souter; and twenty-six seamen from the Scottish east-coast whale ports (the majority from Dundee) with their numbers made up by two Shetlanders, all on £60 a year, making a total ship's company of forty-three.[56]

For Jackson this was all something of a new experience. In Dundee and later in Hobart he found that most of the crew were busy getting blind drunk. Three naval cruisers took turns to tow them on their express mission, faster than a mail boat. Leaving Dundee on 20th August, they arrived in Hobart on 31st October 1903 in record time and then, ironically, had to wait eight days for *Morning* to arrive from New Zealand. Colbeck was still smarting from the way he had been treated by Wharton in London. The Admiral had sent him back to New Zealand on a disgustingly slow boat, using up what Colbeck had hoped would have been three weeks' leave with his fiancée. On arrival back in Wellington, he avoided his ship in Lyttelton and went off to stay with friends on North Island. He then put *Morning* in

54. J.D.Morrison, Antarctic Diary, entry for March 22 1903.
55. A.P.Jackson, Diary of a Voyage in Antarctic Regions on the ship *Terra Nova* 1904, 20 August 1903.
56. *Terra Nova* Crew List 1903–04. Voyage Dundee to the Antarctic returning to Sheerness.

dry dock contrary to Wharton's instructions and was clearly in no mood to reach Hobart quickly. He declined to take much of the gear brought by McKay, and when the expedition coal arrived, the mix-up over the stowage of gear greatly reduced the amount of coal that McKay could load. This led to complications later. On December 6th it was more important to leave without further delay than to sort out their coal problems. So the ships sailed with *Terra Nova* bedecked with carcasses of mutton hanging between her boat davits and the coal badly stowed. Before departing for the Antarctic, Colbeck had a frantic exchange of letters with the Admiralty over the supply of explosives for the two relief ships. A bemused Morrison examined the supplies sent by their Lordships from Sydney and observed with typical doleful humour:

> they sent a hundred ball cartridges 25% of which misfire and a hundred blank cartridges for which no-one has been able even to guess a purpose, unless they are for firing at burial parades![57]

Round In Antarctic Circles

Some recent commentators have attempted to discredit McKay by implying that he and Colbeck did not see eye-to-eye on the voyage to McMurdo Sound. In fact this was not so. Some foolish schoolboy pranks were played by the Dundee men, but it is important to realise that they were just relieving boredom and why they needed to do so. Capturing a white seal alive, then painting it in exotic colours before setting it free in the path of the *Morning* can be interpreted as a message that the Dundonians had time to spare as they escorted Colbeck south. Much fuss has been made of a near collision between *Terra Nova* and *Morning* but this had nothing to do with McKay, and it was Jackson who put the engines at full speed ahead at the very last moment.

The difficulty facing *Terra Nova* was not appreciated by anyone on the ·*Morning* apart from one solitary ordinary seaman, Len Burgess, who wrote:

> It is splendid how well the two ships keep together during such bad weather for so long.[58]

Initially *Morning*'s ship's company and captain did not appreciate why McKay appeared to be running rings round them. The faster ship was now ahead of them and then behind them, which they took to be just

57. J.D.Morrison, Antarctic Diary, 1904.
58. Len Burgess, Antarctic Diary, entry for 19 December 1903.

showing off her superior power and speed, but they had not the least idea of the embarrassment that they were causing to the Dundonians as they made their dreadfully slow progress, forever stopping in the most alarming situations in thick snow and amidst very large bergs.

Jackson's diary recorded mounting frustration as the men of the *Terra Nova* came to realise that the *Morning* was painfully, even dangerously, slow:

> No wonder she could not do much last year. She has not enough power to get out on her own way. The work is awful hanging back all the time. Morning sails better than she steams! She has stopped engines! Waited two days for Morning to start. Tired of hanging back. Lost sight of her in fog. Hope we have lost her so we can go on our own.[59]

So each day, in order to move safely without leaving *Morning* behind, *Terra Nova* continued to describe a circle round her. Although the two ships' captains remained on very good terms throughout the expedition, Colbeck had no real appreciation of McKay's ice skills. On those occasions when the ships came close, Jackson joked:

> Mind the mutton![60]

But although Colbeck was unamused by their pranks later in the voyage, he recorded that they were most amusing and that *Terra Nova* made *Morning's* task much lighter.[61]

Through the Ice in Record Time

As the ships entered the pack ice, McKay went ahead to clear a way. Even with this work to do the *Terra Nova* continued to experience the same frustrating delays and continued to circle round the *Morning* to break the ice. Len Burgess appreciated what the *Terra Nova* was doing and he recorded in his diary:

> Terra Nova getting through the pack ahead of us, breaking it up a bit as she has more power than us. Better than the last voyage. Made good progress since yesterday.[62]

59. A.P.Jackson Diary of a Voyage in Antarctic Regions on the ship *Terra Nova*, 8–13 December 1903.
60. Gerald Doorly, *The Voyages of the Morning* (1916).
61. William Colbeck, Private Papers, MS 212 Item 13, December 1903.
62. Len Burgess, Antarctic Diary, 27–29 December 1903.

The Second Engineer on *Terra Nova*, William Smith, gives a matter-of-fact description of how they effected this work through the pack ice on Boxing Day:

> We made a few round turns in front of her to break up the ice and started at full speed smashing everything that came in the way, the Morning coming on behind until she got fast again, so there was nothing else but to go back and fish her out. On 28th December the ice was pinching up all round but it took a lot to stop the Terra Nova and at noon we were fairly teeming through it.[63]

With his considerable ice navigation experience, McKay knew what he was about. Jackson's diary, far from revealing any stupidity on their part, records mounting incredulity after just one day in the ice and fog when Colbeck, who was in command, ordered the ships to halt and wait for the fog to clear. Waiting for fog to clear was a novel experience for the Dundee whale men. But frustrations were tempered as Hogmanay descended on *Terra Nova* and diary pages were soon left blank. Once through the ice, Colbeck was surprised to find perfect calm and cloudless skies over the Ross Sea. The tedium and annoyances of the journey then gave way to a delightful P & O-style cruise in the land of the midnight sun.

On 1st January Colbeck passed Cape Adare in record time compared to the year before, saving ten days. This was partly because the pack ice was less formidable than the year before, and the *Morning's* good time was also claimed to be due to the fact that they had followed a course further east than the year before. But the engineers of *Terra Nova* would not have been amused to hear these explanations. The men of the *Morning* genuinely believed the speed had resulted from their own unaided efforts, and McKay was given no credit for clearing the way in any of the written accounts. Colbeck justified the long waiting periods, some of them as long as 36 hours, as a way of saving coal for Commander Scott. When McKay found himself in pack ice, he was accustomed to smash his way through as quickly as possible: in his view it was a far safer way of saving coal. He remarked to Colbeck that he wanted to get all the guncotton used up as quickly as possible and away from the ships, for the safety of all concerned.[64]

63. *Dundee Advertiser*, Article by William Smith of the *Terra Nova*, 11 May 1904.
64. William Colbeck, Private Papers, MS 212 Item 13, January 1904.

PART TWO

The Rescue

CHAPTER NINE

'Dear Mum, There are Two Versions!' Week One: 3–9 January 1904

Twenty Miles of Ice

William Smith, second Engineer of the *Terra Nova*, writing a letter home to Dundee when his polar trip was over, enclosed some New Zealand newspaper cuttings. He explained to his mother that although she would find two quite different versions of what had happened in McMurdo Sound in early 1904, he was confident that she would know which to believe.[65] When Colbeck left Scott on 2nd March 1903, the *Discovery* was locked in only five miles of solid ice, but when he returned on 5th January 1904 there were some twenty miles of all too solid ice between *Discovery* and the freedom of the open water where the two rescue ships lay anchored. This was no ordinary relief expedition. It was a rescue to ensure that the men returned home safely, that the results of two years' work in the shape of scientific collections and records were saved, and that a very expensive, brand-new, purpose-built expedition ship was not wrecked by the destructive powers of ice. But an alternative version of events was being created in early 1904 – it was essential to refer to the mission as the 'Second Relief Voyage' and to avoid the term 'rescue' at all costs. Heroes don't need rescues.

From 5th January the rescuers had only seven weeks in which to free *Discovery* before the summer conditions began to give way to winter. They would have to progress at an average rate of some three miles of ice per week, a feat which had never been achieved before, though the wildman Jackman had once nearly matched it in the Arctic. It was a task which both Scott and Colbeck pronounced at the outset to be quite impossible. Nevertheless Colbeck kept an open mind, since he was not yet schooled in McKay's techniques, but Scott sank into a seven-week depression.

A study of the men's diaries and articles written on the spot and interviews given in New Zealand months later reveals a fascinating chain of events and some contrasting attitudes. Only by taking the evidence one week at a time does the truth become clear. The published version of events which has

---

65. Second Engineer William Smith, letter in *Dundee Advertiser*, 15 May 1904.

been copied repeatedly since 1904 as the official storyline is a fiction resulting partly from Scott's refusal to go out and see what was actually happening, and partly from a desire to save face by being economical with the truth.

Scott was not the only man who recorded what happened. No fewer than twenty-six sources have now come to light, half of them in the 1990s, and these 'new' diaries depart from Scott's official version of events and give accounts which differ fundamentally from his.

'A Fearful Waste of Time'

Scott was returning from his western sledging trip to the Plateau – the high gateway to the south where he had found mountaineering at high altitudes in fiercely low temperatures was not an easier way to the Pole. The season was coming to a close, the South Pole had not been conquered, the *Morning* would probably arrive at the end of the month and the wrath of the Joint Committee might soon descend upon him.

So Scott had instructed Armitage to make another token gesture and establish a large ice-sawing tent, with two partitions, one for three officers and the other for thirty men. Armitage was ordered to locate it between *Discovery* and the open water, but not knowing where the ice front would be by the time he returned, Scott guessed that it would be the same place as when he left in 1903. It wasn't. It was a further fifteen miles away. Not surprisingly, by this time Armitage was in no mood to take the sawing seriously. He knew that the stupidity of getting thirty men to saw a channel at the rate of twelve yards a day in the middle of a vast icefield would be plain for all to see. To saw twenty miles of ice would take eight years at the rate they were managing and, of course, that assumed that the channel would not freeze over. But it froze again before they had even cut half a mile.

Armitage wrote a report to Scott, characterised by Bernacchi as 'an absurd, sanguine and exaggerated description of our progress.'[66] Skelton called the sawing:

> the most fearful waste of time one can possibly think of. One would think Armitage was entirely devoid of common sense, but he is just carrying out orders![67]

Wilson, obviously in a state of severe depression, commented:

66. Louis Bernacchi, Antarctic Diary, entry 27 December 1903.
67. Reginald Skelton, Antarctic Diary, entry 17 December 1903.

One begins to wonder whether life is worth living. Certainly the work isn't worth doing, for we are attempting a task which is totally impossible and obviously so.[68]

One of *Discovery*'s seamen recalled the scene three months later:

> A start was made to cut a channel to the ship. Two saws were working parallel 50 feet apart, and sawing was continued day and night for a fortnight, officers and men doing the work in shifts. At the commencement of operations there were six men to the shift, but when the sledging parties returned just before New Year this was increased to ten. Each shift, of which there were three, consisted of four hours' work and eight hours off. They had a mile and a quarter to walk from the camp to the work.[69]

Cutting the Ship Free

When Scott returned from his sledging trip, he praised Armitage for following his orders, which he openly admitted were stupid!

> There could have been no officer or man amongst them who did not see from the very first how utterly useless it was, and yet there has been no faltering or complaint simply because all have felt that, as the sailor expresses it – them's the orders.[70]

The Commander was fond of inventing exercises to keep men busy to ensure that discipline was maintained. The lower ranks had already endured scrubbing the mess deck every week in temperatures well below freezing and waiting for hours on deck in a gale for the Commander to inspect the men. The time had come to stop sawing and order everyone back to the *Discovery*. So, one might imagine, there would be no more sawing. But one would be wrong. Scott supposed that sawing was a technique for cutting escape canals to free an ice-bound ship, but in polar work it was more effectively used to cut away the ice that was threatening to crush a ship. It was true that the crew of the *Belgica* had made a successful Antarctic escape in March 1899 by digging a 600-yard channel to release their ship after a year's imprisonment, but the correct technique of sawing seems not to have been

---

68. Edward Wilson, Antarctic Diary, entry 27 December 1903.
69. 'Ice Sawing', article by a member of the *Discovery* crew in the *Press*, New Zealand, 2 April 1904.
70. Robert Falcon Scott, *The Voyage of the Discovery* (1905), Vol.2, Ch.XIX, pages 315–6.

known to anyone on *Discovery*. Sawing is not futile if it is employed at an appropriate stage, for even when saw cuts appear to freeze up again this may be only superficial. The important thing was to open the ice to the sea and to keep the ship free from tidal ice piling up.

When McKay arrived on 5th January, his men were asked to help with more sawing 'experiments' but they managed to decline the invitation on the grounds that it was, as Scott had admitted, a useless exercise at that stage. *Discovery*'s block and tackle gear had two men holding and guiding the saw and six men pulling the tackle. According to McKay's whaling men who were familiar with ice sawing, the tackle was not being used properly. To work effectively it needed a man to guide the saw at the bottom of the ice pit, but that would have been a very dangerous position and nobody volunteered to fill the breach. The men on *Terra Nova* knew that the ice was too thick for sawing and was not under pressure, so not surprisingly none of them was keen to make the saws work. Instead they were busy with more effective ways of freeing the *Discovery*, testing the ice front for the weakest areas. Their efforts were accompanied by sarcastic but amusing remarks from the *Morning* where instant results had been expected:

> we had heard that anything up to eight feet thick was game so perhaps this five foot ice was not worth breaking.[71]

A Chill Reception

On 4th January Scott and Wilson had walked to Cape Royds and camped. Next day they were having what Jackson described as 'a picnic at the seaside' when they saw two ships arrive. Scott sent a message to the men at the sawing camp to start killing penguins for the ship's larder. These birds were food for another year's stay but they were also intended to make the point that the expedition had been living off the country and was not in need of more food supplies.

In his book *The Voyage of the Discovery* Scott devoted a chapter to describing the ship's company in happy holiday mood, enjoying fresh air and exercise, sunburned and in rude health, well fed and free of scurvy when, suddenly, two relief ships arrived. He mocked the idea that anyone could for a moment imagine that they needed relief, let alone rescue. They were always pleased to see Colbeck with the mail bags but were not pleased to see the *Terra Nova*, which was not required. Nobody wanted to leave, everyone would volunteer to stay another year, two years if they were asked.

71. J.D.Morrison, Antarctic Diary, 5 January 1904.

(Of the hundred men with Scott that day only five did volunteer to go with him again on his Antarctic expedition of 1910-1913, and only one of them was an officer.) The pay was good and the duties were comparatively light, especially for a stoker on a stationary ship which her commander did not want to see released.

Scott and Wilson reached the *Morning* in the early evening of the 5th and after two hours with Colbeck they very briefly paid their respects to the Captain of the *Terra Nova*. From Colbeck, Scott learned about the Admiralty's orders:

> If the Discovery cannot be got out of the ice, you will abandon her and bring your people back in the relief ships as my Lords cannot under existing circumstances consent to the further employment of officers and men of the Royal Navy in the Antarctic Regions.[72]

Scott went back to *Discovery* and spent days pondering what he called the 'Admiralty's blunder'. He was unable to come to terms with it:

> With the advent of the relief ships there fell on the Discovery the first and last cloud of gloom which we were destined to experience. As day followed day without improvement in the ice conditions, the gloom deepened until our faces grew so long that one might well have imagined an Antarctic expedition to be a very woeful matter.[73]

In a rare moment of insight he concluded that it must all somehow be the result of his own actions.

The Admiralty's Blunder?

Scott felt that he had brought the unwelcome orders from the Admiralty upon himself. It was completely unexpected, he never for one moment thought that the Admiralty would want to bring the officers and men of the Royal Navy back so soon, or take over the Second Relief operation. As he himself put it:

> No such thought ever entered my head and the first sight of the two vessels conveyed nothing but blank astonishment.[74]

72. Admiralty Orders to Scott, 27 August 1903, quoted in R.Huntford *Scott and Amundsen* (1979), p. 183.
73. Robert Falcon Scott, *The Voyage of the Discovery* (1905), Vol.2, page 328.
74. Robert Falcon Scott, *The Voyage of the Discovery* (1905), Vol.2, page 326.

He should never have implied in March 1903 that Shackleton was being sent home because of scurvy giving the impression that he did not know how to prevent it. Nor should he have given their Lordships and the Joint Committee the impression that he expected the *Morning* to be sent again in January 1904. He should not have assumed that the popularity of his expedition, not least with the King, would ensure that a successful financial appeal could be mounted. He hadn't realised that Markham had offended Longstaff, the expedition's principal benefactor, who wanted his son Tom to join Scott, and that when Sir Clements refused to consider this he closed the door on the most likely source of private funding. Markham then had insufficient time to mount an appeal and had no option but to go on bended knee to the government. All this, Scott thought, had probably caused their Lordships to panic.

Now, as he read in the London papers brought by McKay about Markham's clash with the Prime Minister, he guessed that the Joint Committee of the Expedition and Sir Clements would not be best pleased with him. He was still deeply stuck in the ice and, despite the expense, Colbeck's 1903 expedition had not succeeded in extricating *Discovery* that year, or bringing everyone home.

Scott was also amazed to read that his expedition was not as popular as he thought, and he was upset to find critical newspaper reports of the expense, not least the extra expense voted by the Government for this rescue expedition. And so it came about that he hit upon a plan that, in order to justify his actions, he must deny altogether the need for *Terra Nova* and create firstly the myth that *Morning* was perfectly capable of doing all that was necessary to free him and later the myth that neither of the two relief ships had helped at all. To anyone on the spot these were ludicrous assertions to make but he knew that he could be convincing if the facts were carefully marshalled. In New Zealand he would have to convince himself and others that *Terra Nova* and *Morning* had done nothing at all. The government had made a blunder and was guilty of waste.

The Threat Posed by McKay

At the end of the week Scott was still trying to understand the blow that fate had dealt him. Walter Marsh on the *Morning* described Scott's indignation:

> in spite of his orders, Scott was not going to abandon his ship without a fight.[75]

75. Walter Marsh, The Release of the Discovery, as recorded by Edward Gibbons in 1971.

The Commander was well aware that McKay was going to butt the ice, and at first sight it seems as if Scott welcomed McKay's efforts, but a few days later when he was discouraging Royds from going to visit McKay on the *Terra Nova*, he added that all the whaling captain would do was damage his ship:

> McKay suggests butting the ice – he has little hope of success. McKay points out that he has a powerful ship and may accomplish something. He might as well try to butt through Cape Royds![76]

Scott had made it clear: there would be no fraternising with the *Terra Nova* men. Gradually he found a way of resolving all the difficulties which now faced him. He knew that the *Morning* could not free him. He was not sure whether McKay could do so. Yet all the officers on *Discovery* were aware of McKay's reputation and to them it was obvious why Admiral Pelham Aldrich had chosen McKay of all people. Scott must have heard of McKay's reputation at the launch of *Discovery* but he took care not to mention any of this in his book.

From a career point of view he faced a potential disaster. What could he do to save his own reputation if the whaling captain did succeed? Slowly the new strategy evolved: either the *Morning* must be credited with freeing him, or nobody should be so credited. It would be the work of Providence, God's Great Ocean Swell. Whilst this was a very satisfying solution to the problem, it had the major drawback that, as the weeks went by, nearly a hundred other people would see that the relief ships were succeeding and that a Great Swell was not coming like some Hollywood Old Testament epic. The wrong side would be seen to be winning. In later weeks this is exactly what happened. It was then important not to venture out, not to be seen taking an interest in the activities of Colbeck and McKay. So on January 9th Commander Scott returned from the Cape Royds peninsula and his meetings with Colbeck and retired to his own ship where he went into retreat in his cabin for the greater part of the next six weeks. According to Wilson, Scott was always happy to lend a hand with even the dirtiest of jobs, and yet here, with the most crucial job of all, he played no important role and was practically invisible. James Paton on the *Morning* could scarcely believe Scott's total lack of concern for his ship:

> Discovery is completely buried, one can walk on board without climbing over her rail![78]

76. Robert Falcon Scott, *The Voyage of the Discovery* (1905), Vol.2, page 330.
77. James Paton, Antarctic Diary, entry for 5 January 1904.

Visiting Time

In this first week the officers and scientists presented widely different views about the sudden event that had just begun to dominate their lives. Louis Bernacchi thought that the Admiralty's move had capsized the expedition. Edward Wilson, who had just read the Admiralty's orders in full, concluded that the officers and scientists were now relieved, so it was quite in order to go off and see some more penguins. He had only recently been let into Scott's secret plans for 1905, but now these were all null and void, pole-bagging was over for this expedition, and he could get on with his scientific work. Albert Armitage welcomed the news that Colbeck had returned but thought that they should have been more enthusiastic about the arrival of a Dundee whale ship and Harry McKay whose experience he valued highly. In an outburst of satirical wit, he added:

> I am confident that there was not a single man on board who, if given the choice of staying another two years in the Discovery ice-bound, or of deserting her to return safe home, would not have chosen the former course.[78]

Royds had an unpleasant week. Scott had stopped all the sawing on January 1st, and now ordered Royds to start again on the day that the relief ships arrived. Royds communed at length with Skelton and collected his mail in which, as expedition pianist, he was pleased to find some more sheet music, a pleasure soon to be shared with others. Reginald Skelton set off to get mails and unlike his Commander was pleased to find *Terra Nova* and Captain McKay. He commented on McKay's experience and his piloting of the Arctic expedition in

> Barclay Walker's Arctic yacht bought for him for the Baldwin–Ziegler Expedition. The Terra Nova crew are good chaps.[79]

Ferrar helped Royds at the sawing camp but at the end of the week went with Hodgson towards Cape Royds and 'to the Terra Nova to see Captain McKay'.[80]

So it seems that not everyone from the *Discovery* toed the official line of being annoyed by the arrival of Harry McKay, and avoiding all contact with him.

---

78. Albert Armitage, Antarctic Diary, entry for 5 January 1904.
79. Reginald Skelton, Antarctic Diary, entry for 5 January 1904.
80. Hartley Ferrar, Antarctic Diary, entry for 9 January 1904.

The Good News and the Bad News

On 5th January, the great day when the two ships arrived in McMurdo Sound, an unfortunate accident happened on the *Morning*. One of her boiler tubes burst, causing the crown of the boiler to fall in, and as a result she made even slower headway in the last stages of the voyage to the ice front. Lacking in power, *Morning* would be of less use against the ice than the year before, but her captain and crew played a key role in the weeks ahead. Engineer J. D. Morrison, with a wit almost reminiscent of Voltaire, remarked:

> the ignorance and folly of people who manage exploring ships is criminal. They fancy that everything with a funnel is a full-powered steamer and can do a steamer's work. An auxilliary barque like this is a cross between a sailing boat and a steamer and like every other half breed has all the faults of both mother and father and no good points of any sort. I wish the people back home who thought this boat had plenty of power were with us now.[81]

On the evening of 5th January Scott and Wilson were in the company of Captain Colbeck, having a miserable time. At 6 p.m. they went aboard the *Terra Nova* to share their bad news with McKay and his men. Although none of them knew it then this was to prove to be a very rare visit by their Commander and a revealing one for the men of *Terra Nova*. One crew member noted that

> Scott appeared to be broken-hearted over the drastic orders from the Admiralty especially as he had made arrangements to spend another winter on the ice.[82]

According to *Terra Nova's* surgeon, Dr Souter, McKay told Scott that his ship had to come out. Scott again claimed that his crew would volunteer to remain in the Antarctic for another year, that they had not attempted to get out as they were all in good health and that they had not the least anxiety about their food supply, being victualled for another five years (the claim was growing wilder every day).

William Heald was the first man to reach the *Discovery* at 9 p.m. with the news that the relief ships had arrived. One of the *Discovery's* men later described the contrasting scene as the men who had volunteered to stay in the Antarctic received this same allegedly depressing news, calculated to shatter their idyllic lives on board their beloved ship:

81. J.D.Morrison, Antarctic Journal, 5 January 1904.
82. 'How Discovery was got Clear', article in the *Press*, New Zealand, 2 April 1904.

All were delighted with the news and danced around in their glee and the main brace was spliced in honour of the occasion. An hour later a party left for the camp which they reached at 1.30 a.m. and after resting an hour they went on to the relief ships.[83]

Terra Nova *Butts the Ice*

Jackson spent the day after *Terra Nova* arrived measuring the thickness of ice and set up instruments. At the ice front where their ship was tied up, the ice varied from 3 feet to 18 inches in thickness, but Jackson's work was not designed to contribute to the expedition's scientific discoveries, as we shall see later. The Second Engineer, William Smith, recorded that, in the seven weeks which followed, whenever the crew of *Terra Nova* had to stop their work to wait for wind or tide, they passed the time learning to ski, in marked contrast to the *Discovery's* football matches. At the end of that very first week, on Friday 8th January, the ice started to move and the men of *Terra Nova* had to look to her moorings. The following day they could only break the ice a couple of ship's lengths and gave up, the expenditure of coal required being simply too great.

Overall, the first week had been a disappointment to McKay, for although everyone on the other ships seemed to be delighted with the beautiful weather that they were experiencing, it did not help his task of breaking up eighteen miles of ice. Dead calm was not the best condition for butting. McKay needed first to break up the ice edge and then to steer broken floes away with the ship, his men on the ice edge using long boat hooks, skilfully making use of the action of the wind on the floes. Breaking the ice front by butting or ramming with the ship, or by using explosives, was only a fraction of the McKay technique. Here the butting process in Week One is described by one of the *Terra Nova's* crew:

we started butting the ice with the object of breaking it up – an exciting business. In order to start butting you must have a clear way ahead so that the ship can go astern 300 or 400 yards to enable her to get a good way on. When she has got back this distance full speed ahead is given, which means with the Terra Nova eight knots (about 10 miles an hour). Sometimes the effect would be that half the ship's length of the ice barrier would be broken: other times not three yards of progress would be made owing to the ice being too solid with no give or spring in it. The effect on those on board ship varied –

83. 'Relief Ships Sighted', article in the *Press*, New Zealand, 2 April 1904.

sometimes you were toppled off your feet whilst at other times you would hardly feel it at all.[84]

Marsh records how *Morning*'s crew of sceptical spectators were converted:

Harry McKay was a very determined man and the "Morning" joined the "Terra Nova" in this rough and tumble venture.[85]

By Saturday 9th January it was plain to McKay that freeing the *Discovery* was going to be a difficult challenge.

84. 'How Discovery was got clear', article in the *Press* New Zealand, 2 April 1904.
85. Walter Marsh, The Release of Discovery, as told to Edward Gibbons in 1971.

CHAPTER TEN

A Well Kent Captain
Week Two: 10–16 January 1904

Tributes to the Interlopers

Armitage knew McKay by reputation, although they had never met before their paths had crossed on their Arctic expeditions, and there was mutual respect. Armitage wrote a tribute to McKay and his crew and at the beginning it reads somewhat oddly, as if he is contradicting some other version of events. At the end of the passage, it is obvious that this is indeed his intention, though it might seem incredible to anyone not familiar with the true nature of this expedition that there could possibly be an alternative version of events. The comments come in a passage from Armitage's book *Two Years in the Antarctic* which was published in 1905, the same year as Scott's. According to D. W. H. Walton, Scott agreed to Armitage writing this book, but when it was about to be published, threatening letters were sent with the intention of delaying its appearance.[86]

Armitage and his fellow officers on *Discovery* felt strongly that McKay and his men had been very poorly treated and he wished to put the record straight. He described McKay's first contribution to the expedition – that of getting Colbeck safely to McMurdo Sound. He wrote his account on his return home when he knew the full story of how McKay's work had been deliberately discredited. Armitage became the first expedition member to publish the truth:

> Captain McKay was one of the most experienced ice masters of the Northern seas living. On the voyage down from New Zealand he had been of great assistance to the Morning whenever pack ice was met with for Terra Nova was easily able to penetrate it while Morning followed in her wake before it closed up again. This not only enabled Morning to save her coal but it saved much delay to a ship with such a small steam power that, according to rumour, she had to stop when her steam whistle was blown! Terra Nova's crew were nearly all whaling men from Dundee. Theirs was a rather thankless

---

86. D.W.H.Walton [Ed.], Preface to Armitage, *Two Years in the Antarctic.*

task for, rightly or wrongly, they looked upon themselves as, to a certain extent, interlopers who had been forced upon us.[87]

Armitage's vindication of McKay and his men was not directed at Colbeck (who sang McKay's praises for the work he and his men had done in getting them to McMurdo Sound) but at Doorly and Scott. Doorly retaliated later by writing two books which ignored McKay and by entitling his second book of the expedition *In the Wake*, which was meant as a joke.[88] Royds had the same two men in mind when he wrote his defence of McKay:

> He is a good soul and I am afraid he has been treated very badly over this show by several people who were in a position where they could have so easily made it pleasant for him.[89]

Deaf to Explosions

Dr. William Clark Souter, the surgeon on the *Terra Nova*, described the art of blasting which commenced early in their second week:

> Blasting operations were carried out under considerable difficulty, the men often working till midnight. After being turned in for an hour or two they would be called out again to make another start.[90]
>
> On the 10th and 11th January the wind changed and drove pack ice and very large bergs on top of us but as we always had steam up we were ready at a moment's notice. Every day the ice barrier gradually broke away and we daily shifted closer.[91]
>
> A hole is drilled in the ice and a charge of sixteen and a quarter pounds is placed in it: sometimes three charges were put in. In most cases the effect was not noticeable; and in other cases ice would break up, but only in the vicinity of the charge.[92]

Men of the *Terra Nova* knew that on some days the blasting was more or less both a waste of time and a waste of guncotton. When they were using several of the smaller charges of some sixteen pounds they worked effectively only if they could be coupled to explode simultaneously as a group of three. The year before, in 1903, when Scott had tried after just two days to

87. Albert Armitage, *Two Years in the Antarctic* (1905), Ch.X.
88. Gerald Doorly, *In the Wake* (1936).
89. Charles Royds, Antarctic Diary entry, for 15 January 1904.
90. 'How Discovery was got clear', article in the *Press,* New Zealand, 2 April 1904.
91. 'Butting the Ice', article in the *Press,* New Zealand, 2 April 1904.
92. 'Voyage of the Morning', article in the *Press,* New Zealand, 2 April 1904.

explode two very small charges, he had given up altogether, convinced that explosives were not the answer.

Initially Armitage seems to have been the only man on *Discovery* who understood McKay and his methods. He had after all blasted with guncotton before on his Arctic expedition, and then when he had watched McKay's rather more powerful blasting techniques he described all *Discovery*'s efforts as 'amateuristic',[94] commenting that they did not have the necessary circuitry in 1903 to do a proper job. Armitage came to realise that Harry McKay had brought with him more than the Navy's regulation issue of explosive gear. *Discovery* was not equipped to detonate large single charges, or to fire the triple charges which were McKay's fifty pounders – his speciality ever since his early whaling days in the Arctic. The captain of the *Terra Nova* had brought the electrical detonation equipment with him from Dundee, plus the experience of how to use it, a rare combination on this expedition. Harry McKay's men wired up three charges to go off all at once. It is no wonder that their captain was well known! Heald was sent over from *Discovery* to observe the blasting but twenty miles away some were deaf to what was happening and tried to stop it. However, there was some hope that McKay might convert them, and three weeks later Scott wrote to Colbeck asking him to send him some guncotton and explosive equipment.

Sallying the Terra Nova

Jackson had not yet given up butting the ice front and in the second week he used the old whale captain's technique of rolling or 'sallying' the *Terra Nova* as the ship charged the ice front. He describes the method and the frustrations:

> On the 12th January we had another shot at butting but some loose pack jammed us up. On the 13th January we tried butting again. This time we rolled and sallied the ship in addition. All hands, at the word of command 'over!' ran from one side to the other . This produced a roll on the ship which added to the force with which she struck the barrier and had the effect of breaking it up. By this method good progress was made. Heavy snow fell all next day and night, and owing to the continuous breaking of the ice the moorings had to be continuously altered.[94]

For the rest of the week *Terra Nova* and *Morning* had to keep altering their moorings each day as they both made progress by butting. It was more

93. Albert Armitage, *Two Years in the Antarctic* (1905), Ch.XVII.
94. A. Jackson, 'Sallying the Terra Nova', article in the *Press*, New Zealand, 2 April 1904.

effective than explosives in the weather conditions that they were experiencing but a change in wind direction could blow all the loose floes that had floated away back in again. *Terra Nova* had to keep the floes moving without getting nipped, which meant McKay had to keep steam up and so a telltale wisp of smoke rose from his ship. Twenty miles away this was seen as a dreadful waste of coal, coal that would be needed when the ice broke up, though in truth it was very seldom seen at all. However, it was obviously reported and coal consumption preyed upon the Commander's mind to such an extent that he became obsessive about *his* coal. Gradually in the course of the next few weeks the use of coal was seen not as a vital safety factor to ensure that the two relief ships kept out of the way of drifting icebergs, or as an essential tool in the release of *Discovery*, but simply as an annoyance. Those who had convinced themselves that *Terra Nova* was superfluous to the scheme of things, that she was doing nothing in the least useful, never understood McKay's tactics.

Scott relied on the reports from his officers but when they reported that a mile of ice had gone out at the ice front he refused to believe it, remarking that if all the optimistic and exaggerated reports were added together the two relief ships would soon be in sight. Instead of encouraging Colbeck and McKay, he was convinced that because there was no obvious sign of his Great Providential Swell, it was all too late.

Scott always remained aloof. He had not the patience to watch the sallying, nor would he demean himself by asking a whaling captain to explain to him what he was doing. It was not a matter of naval discipline, simply a matter of class distinction. He did not want to know about the ways of a Scots whaling captain; they were sometimes amusing, but that was all.

Giving Up Sawing Again

On Monday morning, 11th January, the crew of Colbeck's ship, with some not very enthusiastic helpers from *Terra Nova*, tried sawing the ice again. Their 'experiment' was at the ice front rather than in the middle of the twenty-mile expanse of ice. Royds had also been instructed to try sawing round *Discovery*. He told Scott that he wanted to go off to talk to McKay, whom he had met at the launch in Dundee. But it was not going to be a social call; Royds needed McKay's help with the guncotton. Scott agreed to his going for the better reason that he should supervise the sawing at the ice front. In granting permission to blast, the Commander cautioned Royds not to use too much explosive and to find out exactly how to set about the work when the time comes, if it ever does come.[95]

If they had waited for Scott, the time would never have come, for less than a week later Scott was writing to Colbeck to call a halt to the rescue operations:

Scott wants my opinion of blasting and wishes it discontinued.[96]

Royds' short training course with McKay was only one of several provided in the coming weeks for the men from the *Morning* and *Discovery*, and here one can detect a growing note of optimism. Men were learning that waiting for Providence to free a ship from the grip of the ice was an interesting theoretical technique, but in the verdict of the Dundonians it was 'not proven'. After three day's work Scott sent a note to everyone telling them to stop sawing as it was a 'waste of time'. Royds stayed overnight in McKay's cabin on 15th January and was shown how to blast on the following day by McKay himself. It was apparently an eye-opener:

Blasting with McKay. Three charges in a triangular crack 60 feet apart and four to five fathoms deep. Explosions more than I expected! Broke up the floe in all directions, opened up the original crack to the original ice edge, the whole lot went out shortly after. 150 yards of ice. Went aboard "Terra Nova" to yarn with McKay and dined on the "Morning", McKay came aboard with Wilson and Colbeck. Yarned to 3 a.m.[97]

The Saturday gathering on the *Morning* hosted by Colbeck was turning into an officers' and scientists' club. Ferrar had been helping the surgeons of the *Discovery* and *Morning*, Wilson and Davidson. All three shared an interest in natural history. They had collected a specimen of a sea elephant and, being unable to lift their trophy, they went to seek Colbeck's advice. On the voyage home, the sea elephant became better known in the tropics than it was in the Antarctic, as the odour filled every corner of the ship.

Working with Nature

Jackson noted every day of the second week how much ice had been shifted by their various efforts and he was satisfied with progress. He said that sawing was not given up because of Scott's instruction about its futility:

95. Robert Falcon Scott, *The Voyage of the Discovery* (1905), Vol.2, Ch.XIX, page 331.
96. William Colbeck, Diary entry for 23 January 1904.
97. Charles Royds, Antarctic Diary, entry for 16 January 1904.

We gave it up because the ice was wasting away slowly but we have to watch our moorings as bergs drift in with the current. No joke if one caught us between it and the floe.[98]

During the week, the *Terra Nova's* Surgeon, William Clark Souter, a man with no previous experience of the Antarctic, fell out with Royds who recorded some unrepeatable remarks about the doctor in his diary. What seems to have occasioned the outburst was a criticism of Royds' work when Souter remarked on what he called the ineffectual activities going on around him. In fact he thought that Royds' and McKay's efforts were pointless and said that little ice had been broken away by either butting or blasting, or for that matter by Nature, in the course of the week. This observation, or rather the lack of observation, is telling. Of the one hundred people on the ice of McMurdo Sound that summer, only the few who worked on the rescue operation on a day-to-day basis really understood what was happening. Souter did understand eventually and then became one of Royds' and McKay's staunchest supporters. Ironically, Souter's camera recorded what actually happened in the weeks that followed. Those who took an interest and were permitted to see for themselves might watch a single explosion, note that it made no impression and then go away convinced that nothing had happened. With the exception of Burgess, the diary writers on the *Morning* saw no progress by mid-January, but the *Terra Nova* men knew better. They saw the effects develop several hours after the explosions as they moved in quickly to begin the all-important second stage of shunting the pieces about, easing them northwards. Even Royds took a long time to appreciate that one had to be quite patient before jumping to any conclusion about success or failure. Ferrar, with his knowledge of ice, displayed a sort of quiet confidence in McKay and Colbeck; he appreciated how they were working together with Nature and realised better than most that, left to its own devices, Nature would not free *Discovery*:

> I went out to see how the ice was thinning and then went over to the Terra Nova with Captain Colbeck and Hodgson to pay our respects to Captain McKay. He was very pleasant to us.[99]

According to his crew, McKay had no time for scientists but he got on well with Ferrar and Hodgson, perhaps because all three were fond of making holes.[100]

98. A.P. Jackson, Diary of a Voyage in Antarctic Regions on the ship Terra Nova, entry for 11 January 1904.
99. Hartley T. Ferrar, Antarctic Diary, entry for 10 January 1904.
100. Edward Wilson, Antarctic Diary, entry for 17 January 1904.

Sledging as a Sporting Pastime
Week Three: 17–23 January 1904

We Will Do Without

When Colbeck met Scott on 5th January 1904, they withdrew into a private meeting where they were overheard by First Officer and expert eavesdropper, Gerald Doorly, who reported that Colbeck asked Scott what he thought were the prospects of *Discovery* being freed from the ice that year and Scott replied:

Not a cat's chance![101]

Colbeck then showed the Commander the newspapers which McKay had brought from home with their criticisms of the expense of his over-large expedition. Scott's reaction was that he would not take any government stores from the *Terra Nova*:

What we haven't got we will do without.[102]

This remark greatly impressed Gerald Doorly. However, by the beginning of the third week Doorly was more interested in the amount of ice around him than in Scott's conscientiousness, and he seemed quite unaware that on Sunday 17th January a start had been made to sledge eight hundred cases of government stores from *Terra Nova* to the *Discovery* where, of course, they were not wanted.

The *Terra Nova's* Surgeon, Dr. Clark Souter, was now becoming an enthusiastic sledger and he was also keeping an eye on the men's health:

Sledging stores to the Discovery and bringing back from her the nautical and scientific instruments in view of the probable abandonment of the ship. The Morning and Terra Nova parties went as far as a half-way camp which took a day to reach. There they were met by the Discovery sledging party who took their sledges on, whilst they took over the Discovery's sledges.[103]

101. Gerald Doorly, *The Voyage of the Morning* (1916).
102. Dr. W.Clark Souter articles: 'Admiralty's Orders', and 'Dr. Souter's Sledge Journey'.
103. in the *Press*, New Zealand, 2 April 1904.

Apparently Scott did not notice all these government stores being moved into his ship, even though he had initiated the sledging operations himself. Now that the sawing season had ended somewhat abruptly, sledging was the new task which could fully occupy his men whilst they were waiting for the Great Swell to come. It was a most excellent substitute. The system was designed so that the chaps from *Discovery* shuttled their way between their ship and the halfway camp and back again to their own ship and consequently never reached the other ships where they would have found themselves in bad company, as Royds had done.

The Hopeless Prospect

A sailor on *Terra Nova* commented favourably on what the men on the other ships regarded as 'bad' weather and recorded the progress that his shipmates were making:

> On the Wednesday the temperature fell to 19 degrees Fahrenheit and it was blowing hard. By 10.30 p.m. it was a regular blizzard from the south. This resulted in a large amount of ice breaking away and bringing the relief ships nearer to Discovery. The next day there was more butting at the ice but it was ineffectual. By the end of the week the original ice between the ships had been reduced by one half.[104]

Burgess recorded in his diary on the *Morning* the depressing news which was brought back by his shipmates returning from halfway camp:

> Scott has given up all hope of saving the ship now.[105]

Some months later Scott wrote a story for the *Sphere* newspaper (he probably assumed that it would not be widely read in England) in which he was less dismal in Week Three and was making no gloomy predictions for the future:

> The ice began to weaken between the ships on January 20th and broke rapidly towards the end of the month.[106]

Skelton recorded his conviction that the ice was being broken at the rate of 100 yards per day and that McKay would make it to *Discovery*. Royds spent the week noting that sometimes a hundred yards of ice went away in the

---

104. Article, 'Butting the Ice', by an officer of the *Terra Nova*, in the *Press*, New Zealand, 2 April 1904'.
105. Len Burgess, Antarctic Diary, entry for 17 January 1904.
106. Robert Falcon Scott, article in the *Sphere* Supplement, 25 June 1904.

evening and sometimes none at all. On the Tuesday, gaining noticeably in confidence, Royds tried a McKay special – a six-charge circuit – but although the cracks produced were most impressive, there was no immediate movement of ice at all.

Ferrar and Bernacchi showed up with more dismal news. Scott was becoming very impatient and so they had found an excuse to escape and go over to the Cape Royds penguin rookery for the day to break up the camp that Scott and Wilson had left. Lo! By the time they returned, the blasted ice had all gone out. Royds, after a sleepless night worrying about his responsibilities, was happy to see that the ice was moving out well now. Burgess was suffering from the movement initiated by the blasting as they had to keep moving their moorings:

> killing work carrying these blessed ice anchors about 200 yards, then boring a hole in the ice to knock the anchor in.[107]

Antarctic Asylum

Royds and McKay were getting to know each other. Royds recorded in his diary that one evening when they were imbibing together on the *Terra Nova* Harry McKay confided:

> He loathes this place and wants to be away north again. I said thirty-seven days and he said he hoped it would be before that.[108]

Next day, with renewed faith in their abilities to win through, Royds and McKay set off six charges before lunch and by 2 pm all the ice up to the explosion area had gone out. At 8 pm a further 400 yards of ice went out.

Skelton and Bernacchi paid a visit to McKay on Friday and got filled up with rum. Skelton had come to watch operations. He saw Royds make a triple charge but, like many others, he observed that the ice had not moved after the explosion. Skelton reported back that a *Discovery* man, Whitfield, had escaped to the *Terra Nova*

> without leave and he will be kept on Discovery until he recovers.[109]

Whitfield was by no means the only man to seek asylum on the *Terra Nova*: it was an obvious choice of refuge for officers on a regular basis. That Friday a mile of the excavated ice went out in the night but if Skelton noticed this

107. Len Burgess, Antarctic Diary, entry for 20 January 1904.
108. Charles Royds, Antarctic Diary, entry for 21 January 1904.
109. Reginald Skelton, Antarctic Diary, entry for 23 January 1904.

. Whale ships in Earl Grey Docks, Dundee 1880. By the 1880s Dundee had become the premier whaling
rt of Britain and had developed expertise in building ships for work in polar areas and a reputation for ice
cue techniques using the new high explosive of guncotton. Dundee built more polar expedition ships than
y other British port; the two most famous are *Discovery*, for Scott's 1901-04 expedition, and McKay's *Terra
va*, which rescued Scott in 1904. In 1986 *Discovery* was brought home and interpreted at the new Discovery
int Centre. The light on the right of the photograph can still be seen and was part of a maritime trail until
s was blocked by a hotel built across the riverside route.

2. Left to right: Dundee whale ships *Active*, *Balaena* and *Diana* on the Dundee Antarctic Expedition of 1892-3. Painting by W. G. Burn in McManus Gallery, Dundee.

3. Scientific staff of the British Antarctic Expedition of 1898–1900. Louis Bernacchi (far right) also joined Scott's first expedition. William Colbeck (3rd from left) helped Royal Geographical Society President Clements Markham to plan Scott's expedition. Colbeck also commanded the 1903-04 rescue bids to free Scott.

4. The devious Clements Markham(left), greeted by a suspicious Prime Minister Balfour who later accused m of concealing his plans for sending relief expeditions to the Antarctic. Drawing by A. S. Boyd, for the *ustrated London News*, 23 June 1899.

5. *Discovery*, specially built in Dundee for the 1901-04 British Antarctic Expedition, sets out on her trials on e Tay.

6. *Discovery* called at Cowes on 5 August 1901 where Markham's chosen naval officers were presented to King Edward VII and Princess Victoria. Cowes is, as everyone knows, directly en route for the South Pole and promotion. Drawn by S. Begg.

7. Facing page top: the officers and scientists of the *Discovery* on their way to the Antarctic. Left to right: Wilson, Shackleton, Armitage, Barne, Koettlitz, Skelton, Scott, Royds, Bernacchi, Ferrar and Hodgson.

8. Facing page bottom: sub-zero theatrical performances by *Discovery* men recommended by Markham as sure fire way of preventing scurvy. Sadly, as Cook and Nelson knew but Scott never discovered, such advice was out of date or just silly.

9. Above: Officers of Colbeck's relief ship *Morning* in 1903. L-R Back row: Sommerville, Pepper. Main row: Doorly, Evans, Morrison, England, Captain Colbeck, Mulock (later transferred to *Discovery*), Davidson. All but two (Evans and Mulock) of Colbeck's ship's company (sent to relieve *Discovery* beset in ten miles of ice in 1903) were Merchant Navy men. Discouraged from freeing *Discovery* by Scott who wanted to stay another year, Colbeck's visit made it possible for Scott to remove all but two (Armitage and Weller) of his original fifteen Merchant Navy men from the expedition and make it a Royal Navy affair. Photograph by J.D.Morrison.

10. Facing page top: men of the *Morning* in 1903. Back row: Parkins, Riley, Rolfe, Cheetham, Sullivan, Bilsby, King. Mid row: Hender, Burgess, Noyon, Burton, Wainwright, Beer, Coelho. Front row: Taylor, Pepper, Leavy, Chester.

11. Facing page bottom: ship's company of the *Terra Nova* sent to join Colbeck's *Morning* in 1904, by which time *Discovery* was beset in eighteen miles of ice. Back row: 1st left Elms, 2nd left Souter, 3rd left Jackson, 4th left Captain McKay; 2nd row, 1st left, Aitken, 3rd row the two cooks, Grant and Clark. Dundee's McKay was chosen by the Admiralty to rescue Scott, as, since the death of Captain Adams in 1889, he was the most experienced ice master in the Arctic. Colbeck came from Hull and, in addition to experience as a first-rate seaman, he had colluded with Markham to plan Scott's over-wintering in the Antarctic. Theirs was no relief expedition but an Admiralty rescue mission ordering the expedition to return in the *Morning* and *Terra Nova* if *Discovery* could not be freed. If she could be freed, Scott was forbidden to do further scientific work in the ice from his ship.

12. *Terra Nova* Officers, anticlockwise from the top: 2nd Engineer W. Smith, Captain H. McKay, Chief Engineer A. Sharp, 2nd Steward W. Shearer, Boatswain A. Aitken, 2nd Officer A. J. Elms, 1st Officer A. P. Jackson. Photographed in New Zealand by Dr. William Clark Souter.

3. This picture is captioned in the book *The Voyage of the Discovery* 'party in deep snow'. Note how it most comes up to the men's ankles and typically is what journalists even today call gruelling conditions.

4. In contrast to the above shot of men practising Pole bagging there were no pictures in the book of any entific activity. However, Shackleton (who was sent home early in 1903 for being an officer unsuited to oyal Naval discipline) managed to record the biologist Hodgson at work. Hodgson used a dragnet under e ice, toiling in summer and winter alike. Drawing by *Illustrated London News* artist A. Forestier.

15. The London artist, Forestier, given more free rein! Armitage, who discovered the Polar Plateau, is suspended in thin air over the proverbial bottomless crevasse. With a rope round his chest he would almost certainly have expired in a few minutes. Scott insisted on rediscovering the Polar Plateau the following year, fell in a big crevasse and wrote it up as an even greater epic.

6. The *Discovery* beset miles from the ice front in McMurdo Sound, swept by heavy snowfalls and frequent
zzards and in considerable danger.

7. Despite the construction of awnings, drifts threatened to bury the ship. Colbeck reached Scott in 1903
returned to winter in New Zealand where he reported on the plight of *Discovery*, which led to the
unting of a rescue by the Admiralty in 1904.

18, 19. Dr. W. Clark Souter, surgeon on McKay's powerful rescue ship, took these two pictures of the expedition's plight, early in 1904. In 1903, when Colbeck left Scott at the onset of winter, *Discovery* was iced-in five miles from clear water. Here, *Discovery* is photographed by Souter in 1904, by which time she was some twenty miles from the sea and held firmly in a cradle of ice fifteen feet thick. The lower picture shows a blizzard with heavy drifting threatening to bury her and emphasises the need for a rescue.

20, 21. En route to Antarctica, McKay's *Terra Nova* cleared the way for Colbeck's ship through pack ice. Above: Souter's photo of a large iceberg. Below: his shot from the crow's nest of *Terra Nova* looking back to *Morning* following in their wake.

22. Colbeck's photo of man–hauling sledges with equipment from *Discovery* to the *Morning* in the best Markham Royal Navy tradition with flags (essential) – Markham had designed coats of arms for all the office to fly on their expedition sledges.

23. Morrison picture of a dog team from *Discovery* reaching *Terra Nova*. The other ships did not bring dogs The cable from the ship leads to charges of guncotton.

24. *Terra Nova* sledge party reaching the Halfway Tent where they took over the sledges from *Discovery* and turned. Photograph by Dr. W. Clark Souter.

25. Souter worked on sledging parties between the ships and photographed the large Halfway Tent with its stovepipe. When *Discovery* officers used the tent, a division was made inside to separate officers from men. Photograph by Dr. W. Clark Souter.

26 (top left). a sledging party sets off on skis – men of the *Terra Nova* were competent skiers.
27 (bottom left). two sledge parties with *Terra Nova* in the foreground, showing footprints, ski and sledge
acks at the ice edge. J. D. Morrison photographs.
28. Above, a great portrait of his ship, the *Morning*, by her Chief Engineer J. D .Morrison.

29. McKay's *Terra Nova*(top), being more powerful than the *Morning*, was much exercised in butting ice which was then pushed away by men on the ice. Photograph by Dr. W. Clark Souter

30. *Morning* in the foreground is beset in the ice whilst *Terra Nova* is working at the ice front in the distan *Discovery* is twenty miles away. Photograph by J. D. Morrison.

1. Heavy pack-ice butted by *Terra Nova*. The ice anchor and tripping line hang from the jib boom - ice
netimes drifted back as well as drifting out to sea, so the anchor was constantly being shifted and the ship
to keep steam up in order to escape being nipped in the ice. When Scott was informed of the near-
stant coal consumption, he was not appreciative. He had no desire to be rescued by a whaling captain and
played no useful part in the operations and ordered them to stop. Fortunately for him his orders were
obeyed. Photograph by Dr. W. Clark Souter.

32. Left: J.D.Morrison's picture of the *Terra Nova* butting her way to the rescue is a photograph which says all. As the two ships got closer to *Discovery,* they presented, on the one hand, increasing hopes for the imprisoned ship's company and, on the other, a growing threat to those who had no wish to have their Royal Naval careers spoiled by the ignominy of being rescued by men of the Merchant Navy. It seemed impossible to be rid of these people and unbelievable that the *Morning* had come back from New Zealand with a bunch of whaling men from Dundee! There was but one explanation open to the Commander of *Discovery* - to invent a mystical swell capable of removing eighteen miles of ice at a stroke. Thus did Providence and Nature come to the rescue of his ship on 14 February 1904! Photograph by J. D. Morrison.

33. Above, Souter's historic photograph of the *Terra Nova* reaching the Halfway Tent after blasting through some nine miles of ice. Compare Plate 25. McKay and Jackson of the *Terra Nova* made regular progress - three miles of ice per week - and they accurately forecast when they expected to reach *Discovery*. Scott was convinced that only a great providential swell could free his ship.

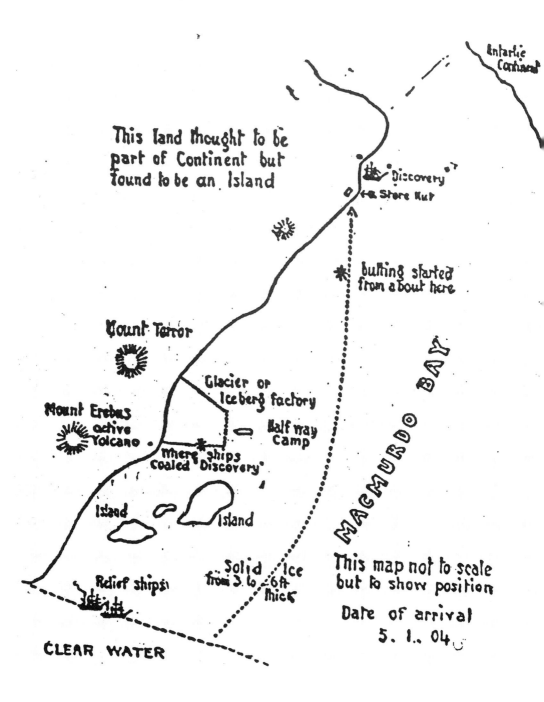

Antartic Continent

This land thought to be part of Continent but found to be an Island

Discovery

Store Hut

burning started from about here

Mount Terror

Glacier or Iceberg factory

MACMURDO BAY

Half way Camp

Mount Erebus active Volcano

Where ships coaled Discovery

Island

Island

Relief ships

Solid Ice from 3 to 6 ft thick

This map not to scale but to show position

Date of arrival 5. 1.. 04

CLEAR WATER

34. Sketch of the 1904 rescue from a letter sent to his mother in Dundee by William Smith, the Second Engineer on the *Terra Nova*.

35, 36. Morrison photographs of a blasting team and tent. Royds and Heald were two men from *Discovery* who joined in McKay's blasting on their own initiative. The *Terra Nova* and *Morning* men worked round the clock in the Antarctic summer.

37. Royds preparing the battery and electrical leads to blast the ice with guncotton, using the techniques learned from Captain Harry McKay. Admiral Pelham Aldrich and hydrographer Admiral William Wharton chose McKay particularly for his experience and skill in the use of guncotton to free ships beset in ice. Photograph by J.D. Morrison.

8. Scott's photo opportunity taken for his book *The Voyage of the Discovery*. It shows two so-called expert plosives men wiring up a little can of propellent explosive whilst reading the instruction manual, apparently aware that they should be using a Brisant explosive instead. Not surprisingly, Scott, referring to his own orts, said that explosives were a complete waste of time.

9. McKay and Royds blasted the ice with very large 16½ pound charges. *Terra Nova* in the background is the ice edge. Photograph by J. D. Morrison.

40. The 16½ pound charges of guncotton were exploded from pits dug into the ice. The break-up of the ice took several hours to manifest itself. Very few observers had the patience to wait and see the full effects. Indeed several observers came from *Discovery* and saw no visible effects in the ice and reported back that it was all ineffective, whereas in the following six hours half a mile of ice could drift out. The Halfway Tent was the main landmark indicating McKay's progress. Photograph by Dr. W. Clark Souter.

1, 42. In addition to Morrison, Dr. William Clark Souter, surgeon on the *Terra Nova*, also took an interest photographing the progress of blasting with guncotton. Note the small blasting tent on the left of the per of these two Souter pictures.

43. A McKay special(top) - a large simultaneous triple explosion lifts the ice high in the air and is captured on film by J. D. Morrison, Chief Engineer of the *Morning*.

44. Scott described the coming of a providential swell which cleared miles of ice away instantly! On the British Antarctic Expedition of 1898-1900 Louis Bernacchi photographed this big swell which brought in a massive 60-foot wall of ice. *Discovery* would never have survived it. Fortunately Scott's prayers for a swell weren't answered.

5. The moment when the rescue ships *Terra Nova* (centre) and *Morning* (right) finally reached *Discovery* (left). This photograph by Skelton shows clearly that *Terra Nova* had butted her way to reach Scott's ship and the little *Morning* again followed in her wake. The moment was also recorded as a cartoon in the *Weekly Press*, Christchurch, New Zealand by W. Bowring (see the frontispiece), showing McKay plucking *Discovery* out of the ice of McMurdo Sound. On the ships' return to New Zealand a cover-up story was broadcast in the press with the help of Markham's brother-in-law, the Hon. C. C. Bowen. The cartoon and this photograph are the first clues that the official account of the expedition being released by a great providential swell had deleted from the records all mention of the extraordinary rescue feat by McKay and Colbeck and their men. The newspaper men were in no doubt about the true story of the rescue but their version of events was suppressed and it was never published in Britain, apart from in Dundee, which doesn't count.

46, 47. Men of the two rescue ships coaling *Discovery*, taking coal which had been stored temporarily on glacier by Captain Colbeck the previous year. They were then ordered to give up their own fuel supplies. This obliged *Terra Nova* and *Morning* to go through the pack ice to New Zealand under sail without auxili steam power. When the *Morning* gave up her coal, she then lacked ballast and was described by her Captain unseaworthy. Both photographs by J. D. Morrison.

3. Dr .William Clark Souter was fond of grouping his pictures thematically. Here is his pictorial triptych, published in a New Zealand newspaper, and captioned (a) DESPAIR (b) HOPE (as *Discovery* is reached) (c) (as *Discovery* is freed).

49. *Discovery* (top) blasted free of her ice cradle. But after six long weeks of inactivity due to the belief that she would never be freed, she had not been made ready to sail. Men from *Terra Nova* worked with *Discovery* Engineer Reginald Skelton all hours to effect yet another rescue. Photograph by William Colbeck.

50. Robertson Bay. An exasperated Captain McKay in *Terra Nova* (right) waiting for *Discovery* (left) to change her rudder which was damaged when she ran aground after the rescue. Then, leaving for New Zealand, her pumps failed and, according to Louis Bernacchi, she was nearly lost for a third time. Photograph by Reginald Skelton.

next morning, he didn't record it. *Terra Nova* and *Morning* were now almost at the tent which was formerly designated as Halfway Camp. Lieutenant Mulock, the surveyor, arrived to take over from Royds who gave him a quick training course in explosives, McKay-style. Each of the two rescue ships had seven tons of guncotton remaining (there was none on *Discovery*) and the crews calculated that this should be sufficient – no need to be too sparing in the coming weeks.

Jackson had been thinking about the *Discovery* and he was not impressed with the lack of support for their rescue bid from a certain quarter. He had already begun to think the unthinkable. What if the *Discovery* should not be released,

or should meet with some mishap after her release?[110]

At least all the gear, instruments, specimens and records of her two-year sojourn in the ice would soon have been sledged over to the edge of the ice floe and safely stowed on the two rescue ships. Jackson didn't take part in this work himself because he and seven men from the *Terra Nova* were busy blasting at the time.

To the Sledge Camp

Ironically the best account of sledging to the Halfway Camp was given not by the master sledger and expert writer from his desk in the bowels of his ship *Discovery*, but by two complete sledging novices on the much-despised relief ship. The first description comes from Dr. Clark Souter, Surgeon on the *Terra Nova*. It was made at a time when men from *Terra Nova* and *Discovery* had equally far to go. The second account was made when Halfway Camp was no longer at the mid point:

> It was arranged that all instruments, records, apparatus, collections of speci-
> mens and all valuable books should be transferred in the first instance, while
> personal gear was to come later on. As the distance was so considerable and as
> congestion was to be avoided, a home-made sail cloth tent fitted with
> reindeer sleeping bags, tarpaulins, stores and cooking utensils was erected on
> the ice near the glacier, half-way between the ships. The Discovery's party
> was to pull the precious loads down to the tent, sleep there all night and
> return next day while the united party from the relief ships came up to the
> tent with more or less light loads and returned to their own ships with the

110. A.P.Jackson, 'The Relief Ships', Article in the *Press*, New Zealand, 2 April 1904.

sledge loads left waiting. In this way the two ships' companies were never at the tent at the same time.[111]

On Sunday 17th January the first sledge party left the relief ships heavily laden with frozen beef and fresh potatoes for the Discovery. Camp being reached about 7 p.m. the party, feeling rather fatigued with the unwonted exercise, had a good meal of seal steak, biscuits, butter and cheese with plenty of tea or cocoa. After a copious repast we turned into our reindeer sleeping bags which we had laid on the tarpaulin spread on the ice, some to read, some to sleep, some to talk, but most, of course, to enjoy the greatest of Antarctic luxuries – a really good smoke.[112]

Souter is one of the few commentators to record the interest shown by the men of the *Discovery* in what McKay and Royds were doing:

Next morning about nine o'clock when the cook – a man from Discovery – roused us up, our first consideration was not our breakfast but we went out at once to see how much the ships had come in during the night. After a big tin plateful of solid porridge and some tea, we set out on our return to the ships and it was a matter of everyday observation that the Terra Nova was always the nearer ship to our tent, and usually we made for it. On the march we suffered badly from thirst which we quenched by drinking lime juice whenever a halt was made.[113]

In this way did government beef and potatoes find their way on to *Discovery*.

A Novice Sledger as Happy as Harry

William Smith, the Second Engineer of the *Terra Nova*, wrote an account of his sledge journey:

Sunday 17 January 1904.

I shall remember this day all my life. A sledging party started for camp, supposed to be halfway to the Discovery, to bring down some cases of instruments. There were four sleighs in all. We got half roads all right and then the fun started for after that we were up to our knees in snow and I can assure you that it takes it out of a fellow. First one man dropped out and had to be put on a sleigh, then another dropped out but he had to fall behind taking it easy – this all happening within ten minutes of our reaching our goal.[114]

111–113. Article by Dr W.Clark Souter in *Dundee Advertiser* 11 May 1904.
114. William Smith of the *Terra Nova*, article in *Dundee Advertiser*, 11 May 1904.

We got there all right pretty fagged out, but after a good tuck in felt not so bad. The next item on our programme was to get our sleeping bags ready. Getting nicely ensconced into it we all felt as happy as Harry! Just fancy sleeping inside a hut in five degrees of frost!

On Monday the return journey was safely accomplished.[115]

There was one other refugee. Dr Edward Wilson visited the *Terra Nova* in that third week and he too enjoyed the company of the Dundee Captain. In January and February 1904 Wilson was engrossed in his natural history studies, particularly of penguins, and seems to have taken very little notice of the people and events all around him, although in company with most officers from *Discovery* who had paid a visit to the *Terra Nova* he did notice McKay this once:

Long talks with Colbeck and Davidson on the Morning and then went over to see McKay with Colbeck. We brought McKay over to the Morning and he remained spinning yarns of the north until 3 a.m. He was most amusing and entertaining having been north whaling for thirty or forty years. He knows most of the northern explorers and was on one of the Greely Relief Expedition ships. He had the most profound contempt for scientists as a class and certain of them in particular.[116]

Sadly, Edward Wilson tells us no more of this conversation but it fills in more detail in the picture of McKay who, although he was ill-treated in some quarters, seems to have been much appreciated by the majority of officers and scientists from all three ships, which suggests that there really was only one person who was 'treating McKay badly', to quote the words of Charles Royds, the only person it would seem who had any motive for doing so.

115. William Smith of the *Terra Nova*, article in *Dundee Advertiser*, 11 May 1904.
116. Edward Wilson, Antarctic Diary, entry for 17 January 1904.

CHAPTER TWELVE

An Agreeably Disappointed Man
Week Four: 24–30 January 1904

The Prisoners of Discovery

Whitfield was brought back from his runaway trip to the *Terra Nova*. But nobody considered what ought to be done, which sheds light on the attitude of naval officers to the men serving under them at that time. There was, for example, no suggestion that Whitfield should visit one of the four doctors who just happened to be on the expedition. Ships' doctors were employed to check out men when they were signed on, not when they were ill. There was no suggestion that perhaps Whitfield left this much-loved ship because he wanted to, or because a constant stream of officers were being allowed to run away from *Discovery* to *Terra Nova* every week. It can hardly be a coincidence that from this time onwards the frequency of officers' trips to the *Terra Nova* declined suddenly.

Scott was himself a prisoner in *Discovery* and had been so for several weeks. He felt hemmed in during this particular week and decided to take a short walk up the hill just behind the ship where he interpreted everything that he saw as bad news.

Looking out towards the *Morning* and *Terra Nova*, he could see across Erebus Bay to two major landmarks – ten miles away was the glacier tongue which came down the slopes of the active volcano of Mount Erebus on Ross Island, which was the site of their coal depot. He could also make out the nearest of the small Dellbridge Islands behind the glacier tongue just over a mile further on. In the course of the week these proved to be useful features which served to mark plainly the progress that was now being made by McKay. But Colbeck's ship was in difficulty and had stopped; as Burgess recorded, they were beset in the ice again. The sledging parties between *Discovery* and *Morning* were prevented by sudden movement of the ice from reaching four sledges which should have been exchanged for Burgess' sledges, but they had been abandoned rather hurriedly by the men from the *Discovery*:

> We can do nothing. The Terra Nova is closer to the main ice than us so we signalled her to get to the ice and send a party out to fetch the sledges. McKay

sent a party of fourteen and retrieved the sledges and next day he sent the sledges over. All morning on the 29th we were trying to get clear of the pack. We have had only eight hours sleep in the week.[117]

Colbeck's diary takes up the story of the tent which had drifted some long way out to sea:

the tent and primuses loss bemoaned – but Evans went to see McKay and was overjoyed to find that he had picked them up. Went to dinner, back at 11pm.[118]

Why Guncotton is Useless

On his trip up the hill at Hut Point Scott could not understood why the ice was breaking along the Erebus coast first because he could not accept the truth that a great deal of explosive effort was being employed there. It was not long into Week Four before Scott elaborated on this his favourite theme, that of explosives, which by then seems to have become a metaphor for McKay and *Terra Nova*. Explosives had now begun to symbolise a rude and shattering intrusion into Scott's pure, white, idyllic world of Nature and Providence:

Everyone agrees that explosives are useless and only tend to forestall nature by an hour or two. I learn that Terra Nova's butting came to naught, as I expected.[119]

He had never waited 'an hour or two' to see how guncotton should be used properly but it would not have made any difference even if he had, for he now had no alternative but to insist that his ship could only be released from the ice by Nature herself. Gone was the thought that Colbeck was useful. As there was so much work for Nature still to do and as there was so little time in which she could do it, all Scott could hope for now was that the Great Swell would come soon, like a tsunami or giant tidal wave that occurs after violent submarine volcanic eruptions or earthquakes. Fortunately for everyone concerned, his prayers were not answered and the active volcano Erebus just fumed away quietly in the background and nothing violent happened.

Armitage, who was on *Discovery* at the same time, commented during this week on the use of explosives by the rescue ships, and his remarks could hardly have been more in contrast:

117. Len Burgess, Antarctic Diary, 27 January 1904.
118. Colbeck Private Papers, MS 212 Item 24, 30 January 1904.
119. Robert Falcon Scott, *The Voyage of the Discovery*, vol.2. page 336.

Explosives were again brought into play and had a good effect in shaking up and cracking the ice in readiness for the ocean swell when it came along. At times it seemed as though our boundaries would never narrow; at others quantities of ice would separate from the main body and float away. Often after a charge had been fired there was no change in the appearance of the ice for some hours; then suddenly and quietly, a large flat piece would detach itself from the parent floe and set out on its voyage of discovery and dissolution.[120]

Royds, who was also on the *Discovery* at this time, began the week by observing that the ships had not yet reached the place where the *Morning* moored during the 1903 Relief Expedition, but he was not depressed. In fact he was cheered with the progress reports from *Terra Nova*. *Morning* was still beset in the ice all week but her crew were still working excessively long hours at the sledging.

Creaking and Groaning on Discovery

It is amusing to find that Scott's ups and downs now began to correlate with the movements of the tide. Beginning on Thursday, we can witness one typical rise and fall. The results of the blasting away of over half of the eighteen miles of the ice between Colbeck and Scott were allowing the tidal effects to be felt by the Commander even when he was tucked up in his bunk:

> This morning as I lay in my bunk I was astonished to hear the ship creaking. On getting up I found that she was moving in the ice with a very slow rhythmic motion. After breakfast we all went to Hut Point and found that the whole ice-sheet was swaying very slightly under the action of a long swell.[121]

Ferrar (who doubtless had never seen an ice sheet swaying before) rushed out to cast his scientific eye on the Hut Point phenomenon and calculated that a swell of twelve inches had broken away an area of ice 50 by 200 yards. Scott, seeing this cheering sight, set off up the hill at once to get depressed:

> One feels immensely cheered till one goes up the hill and looks out on the long miles of ice and misty screen which hides the sea.[122]

Scott then let slip an amazing and revealing turn of phrase:

> Went up the hill shortly after Koettlitz and was most agreeably disappointed to find open water just round the edge of the glacier.[123]

120. Albert Armitage *Two Years in the Antarctic*, (1905).
121–123. Robert Falcon Scott, *The Voyage of the Discovery*, vol.2.Ch.XIX.
    p. 336

So, at the end of a very effective week with good reports from the two relief ships, Scott still managed to stay depressed. Fortunately the men of the *Terra Nova* carried on relentlessly, paying no regard to the antics around *Discovery*.

From this point onwards the story of blasting is sometimes rather difficult to disentangle and a number of later commentators have misinterpreted the contemporary reports, confusing the blasting operations near *Terra Nova* by Colbeck and McKay with the blasting operations around *Discovery* by Scott's men, just as some have confused orders from Scott to stop the blasting round his ship with a request to stop all blasting. Others have further confused Scott's orders to stop the sawing with his orders to stop the blasting. There had been no blasting at all around Scott's ship in the first four weeks of the rescue operation but Royds was just beginning to think that if one had eighteen miles of ice to move it might be quicker if one worked at both ends simultaneously during February and maybe the Commander should be told.

Always Look on the Gloomy Side

During January and February 1904 Scott always looked on the gloomy side first:

> One can see the ships distinctly with their hulls but this is probably due to a mirage . . . I grow a little sceptical of reports which tell of the departure of a mile or half a mile of ice.[124]

He was convinced that there was an irresistible tendency to exaggerate the amount of ice breaking away[125] but he could not risk going to the ice front to find out for himself. In the last three days of that week Royds took a very different view of the situation:

> All last night, and today [Thursday] the Terra Nova has been working the ice and everything is on the creak, most extraordinary breaking up at Hut Point. [Friday] Swell continues, spirits go up and down. [Saturday] Hopes very high but swell died down.[126]

Other *Discovery* officers were excited by the movement felt on the ship. Armitage, Royds, Ferrar and Skelton now fully understood what Scott could never see, that McKay was working with the swell. If the relief ships had not assisted the natural break-up of the ice and had not moved the broken ice out of the way, often working day and night to do so, the tidal

124–25. Robert Falcon Scott, *The Voyage of the Discovery*, Vol.2 Ch/XIX.
126. Charles Royds, Antarctic Journal, 28 January 1904.

movement or swell could not have come in. The creaking of *Discovery* had nothing to do with Providence, it was the result of the carving up of the ice field. McKay was not trying to cut a canal to *Discovery*, he was paring off the ice front and shunting it out to the north.

Nor was there going to be that one Great Ocean Swell that Scott still believed in. They could see now that it was the little swells that really mattered. However, there was a long way to go: still ten miles of ice. As the ice breakers got nearer to the *Discovery,* things got thicker, in more senses than one. Butting and drilling ice which was fifteen feet thick was going to be more difficult. Jackson on the *Terra Nova* was not quite so full of joy as Mulock that week. Good work had been done to let the swell in, and this had cheered the officers on *Discovery* watching from the hill. However, the temperature was too low, with thirty degrees of frost, for any spectacular progress. It was still possible to break the ice using the *Terra Nova's* engines and ramming the ice front with the ship but Jackson was less hopeful that the floes would continue to go out so effectively at the end of that week.

On the Saturday all the ice that had been broken that day drifted out until midnight, but then it all drifted back in again. This was typical of the job; it was nothing to get despondent about. McKay had got to the halfway point in four weeks. True, he only had three weeks left. He would have to put on a spurt.

CHAPTER THIRTEEN

Taking an Interest
Week Five: 31 January–6 February 1904

Someone Should Do Something Now!

By the beginning of Week Five even the most reluctant observer of the scene at Hut Point should have noticed that the sledging parties were only taking half the time to complete their journeys, because the distance between *Discovery* and the rescue ships had been so much reduced. Scott did notice, so he decided to go across to the *Morning* to stop the men sledging. There were some other little indications of change: noises such as more creaking of ship's timbers and the sound of cheerful officers on board the *Discovery*. There was also a fleeting thought crossing some men's minds that perhaps the two captains, Colbeck and McKay, would be able to achieve the impossible and get their ship out after all. It seemed that even the ship's cat might have a chance now.

To their Commander, what mattered much more than getting the ship out was the manner in which *Discovery* was extricated from the ice. It would be a complete disaster for him if credit went to McKay and the *Terra Nova* for the release of his ship. The time had now come to do something positive near the ship, as Royds had already hinted; after all the Commander was a naval torpedo officer, and despite what he had just written about explosives the previous week, he ought not to return home with the relief ships' supply of guncotton still virtually intact and so risk being accused of not really trying to get out by every means at his disposal. Shackleton, writing in Dundee, had assured everyone that Scott would get free.

Scott had, of course, tried blasting the year before, which is how he had discovered that explosives were so absolutely useless. The conditions in February 1904 were not really similar to that last escapade in February 1903 when *Morning* came to within five miles of his ship. Now *Morning* was still seven miles distant from Hut Point and the ice that held *Discovery* in its grip was fifteen feet thick. It was moulded around the ship like a plaster cast and held her fast. One could not be sure that *Discovery* would be freed from the grip of this ice cradle. The good news was that everyone on *Discovery* had just experienced this movement in the ice, and now that it had moved one ought to do something, even if it wasn't easy to think what. Scott believed that it was simply a race against time, a race between the coming of the Great Swell and the coming of the Long Winter. This was a view which he managed to abandon by the end of the week but was able to resurrect when he came to write his book.

That was his creative genius.

A Torpedo Officer's First Lesson

Scott spent Thursday 4th February with McKay. It was an important event, for the meeting was in reality a training course; McKay's 'yarns', as they called them, were accounts of the Captain's adventures designed to give Scott a distillation of the whaling captain's working experience in the ice, and Scott emerged miraculously converted. But he was no mere convert to guncotton, he had become the officer who introduced guncotton and it was now *his* idea!

It was Scott's first visit to the relief ships for a month. The *Terra Nova* crew demonstrated to the Commander what he had been missing – how blasting should be done. Scott was critical of their efforts and, according to Doorly, he made his standard remarks about the ice going out too slowly to have any effect. Nevertheless his attitude was changing even as he watched.

On the following day he tried to give the impression that he had personally taken command of all blasting operations, first at the *Terra Nova* and then initiating blasting at *Discovery*. What actually happened was slightly different. Heald, with two men from each rescue ship, after showing off the McKay blasting techniques with three simultaneous detonations using *Terra Nova's* long cables, demonstrated why and how the ice cracked, when ice cracked, and when it could be expected to move out. No wonder that this day changed Scott's attitude to cracks in the ice and the importance of helping ice to move out. From this point onwards he began to preach in his usual fashion, as if it was something that he had just invented. He then took Heald and his four *Terra Nova* and *Morning* instructors to the *Discovery* to show his chaps how to do it.

When Scott wrote his beautiful prose in *The Voyage of the Discovery*, the crews of the *Terra Nova* and *Morning* were suddenly re-cast as navvies who were there to dig holes for his Royal Navy experts. Not even his Journal acknowledges their work. But the most extraordinary part of this whole fantasy is Scott's invention of a special party of experienced torpedo officers drawn from his team of old shipmates on the *Discovery*, who are conjured up in his imagination to begin the blasting operations:

I have sent to the Discovery for a party of our special torpedo men who will continue to fit, place and fire the charges whilst the men of the relief ships go on digging holes.[127]

But Len Burgess tells a different story of five gangs of three seamen blasting:

Leaving four hands on board to work the ships we are going on all day. It was 7. 30 when we knocked off tonight blasting this end and a blasting party at the other end.[128]

Explaining How He Did It

It is typical of the way that Scott's fictions have been written and have then found their way into the official records as non-fiction, that the month of largely successful blasting done by McKay and Royds between 5th January and 6th February was edited out of the records at a stroke by this extraordinary claim, the simple half-truth of this one incredible entry:

Took charge of the blasting on 6th February and the work was carried out with great vigour.[129]

Blasting was then going on at 'both ends' but Scott's writings show that he had considerable difficulty in composing his narrative for his Week Five Fantasy. Somehow he had to transpose the gloom of his Journal (where there was no progress, where everything was now entirely dependent on the coming of the Great Swell, and where he was suffering from what he called his irritation over the absence of a swell) into a different story to be told with enthusiasm – the idea not just of working with Nature but much more than this. He had to adopt McKay's theme: if you don't move the ice out, working round the clock by taking advantage of the midnight sun, then you really cannot expect Nature to come in and free your ship for you.

It was tricky to explain his change of attitude which had switched so violently from total lack of interest in blasting to this sudden enthusiasm. He could not admit that other people had contributed much before 6th February. He had to create the myth that all the blasting of the ice had been *his* blasting. He had to show how single-handedly he had suddenly taken the initiative in the fifth week. He could, of course, have claimed that as he was in sole command of the expedition, any successes that had been achieved in January by the relief ships should be credited solely to Royds

127. Robert Falcon Scott, *The Voyage of the Discovery*, Vol.2, page 340.
128. Len Burgess, Antarctic Journal, 6 February 1904.
129. Robert Falcon Scott, quoted in the *Press*, New Zealand, 2 April 1902.

who was in command 'down there'. This would cut McKay out of the picture and at the same time it could imply that Royds had just been sent to experiment with the explosives until his Commander came along to show him how to blast the ice front properly.

But Scott had a more daring plan to explain why he started blasting on 6th February and why nothing had happened before Week Five:

> I did not want to begin explosions whilst the distance was so great, but on considering the stagnant condition of affairs I decided to make a start today. [6th February 1904].[130]

What would he have written had he known about the twenty-five other diaries being recorded at that time, including several by his so-called navvies?

How To Write an Ice Manual

So much for Scott's respect for his 'old acquaintance, Captain McKay' who had proved so useful to him. One is reminded of a remark made by Armitage:

> Scott would, apparently, make a great friend of a man and throw him to one side.[131]

Armitage had served his purpose until his discovery of the Polar Plateau posed a threat. He had found a possible route to the Pole but this just had to be Scott's route. Similarly, McKay and Royds posed threats as they blasted their way to *Discovery* without their Commander taking any of the credit. When Scott sat down to compose his official book version of these events, he collected together all the points he had picked up about the use of guncotton. But once again the version for publication presents a story in which he appears as the hero and there is not the least hint of his sudden conversion to blasting. A more candid version might have been more entertaining and would have read like this:

1 Do not imagine guncotton is useless (forget what I said last week).

2 It has been evident to me for some time (since yesterday) that if explosives are to be of any use they must be expended freely (not sparingly as I told Royds last month).

3 Don't think that if no cracks appear after an explosion that they will not develop later (as I used to think).

130. Robert Falcon Scott, *The Voyage of the Discovery*, Vol.2, page 339.
131. Albert Armitage, unpublished memo to Hugh Robert Mill, 24 May 1922.

4 We need to get ahead of Nature by forming transverse cracks (not waiting for Nature's Great Swell to come).

5 It is essential to have the proper electrical circuitry so that several charges can be detonated simultaneously (Royds didn't bring ours).

6 The process needs a good officer with proper organising ability – a torpedo officer is the best type of person. (Without such a man one might hang about for five weeks and achieve nothing at all).

Commander Scott's sole contribution to the blasting operation was to place little wooden sticks to indicate where Colbeck and McKay's chaps ought to dig the holes in the ice. The rest is fiction.

The Two Experts

It did not matter to McKay who should be credited with the job of releasing Scott's ship; he had no interest in bronze medals. His attitude would doubtless have been similar to that of the great Arctic explorer John Rae. When Rae came from Canada to visit his old home in Orkney, he failed to collect his Royal Geographical Society medal in London, thereby missing a rather good speech by one of Clements Markham's predecessors, the geologist, President Sir Roderick Murchison. The idea of Rae traversing the leafy London squares to discover Savile Row and accepting a medal for his Arctic skills does seem rather bizarre. By the same token, McKay needed no end-of-term report from Scott or even one from Colbeck. Bronze medals were given to the majority of the rescuers and silver medals awarded to those who were rescued because the distinction between bronze and silver rested not on a man's merit but on the length of time he spent away from home.

The leader of the expedition was faced by a profoundly difficult dilemma. Which myth should he construct? He could claim credit for freeing *Discovery* with explosives, on the grounds of being an expert and fully trained torpedo lieutenant. Alternatively, he could boldly assert that explosives, sawing and butting were all completely ineffectual and that *Discovery* was released in a matter of a few hours by a Great Swell. But in Week Five the disadvantage of both these ploys was that Scott couldn't be sure that *Discovery* would be freed. So the two myths had to be capable of explaining failure as well as success and they must do so without reflecting badly on the leader of the expedition. The advantage of both myths was that whether *Discovery* was freed or not, Scott could claim that Colbeck and McKay played no role in the rescue whatsoever. The Commander could tidy up the book version of what happened later, but he would need to be careful about what he wrote in the next few rather critical weeks in his Journal. For the most part he was very careful.

Until now nobody has ever suggested that a Royal Navy torpedo man might actually have no knowledge at all about blasting holes in ice with guncotton and electrical detonators. But Scott and McKay were different types of explosive expert, used to two quite different types of explosives and familiar with different ways of starting their explosive charges. The Royal Navy officers understood Propellent Explosives and they understood their propulsive effect in such missiles as naval torpedoes. By way of contrast McKay was an expert in Brisant Explosives with their shattering effect of heaving large floes of ice up into the air. A torpedo is initiated by percussion but an ice-breaking blast is initiated by an electrically operated fuse head. Although Scott had seen demonstrations by McKay, he cannot have paid very close attention for he writes of using a lead/acid accumulator in his blasting work. This was an unfortunate slip and the product of his literary imagination and it rather spoils his other claims of expertise in this field.

The Souter and Morrison Photographs

William Clark Souter, the young doctor, just qualified in 1902 and recommended by his Professor in Aberdeen University to act as surgeon to the *Terra Nova*, was interested in photography. The young men on all three ships became the butt of jokes and Colbeck, quoting Harry McKay, wrote:

> Souter has only taken a dozen photographs since he left England, McKay says he is a thorough Aberdonian![132]

But the joke was on them, for McKay had no camera and Colbeck's pictures were poorly processed in New Zealand, but both Souter's *Terra Nova* coverage and Chief Engineer Morrison's *Morning* coverage have given us the finest collection of pictures of the 1904 rescue operation. The men of McKay's ship had no need of a doctor, they suffered only from the occasional hangover, so Souter found himself under-employed and he obtained McKay's permission to attach himself to the sledging and blasting parties and always had his camera at the ready. Lacking polar experience, he was often teased by the *Terra Nova* officers, but fellow Scot J. D. Morrison from the other relief ship seems to have befriended him (an odd partnership

132. William Colbeck, Private Papers, MS 212 Item 13 27 December 1903.

in view of the Chief Engineer's acidic wit), perhaps because they shared this interest in photography, and together they recorded the blasting. After the expedition was over, when they returned to New Zealand, both Souter and Morrison were sought out by reporters from the *Weekly Press*, and so it came about that for three consecutive editions that newspaper featured their pictures of the rescue, no doubt to the surprise and embarrassment of the leader of the National Antarctic Expedition.

Their most revealing pictures are of explosions. Anyone attempting to promote the fiction that Colbeck and McKay played no part in the rescue and that blasting and butting were ineffectual would now have to explain the pictorial journalism of these two photographers. However, those who were busy creating the Great Swell story were doubtless much relieved to learn that the copyright of these pictures would remain in New Zealand. In order to answer such awkward questions as why *Discovery*'s photographer, Reginald Skelton, had no pictures of blasting, a very strange photo was mocked up and found its way into a rival New Zealand newspaper and finally into Scott's book in 1905. It shows two men from the *Discovery* sitting on a small sledge beside three pint-sized cylinders together with an accumulator and some wires. This equipment has no connection with the blasting done by Colbeck and McKay, whose sixteen-and-a-half-pound guncotton charges are shown in a Morrison photo as metal kegs, like two-gallon beer barrels, with some very convincing follow-up pictures.

CHAPTER FOURTEEN

Abandon Ship!
Week Six: 7–13 February 1904

Return to the Gloom

At the beginning of the week the weather was fine with some of those balmy days which in the previous month Scott would have welcomed whilst cursing the days of strong northerly or southerly winds. It is a measure of his recent contact with the blasting fraternity from the rescue ships that he now complained about clear blue skies and calm, convinced that the ice was not breaking up and even daring to think that the Great Swell was not going to come. On Monday the 8th he lamented:

> Wretched luck today. It is quite calm and the swell has almost vanished; the floes that broke away last night are still hanging about the ice-edge and damping what little swell remains.[133]

From this observation it would seem that he had at last grasped the reason for moving floes out as soon as possible, but in his state of despondency he plodded the six weary miles back to his ship. Again he retreated into the inner sanctum of the *Discovery*, observing that hope had fallen to a low ebb. Explosions were continuing but he was sure it was too late for it was now only a matter of days before the season closed altogether. For Wednesday 10th his book records:

> Everyone now is making an effort to be cheerful, but it is an obvious effort. I have made every arrangement for abandoning the ship. . . . I don't think I ever had a more depressing evening's work.[134]

Thursday dawned dismal grey with a snowstorm to add to his gloom. Colbeck's men were in high spirits and he had the temerity to ask Scott to help them:

133–134. Robert Falcon Scott, *The Voyage of the Discovery*, Vol.2, pages
    343, 345.

Scott thought things looked black. It was a glorious day at the ice so I sent Doorly to ask Scott for extra men.[135]

Royds was duly dispatched with six men to help dig holes. At this late stage of the rescue other officers from *Discovery* volunteered to dig and they suffered from snow blindness in the glare of the long hours of Antarctic summer sunshine. Snow blindness was a common ailment on *Discovery*. Quite senior officers suffered from the ailment but no explanation is given. It is easy enough to lose one's snow goggles especially when working energetically digging a snow pit which is filling to the brim with sea water. The heavy work produced perspiration but their goggles did not steam up as they were made of wood on the Inuit pattern. We are left wondering why it was exclusive to *Discovery*.

Hope Gone to Zero

Although one might have thought that Colbeck's request for more men to help should have raised Scott's hopes on 11th February, quite the reverse was true and the following day he recalled his six men to *Discovery* to the utter amazement of the crews of the two rescue ships. Once more he concluded that the explosions were ineffectual and yet he recorded the fact that ice around his ship was so rotten that two men fell into the sea. So the rapid melting of the ice did nothing to raise his hopes.

In the course of Week Six, Scott observed that hope had gone to zero, that the whole outlook was depressing, that nothing short of a miracle would free the ship, and lastly, that he had abandoned all hope. He returned to his former beliefs and again thought that the rescue efforts were of no value. The men of the rescue ships were paying no attention to Scott's changes of mood, nor, it would seem, to his extraordinary belief that he was overseeing all the blasting operations, and so his orders to stop blasting were observed only at the *Discovery* end of the operations.

The *Terra Nova* crew recorded a week of continuous blasting activity round the clock. The ship's blacksmith, Colin Macgregor, was fully employed making ice drilling tools for the men of the *Morning*. For some reason Colbeck's men, most of whom came from his home port of Hull, were not familiar with the tools required for the job of preparing the ice for blasting. Jackson recorded that on both the Sunday and the Monday of that week the blasting was helping to move the ice effectively, but by the end of the week his spirits were beginning to waver and there were even times

135. William Colbeck, Private Papers, MS 212 Item 13 11 February 1904.

when it was difficult for him to say whether Nature, or Man, played the greater part. But his loss of faith in the eventual success of his efforts was short-lived compared to some others:

> Ice coming away by blasts, I think guncotton is helping. Looking more like getting Discovery out, though Scott seems to have given up hope.[136]

Events then took another turn that might easily have depressed Scott even further had he been told about it, but fortunately he wasn't. The *Morning* was once more beset, firmly locked in the ice for several days, but her crew continued their all-out efforts on the ice. Jackson and McKay, ignoring orders to stop, continued to blast every day and worked through the light of the Antarctic night with such good results that they had to keep moving their ice anchors. Such was the break-up of ice by the weekend that the men digging holes around the *Terra Nova* had to take great care not to fall through the fast rotting ice, or to suffer a similar fate to the Halfway Tent which had been carried far out to sea on a rapidly melting floe and had to be retrieved by McKay. By the weekend the *Terra Nova* had succeeded in getting to within just three miles of her goal.

'It Could Be Worked Different!'

When the *Morning* was beset in the ice during the week, it should not be imagined that her crew were contributing nothing to the rescue efforts; in fact their efforts were redoubled during the week, as Len Burgess records in some detail:

7th Feb.	Blasting all day. Good success, over half a mile from 9am to 7.30pm.
8th Feb.	Blasting all day. We have got 14 holes done today. As soon as there comes any wind there are five gangs of us, three men in each hole. We wear thigh length boots because the water comes in and we are always wet through. Sometimes we use guncotton to make a hole deeper. Twenty-nine and a half pound charges of guncotton and we blast two holes at a time with double charges, that is 118 lbs each blast.
9th Feb.	The wind shifted the ice in the night so we turned to at 6 a. m. and blasted six charges, then the wind died.
10th Feb.	No blasting today. Digging.

136. A.P. Jackson A Diary of a Voyage to Antarctic Regions on the ship Terra Nova, entry for 7 February 1904.

11th Feb.	Blasting 6 a.m. Colbeck sent to Scott for more men from Discovery who come on at midnight.
12th Feb.	We relieve Discovery men at 6 a.m. and work away to noon. No Discovery men come out. We find Scott is going to send all his men back as she is not going away fast enough. It is something shameful how we are being worked. 15 hours yesterday now 18 hours today. It is killing work, we know it is for a good cause but it could be worked different. The Terra Nova men are not being worked half so hard as us. They have 18 sailors and we have only 9 but the best of it is we are working three gangs (of 3 men each) and the "Terra Nova" only 2 gangs (of 9 men each). So we are a hole ahead of them every time and putting three times the hours in. It is dreadful hard. We have all to come in on account of three of us getting frost bitten. We were all caught in time – the officer going his rounds noticed and sent us in and then they were all sent in.
13th Feb.	The Second Officer [Lieutenant E. R. G. R. Evans] fell in the sea today, he went to examine what damage a blast had done and got rather too far and fell in but he got out again before help arrived but it very near killed him – he was all frozen before he got to the ship.[137]

Burgess' shipmate James Paton added an interesting comment on the *Terra Nova* crew working alongside them and on the effectiveness of blasting:

> They are splendid fellows to work with. We are now much nearer Discovery than we was last year – so much for the blasting.[138]

Conditions Overcast

Discovery's Boatswain, Thomas Feather, returned from helping the teams digging at the *Terra Nova* and reported to Scott that practically nothing had happened since his leader had left after his brief visit on 11th February when he had gone over to recall all his men. Feather's report was no great surprise to Scott; after all, he had ordered the suspension of *all* blasting operations. Still, it was odd that with *Terra Nova* only three miles away, the men on the *Discovery* hadn't noticed the sound of the regular explosions getting nearer day by day. They were either out of earshot in their cabins writing their

137. Len Burgess, Diary, entries 7 to 13 February 1904.
138. James Paton, Diary, entry for 13 February 1904.

diaries and turning them into books, or they chose to ignore these disturbing sounds.

Feather, like everyone else on that ship, told his Commander what he wanted to hear. Scott frequently preferred to rely on information from the lower ranks, rather than from his senior officers and scientists, with the exception of Wilson, and on this expedition he was happiest in the company of leading stoker William Lashly and Petty Officer Edgar Evans who always knew what their leader required and how to deliver it. This explains in part why Scott knew so little about what was happening all around him during these seven weeks and why, whenever he did venture out, what he saw sometimes changed his attitude, except in those vital matters where he could not afford to change his mind.

So, at the end of a week when everyone else's expectations of seeing *Discovery* freed were at an all-time high, Scott's expectations were at an all-time low. When he came to write his own account of the rescue, he combined the events of two different periods of time. From his viewpoint above Hut Point, Scott chose to record the one solitary occasion when *Terra Nova* was *not* working at the ice front (an afternoon in Week Four when McKay was away in his ship rescuing the Halfway Tent), and he conflated this episode with a quite different event (in Week Six when *Morning* was beset in the ice but her crew were all busy blasting at the ice front). He could then record that *Terra Nova* did nothing, and that *Morning* freed his ship:

> From our observation station we could see everything. The Terra Nova was just picking up our large tent, which was a little over four miles from Hut Point, but the Morning was to the westward and quite half a mile nearer, and it was here that the explosive work was being pushed vigorously forward; one could see the tiny groups of figures digging away at holes.[139]

One wonders how he knew that the men blasting were not from both rescue ships. Scott sank back into the general gloom of his dilemma: gloomy at not being released from the ice, or gloomy at being rescued.

139. Robert Falcon Scott, *The Voyage of the Discovery*, Vol.2, page 346.

CHAPTER FIFTEEN

The Vindication of Harry McKay
Week Seven: 14–20 February 1904

A Valentine for Discovery

Sunday, 14th February was the day when one hundred men of the three ships' companies saw Harry McKay smash his ship *Terra Nova* through the ice to reach the *Discovery*. An officer on the *Terra Nova* wrote:

> Of the hundred people there that Sunday night, not one of them will forget it as long as memory lasts.[140]

In the years that followed the great majority of them fell silent and could not even remember that they had described the rescue as one of the most memorable events of their lives. One officer said it was the most thrilling and sensational experience of his life and yet he was the first to write a book completely editing out the event. Fortunately, three men on McKay's ship, Chief Officer A. P. Jackson, Dr. Clark Souter, and Second Engineer William Smith, described independently and in detail the events of that Sunday. Both rescue ships had begun the day early with blasting. Jackson worked with seven men and McKay had to move *Terra Nova* three times before noon. In the early afternoon they continued and Souter described how eight men from the *Morning* blasting the ice were forced aboard McKay's ship as the ice suddenly broke away:

> It was strange to see a number of unexploded newly-dug blast holes drifting gaily out to sea and this too whilst blasting was going on a good bit astern of our ship. About 4. 30 p.m. we began butting and did an hour at it. At 6 p.m. we resumed and Captain McKay remarked that his chance had now come and he would take it. There was a lead of open water off Hut Point and it was our object to burst through the intervening ice and get up there.[141]

Terra Nova's William Smith gives an engineer's perspective:

---

140. 'Discovery Reached'. Article by an Officer of the *Terra Nova*, the *Press*, New Zealand, 2 April 1904.
141. William Clark Souter, article in *Dundee Advertiser*, 11 May 1904.

We backed out slow astern for a hundred yards and flew at the ice full belt tearing a way through and cracking it in all directions.[142]

The crew of the *Terra Nova* began sallying the ship and by 10.00 p.m. they were only a quarter of a mile from the *Discovery*. Burgess and his seven shipmates, who were now refugees on *Terra Nova*, had a grandstand view of the finale as they were put to work sallying on deck by McKay. It was Burgess' birthday:

At 10 p.m. we could see all the Discovery men at Hut Point watching us. It was a grand sight and at 11.15 p.m. we got through to the Discovery.[143]

The Morning *Could not Butt a Matchbox!*

The *Discovery* crowd, as Jackson was in the habit of calling Commander Scott's ship's company, were on the slope at Hut Point watching the final stage of the rescue, which was later described in all official papers as the second relief expedition. A member of McKay's crew wrote:

They saw all hands on board the Terra Nova roll and butt the ship with four men stationed at the wheel. As for Colbeck's ship, she could not butt a matchbox! She tried once, but the attempt was so ludicrous that the crew laughed extravagantly. At the last quarter of a mile the Captain of the Terra Nova remarked to one of his crew who showed signs of fatigue involved by rolling the ship – what's the matter? Hard work, was the reply! Well, said Captain McKay, I'm going through this time. And he did.[144]

Souter gives a more sober version of the events seen from the ship:

The Morning on our port side, and quite unable to butt, was kept busy poking into the cracks which we made when we came full speed up against the solid ice. It was quite obvious that she was anxious to enter the open water first and get the applause but this she could not do by her own exertions. Once indeed she tried to butt and her performance was distinctly amusing and some of the men were constrained to laugh, it was a cruel thing to do but very human. So close did she come to us in her eagerness that we had to cease firing for a while and proceed away on the other side to get room. Hither, however, she followed us but we went on.[145]

142. Article in *Dundee Advertiser*, 11 May 1904.
143. Len Burgess, Diary, 14 February 1904.
144. 'Discovery Reached'. Article by an officer of the *Terra Nova* the *Press*, New Zealand, 2 April 1904.
145. Article in *Dundee Advertiser*, 11 May 1904.

McKay did some really good work and on one special well-remembered occasion broke a big piece off on the port side which opened up a nice crack just ahead of Colbeck giving access to open water beyond. Morning made a brave bid to enter it and we all stood breathless, believing that she would get in before us after all. Our Captain, grasping the situation put the engines at full speed ahead and in a very few seconds, while Morning was still struggling to insinuate her stern into the crack, we came at full speed against the ice, driving it away to port and effectually closed the crack. The Morning was stopped dead and had to retire, while we went on ahead chewing up the ice. Away we went crashing through the last few yards and entered open water at Hut Point.[146]

This was *Terra Nova*'s Gala Day, with something of the atmosphere of a regatta, a sporting occasion to make a fitting climax to the long weeks of round-the-clock effort by the men of all three ships, but principally it was McKay's brilliant gift to his own unappreciated, long-suffering and hard-working crew of the *Terra Nova*. The celebrations went on long into the Antarctic night and the sun did not set.

Three Cheers for Sports Day!

Colbeck also enjoyed the event, and even reported later in the annals of the Royal Geographical Society, no less, that it was a rather unusual 'relief':

> Everyone was wild with excitement and made no attempt to hide it. In after years those last two hours of February 14th will be my happiest Antarctic reminiscence.[147]

Gerald Doorly, *Morning*'s Third Officer, was still suffering from the delusion that his ship had almost unlimited power. He had forgotten that for a considerable part of the seven-week rescue period his ship was beset and was never able to butt the ice and he thought she was just unlucky not to have reached the *Discovery* before Harry McKay who had been leading the way, charging ahead as though the ice didn't exist. Doorly gave his characteristic version of events which differs more than somewhat from most other accounts:

> I can safely state that this is the most thrilling and sensational experience of my life! At 10.30 p.m. the final crack was made and Terra Nova had the good

146. Article in *Dundee Advertiser*, 11 May 1904.
147. William Colbeck, Report in *Geographical Journal*, 1904, page 742.

luck to be charging ahead. The little Morning stuck to it doggedly but her chance was missed by a few seconds.[148]

When *Terra Nova* reached Hut Point, the crew of the *Discovery* came flying down the hill and one of McKay's aborigines from the port of Dundee commented on this rush of English gentlemen:

> Like a mob of savage islanders rushing to meet the first white men on their shores, they came yelling and shouting and boarded our ship and shook hands with all and sundry.[149]

Engineer William Smith remembered the final moments of the sports day:

> By this time the crew of Discovery were swarming all over us shaking hands. A football match wasn't in it. Their officers said they had seen yacht races but nothing half so exciting as the way we bottled up the Morning when she came sneaking up . . . we only backed a few yards and made for the ice again at full speed, crossing right across her bows, showering all the broken ice in front of her and finished her little game.[150]

Dr Souter remembered the cheering from his splendid view of the school sports day shared with William Smith on the deck of *Terra Nova*:

> As soon as we got through, the crowd on Hut Point cheered lustily and hoisted the lovely blue Union Jack presented by Sir George Nares while all aboard our ship gave three ringing cheers for Captain Harry McKay, for the good old ship Terra Nova, and for the Morning.[151]

Nature Did It

The Commander had been in his cabin all Sunday 14th February but eventually he joined his men on the hill on that fateful night where he had to face the reality that he was now in a minority of one. Everyone else saw that *Discovery* would be freed but he still looked for a way out of his dilemma and, incredibly, he was still making disparaging remarks about the work of the *Terra Nova*. However, Colbeck had consistently supported McKay's efforts and would not agree with Scott's proposal to discontinue the blasting and butting; as he said somewhat ruefully:

148. Gerald Doorly, *The Voyages of the Morning*, 1916.
149. Article by *Terra Nova* officer in the *Press*, New Zealand, 2 April 1904.
150. Article in *Dundee Advertiser*, 11 May 1904.
151. Article in *Dundee Advertiser*, 11 May 1904.

> Poor little Morning with her tin pot boiler and coffee mill engine is unable to do this.[152]

Faced by the scenario which he most dreaded – a rescue by a whaling captain – Scott had again made use of two quite unrelated events: the picking up of the blasting teams from the relief ships by *Terra Nova* which, out of context, gave the impression that McKay was not doing anything useful, and the final stage of the breakthrough to *Discovery* which belongs to an entirely different period of time when his description of events gives the impression that *Morning* alone was responsible for the assistance. But he also employed faint praise for the men of the rescue ships and gave all the credit for his ship's release to Nature, falsifying the speed of the natural break–up and so confirming his prediction that only a Great Ocean Swell could conceivably free his ship.

Of course, there was a swell that evening and, of course, it contributed greatly to the release of the *Discovery* but there was only one man on a rescue ship who gave all the honours to Nature. It was Gerald Doorly, the man who believed that the *Morning* was capable of doing anything that *Terra Nova* could do. There were times when he believed that *Morning* was the faster of the two vessels, though in later years he dropped this claim. Together, Scott, Markham and Doorly were responsible for the creation of the myth which barred the work of the Dundonians and their ship from entering the records. One has to admit that Scott's providential Great Swell idea fits heroic mythology better than a rescue by a pantomime collection of frequently inebriated Dundee whaling men led by a breezy captain and his equally amusing chief officer. Scott, in what at first looks like a rare admission of the truth, said that *Discovery* was

> freed without an effort on our part[153]

– but, alas, he meant the crews of all three ships, not just his own; thus he not only edited McKay out of his narrative but also consigned Colbeck and Royds to that same fate. Burgess recorded the last event of that fateful night with unconscious humour:

> Scott sent a case of whisky to each ship for the sailors to drink his health.[154]

152. William Colbeck, Private Papers, MS 212 Item 13.
153. Robert Falcon Scott, *The Voyage of the Discovery*, 1905 Vol.2 Ch.XIX page 348.
154. Len Burgess, Diary, 14 February 1904.

Rising Pressure

As the excitement and celebrations of St Valentine's Day passed into the cold reality of the Monday morning, Jackson and his *Terra Nova* men began a two-day effort to collect glacier ice at the tongue from which only three weeks before they had gazed at a distant ship in need of rescue. But she was not yet ready to leave McMurdo Sound. The ice was being dug to supply fresh water for *Discovery*'s boilers and the men worked on these for two days and two nights. Other *Terra Nova* men were also hard at work, and in the midst of all the activity on the two rescue ships, Jackson was horrified to see the *Morning* suddenly break adrift; she

> fell down on us, slight damage to our sails.[155]

Discovery's Chief Engineer, Reginald Skelton, raised steam in the donkey boiler and praised the efforts of working parties from the *Terra Nova* and *Morning*. By midnight on the Monday they had both port and starboard boilers in action, but the job was far from complete. More pressure was required and Scott obliged by becoming very impatient with the versatile Skelton, who was having to rush everything. Help came from the Dundonians who knew a Gourlay Triple Expansion Engine when they saw one. Skelton was getting very irritated at having to cut corners and he expressed his gratitude to them.

Scott had still not come to terms with what had happened and he admitted that even after seven weeks of inactivity he was still unprepared. Issuing orders to make the ship ready for the voyage to New Zealand, he wrote his usual put down of the *Terra Nova*'s help with the engineering:

> The rapid passage of events has caught us unprepared, and today all hands have been employed in making up for lost time. It has been a busy day; our own men have been on board making things ship-shape and trim, while parties from the other ships have been digging ice.[156]

Discovery couldn't go anywhere; she was still encased in an envelope of thick ice and Scott's mounting impatience now needed a safety valve:

> too restless to go to bed . . . I wandered about to see how the work went and presently mustered an explosion party.[157]

---

155. A.P. Jackson A Diary of a Voyage to Antarctic Regions on the ship Terra Nova, entry for February 1904.

156–157. Robert Falcon Scott, *The Voyage of the Discovery*, Vol.2, pages 350, 351.

The situation was becoming extremely dangerous. The Commander was not a man to leave alone with a large supply of high explosives.

Discovery *Afloat Again*

Jackson and his men spent two days boring holes for explosive charges but Scott, in his impatience, could no longer wait to see how it should be done and decided to beat Jackson to it. There followed what amounted to a mad and highly dangerous blasting competition; as Scott explained:

> I am now all impatience to be away, and therefore contemplate expediting matters by explosions. To make the necessary holes in the ice I have been obliged to call in the assistance of officers.[158]

What happened is an illustration by two officers of how to blast, and how not to blast. Ignoring Jackson's boring strategy, Scott had his men prepare only one big hole fifteen yards ahead of the ship in the early hours of Tuesday 16th February. Having learned that 16 pounds was not a big charge, he placed

> a single charge of 94 pounds of guncotton just ahead of Discovery.[159]

He had mustered a naval explosion party from their beds late on the Monday night, kept them busy digging, and at 1 a.m. they learned just how lucky they were not to be asleep in their bunks. As their dynamic leader said:

> 1 a.m. regardless of the feelings of the sleepers, blew it up. It shook the whole bay and I fear awakened all those who slumbered[160]

Jackson had fired two small charges of guncotton the day before. When woken by Scott's little surprise, he found that *Discovery* was still not freed, although there were now cracks in all directions, much to his annoyance and to the delight of their creator. Souter thought that the Great Big Bang was more effective than Jackson's Little Bangs but Jackson's small explosions were designed to make precise cracks for his triple 16-pound charges which he then placed with accuracy at 11 am next morning in a rift which he had been carefully making across the Winter Harbour. It passed right under the stern of *Discovery*. Scornful of the Big Bang, Jackson noted in his diary with quiet satisfaction:

158. Robert Falcon Scott, *The Voyage of the Discovery*, Vol.2 page 350.
159. Len Burgess, Antarctic Journal, entry for 15,16 February 1904.
160. Robert Falcon Scott, *The Voyage of the Discovery*, Vol.2, page 351.

about midday Discovery afloat.[161]

Souter recorded the cheers, so often their only means of expression:

> Just at noon we could see she was moving beyond all doubt. We ran up our ensign and got all hands aft and gave three ringing cheers for the good ship.[162]

Hurricane Force

The men of the *Terra Nova* were still busily engaged working on *Discovery*'s boilers at 6 p.m. on the night of Tuesday 16th when the officers of the three ships came aboard to dine on penguin and seal meat, now the pride of the Commander's menu. Suddenly, as Second Engineer William Smith recounted:

> there was a shout that Discovery was dragging her anchor. Captain McKay got up on deck and the Chief (Sandy Sharp) and I did likewise and what chaos! Billowing big guns, the two ships drifting apart then coming together and knocking spots off each other. We got aboard our own packet somehow. The Morning had vanished leaving Colbeck aboard the Discovery.[163]

McKay had told Scott when the way to the sea was open that it was not safe to stay in McMurdo Bay a minute longer than he needed to and advised him to 'clear out'. Jackson, Sharp, Smith and McKay, having succeeded in getting back to their ship by 9 p.m., found considerable storm damage to their sails. They let go from *Discovery* and sailed off to the north. Then, by 11 p.m., the wind increased to hurricane force. McKay made for more open water and later the whole bay became choked full of heavy pack. They spent a ghastly night dodging icebergs but the bergs had all gone by the morning.

It had been a wild scramble by Captain McKay and his officers to get back to their own ship, and two of their officers, Elms and South, were left behind on *Discovery* with ten other *Terra Nova* men all of whom were still working there with Skelton to get Scott's ship ready to sail.

Bernacchi, seeing that *Terra Nova* was in an ugly position, observed that McKay

> luckily had steam up and by going full ahead managed to clear us and stand out in the strait.[164]

161. A.P. Jackson Article, 'The Relief Ships', the *Press*, New Zealand, 2 April 1904.
162. Article by Dr. William Clark Souter, the *Press*, New Zealand, 2 April 1904.
163. Article in *Dundee Advertiser*, 11 May 1904.
164. Louis Bernacchi, Antarctic Diary, entry for 16 February 1904.

Unlike most of the other officers, it would appear that Bernacchi still knew little of the ways of Captain McKay: the whaling captain did not rely on luck. Holding her own in the hurricane, the *Terra Nova* had not been visible to the men on the other two ships in the snow blizzard and the hail of ice spiculae. Meanwhile back on the *Discovery* things were already becoming much more critical as pressure was rising and tempers were becoming frayed. Criticised by his Commander for not having steam up in all boilers, Skelton allowed himself the remark:

Scott in one of his impatient moods – the cause of our troubles.[165]

On the Rocks!

Eye-witness Louis Bernacchi described the events on Wednesday morning more fully than anyone else on the good ship *Discovery*:

The port anchor was weighed at 10 a.m. on Wednesday and at 10.30 a.m. with steam up in only one boiler we commenced to move out of our winter quarters. I was standing aft with Dr. Koettlitz and wondering why we were keeping so close to the shore when I heard Captain Scott give the order 'hard-a-port' and the very next moment felt the ship grate on the bottom and saw that she had stopped.

I remarked to Dr Koettlitz that she was aground but a little time seemed to elapse before the fact was realised on the bridge. I suppose it was not thought serious and that we should easily pass over the shoal for the engines were not stopped nor put astern but kept punching ahead for some time. The wind continued to freshen bringing with it a heavy sea which caused the ship to bump heavily on the bottom. Top sails were set and engines put ahead again but with no more success than before. Matters now looked rather grave. The seas commenced to break right over us and against the ice cliff from which we were only 50 feet distance. Large pieces of timber floated up from the bottom and drifted away. Down below one could scarce hear another talk for the crashing noise of the timbers and decks when she bumped, bent like a whale bone, and broke some of the thick glass skylights. The Terra Nova men on board who should know something of this type of ship expressed their opinion she would soon go to pieces if this wind and sea continued and, judging by the quantity of timber being torn off her bottom, I began to think so too. At 6 p.m. the ship appeared to be moving slowly astern. There was a rush at once for the deck. Full speed astern was put on the engines and all

165. Reginald Skelton, Antarctic Diary, entry for 16 February 1904.

hands commenced to roll and sally the ship. In 15 minutes we were afloat, having been aground eight hours.[166]

Dr Souter, one of twelve *Terra Nova* men on board, observed:

with their assistance the sails were bent. Pieces of keel came to the surface and some of us began to think that we would not see the ship float again.[167]

From this day forward there were no more criticisms of Paterson, Manager of the Dundee Shipbuilders, no more charges of poor work. Now it was Paterson's turn to be vindicated as his ship survived the test of the situation into which she had been driven. But naturally it was left to Souter to give the vote of thanks:

Discovery proved a great credit to her builders for few ordinary ships could have stood for five minutes what she stood for so many hours.[168]

Dangerous Coal Shortages

On Thursday 18th February Jackson wrote that his ship *Terra Nova*:

steamed off to the glacial ice tongue where all hands worked coal and gave Discovery 52 tons of coal.[169]

It was at this point in the expedition that Doorly, a great admirer of Commander Scott, had his loyalty severely tested:

Discovery took most of Morning's coal which we could hardly spare![170]

But Scott was still not satisfied and wrote:

Getting a small quantity of coal which the relief ships could spare, 50 tons from Terra Nova and 25 tons from Morning . . . the total quantity was most disappointing, as, together with what remained of our own supply (38 tons) we now had only 115 tons and I knew this would be insufficient to carry out our programme.[171]

166. Louis Bernacchi, Diary entry for 17 February 1904.
167. Article in *Dundee Advertiser*, 11 May 1904.
168. Article in *Dundee Advertiser*, 11 May 1904.
169. A.P. Jackson, A Diary of a Voyage to Antarctic Regions on the ship Terra Nova, entry for 18 February 1904.
170. Gerald Doorly, *The Voyages of the Morning*.
171. Robert Falcon Scott, *The Voyage of the Discovery*, Vol II, page 350.

Colbeck now faced a serious problem. He had to give away coal which he needed not just for fuel but for ballast, and even twenty years after the event he still recalled the nightmare of the voyage back to New Zealand in March 1904:

> In our unballasted condition the ship was, to say the least of it, not seaworthy.[172]

But when Colbeck returned to London he also had to write a report in the *Geographical Journal* where he was obliged to follow the well-formed Royal Geographical Society line, namely, that *Terra Nova* burned more coal than expected. But he knew that he also burned more coal than expected and he admitted that he followed McKay's practice of keeping steam up all the time in McMurdo Sound in order to be ready to escape all the hazards that the Antarctic might throw at them.

Colbeck had been under the impression that McKay had stowed 500 tons of coal in Hobart but *Terra Nova's* capacity was never more than 400 tons, and with the stores mix-up at Hobart, McKay could not stow that much. McKay had reckoned to give Scott 100 tons, and Colbeck relied on this estimate and so took only 250 tons for his own ship's consumption. Colbeck did not realise that McKay did indeed supply *Discovery* with 100 tons although it was so badly stowed that he could only give it in instalments and the final instalments were not given until 23rd and 28th March. However, Scott was not satisfied, and though he did not confront McKay with his accusations, he determined that he was not going to let the matter rest there.

172. William Colbeck, letter to Haggitt 20 February 1925.

CHAPTER SIXTEEN

Outcast in New Zealand

An Unmanageable Ship in a Sea of Complaints

The ships were to rendezvous in the Auckland Islands south of New Zealand. They all waited at Wood Bay for *Discovery* to get glacier ice for drinking water, then, on 21st February, *Morning* was sent off north a week in advance of the other two ships. Jackson on *Terra Nova*, with painful memories of waiting for Colbeck on the journey to McMurdo Sound, could scarcely believe his bad luck at having to wait now for *Discovery* because she wasn't ready. On the night of 22nd February Bernacchi was convinced that *Discovery* almost sank again when her pumps failed and the fires in the main boilers went out. Then they found that the rudder had sprung and again signalled *Terra Nova*: 'Must Stop!' Next day work was finished on the repair of *Discovery*'s engines. On 24th February they removed the old four-ton rudder and replaced it. Jackson, who wasn't finding very much to amuse him on the voyage, was much taken with this because, as he said, they knew they had broken the rudder, but

they don't seem to know why – very funny![173]

McKay was concerned that, having to progress under sail now, with pack ice approaching them on three sides and with the barometer falling fast, he ought to be thinking about avoiding the pack ice altogether; but unknown to him, Scott at that very moment was ignoring his orders to avoid it. He said he was almost unmanageable under sail, meaning the ship. On 28th February *Terra Nova* providentially managed to lose sight of *Discovery* at six in the morning as another hurricane was developing. Two weeks later, on 14th March, *Discovery* was the first of the three ships to reach the Auckland Islands, having been under steam the whole time, and now Scott complained that he had only ten tons of coal left in the bunkers. *Terra Nova* having been under sail all the time, arrived three days later than Scott and Jackson observed with a light satirical touch:

A devil of a passage after losing Discovery, gales one after the other – didn't want to waste our coal on them so we were a long time[174]

173–174. A.P. Jackson, Diary of a Voyage in Antarctic Regions on the ship Terra Nova, entries for 24 February and 19 March 1904.

Scott again made a fuss about having burned all his coal allowance, and Jackson noted incredulously that they would have to give him yet more. On 20th March men started to paint *Discovery* ready for the grand entrance into Lyttelton. They didn't paint over the shovel marks on the ship's boats – which were the result of a Royds working party digging to recover them when they had been lost in snow drifts. This omission had a rather happy consequence as the awful state of the boats was interpreted by the New Zealand public as proof of the extremely rough time they had all experienced on the *Discovery* on their voyage back to New Zealand.

The Great Coal Excuse

Colbeck expected McKay to give *Discovery* 100 tons of coal and he actually delivered slightly more than this, notwithstanding the oft-repeated statement that he didn't, which arises from the omission of one of Jackson's coal deliveries from the official account. Yet Scott was not satisfied, for reasons that were soon to be clear. He had ignored Admiralty instructions to proceed to New Zealand without making any further forays into the ice floes and putting his ship at risk.

He was keen to complete what he called 'our programme', being convinced that he ought to have done more oceanographic exploration. So, before setting a course for the Auckland Islands, he wanted to check the accuracy of the mapping of the American explorer, Charles Wilkes. He managed to correct Wilkes' errors and then he gave Hodgson permission to dabble in a little oceanographic dredging which, according to the crew of the *Terra Nova* who had to follow in his wake, was not very successful as the net came up without any bottom in it. Hodgson, unable to work the gear to his own satisfaction and generally critical of the lack of support for his laboratory research, was often treated as a figure of fun but Wilson had great respect for his scientific work:

> With the single exception of Hodgson we are all intensely ignorant of anything but the elementary knowledge of our several jobs.[175]

On reaching the Auckland Islands, Scott called a two-week halt whilst he prepared his official speeches, his storyline for the New Zealand newspapers, and his journal, all of which edited out the role of Colbeck and McKay. He added a new development to the coal saga. The coal

175. Quoted in George Seaver, *Edward Wilson of the Antarctic*, 1940 edition, page 84.

shortage could be used as an effective excuse to explain why they had not freed their ship from the ice in 1903 and why they had not produced impressive oceanography to compare with Speirs Bruce's work which threatened to steal his thunder. (The simple answer is that *Scotia* was an oceanographic expedition and *Discovery* was not, but this did not appeal to him.) So coal now became a new weapon with which to discredit others. Had it not been for McKay's shortcomings they could have charted the coast round North Cape. With more coal Scott could have freed himself from the ice at any time. With another 100 tons he could have faced any number of hurricanes and bergs. Yet Scott had spared no thought for the safety of Colbeck and McKay and their crews as he took all their coal, putting their ships in great danger. Colbeck never forgot this. Despite all the fine words that Scott could write as the occasion demanded, when it came to the point, the safety of the other crews was of little concern to him. He reported McKay to the Navy's Hydrographer, Admiral Wharton, and revealed what he really thought of the man who had rescued him:

McKay did, I suppose, as much as one could expect from a whaler captain.[176]

The Great Welcome to Lyttleton

On April 1st 1904 the three ships approached Lyttelton and one local paper, the *Press*, recorded the great welcome:

Lyttelton was quickly astir. Messages were speedily sent to town and many who had been long on the look-out for the return of Captain Scott and his crew and the equally honoured men of the relief ships hastened to the railway and by the 8.55 train went through to the Port. The tug Lyttelton was in readiness with the Mayor of Lyttelton, Mr W. Radcliffe, the Town Clerk, Mr G. H. Lewin, and the Harbourmaster, Captain Clarke [twenty other local dignitaries were named], to take up the Christchurch contingent and the Lyttelton Brass Band had been summoned also at short notice to play the explorers home. Cases of apples, baskets of grapes and other nice things were taken out on the tug and just to emphasise the fact that it was Good Friday morning a generous baker staggering under a load of hot cross buns ran down the wharf just too late to get his gift on board and so he had to charter a boat to take his offering out to the ships! The band played "Home Sweet Home".

176. A.G.E Jones, 'Harry McKay, Master of the 'Terra Nova'', in *Antarctic* Vol.6 No.9 (1973) quoting Scott's letter to Admiral Wharton.

Heartiest greetings were exchanged. The three vessels were safely berthed before noon.[177]

The *Press* also recorded an event that evening, the subtle significance of which cannot have gone unnoticed:

> His worship the Mayor entertained Captain Scott of the Discovery and Captain Colbeck of the Morning at dinner.[178]

Nevertheless it was not Lyttelton that snubbed McKay and his men. The officers of the three ships were invited to attend a farewell banquet for his Excellency, the Governor, Lord Ranfurly, Fifth Earl of Uchter, educated at Harrow and Trinity College, Cambridge, Honorary Colonel of the 1st. Wellington Rifle Battalion. But not everyone thought that it was the sort of occasion to which the whaling captain should have been invited and they made sure that McKay was not invited to any future social events. Scott later issued a directive which might well have caused equal offence to his hosts, the civic dignitaries, and his rescuers, when they saw it in the local newspaper:

> Captain Scott it appears would prefer that any entertainment by the citizens should not take place till after the coming week.[179]

The Admirals who drew up the orders for the rescue had altered the first draft to allow Scott to send *Terra Nova* home before the *Morning* should he decide that McKay's services were no longer required. The Commander was hoping that a week should see *Terra Nova* on her way, but was disappointed.

The Cover-Up Begins

There were several major problems which faced the Commander of the English National Antarctic Expedition now all the ships had finally reached New Zealand on 1st April 1904. One was the cost of providing subsistence for all the members of his over-manned expedition on the *Discovery*, and the cost of feeding and accommodating the ships' companies from *Morning* and *Terra Nova*. He did not have the problem which had so worried Colbeck in 1903 – the expense of his decision to send undesirables home by mail steamer. This had cost Colbeck £500 even though he had managed to arrange for some free passages. But now there was the cost of caulking, essential repairs and harbour dues for all three ships and Scott also faced the problem of upholding the English caste system amongst such a motley

177–179. The *Press*, 2 April 1904.

collection of officers and men. Few Chief Officers can have had such tribulations and bad luck.

However, his greatest problem was the one which had most direct bearing on the Commander's own career prospects: how to effect the cover-up of the rescue operation. He could almost certainly keep his own men quiet through a combination of naval discipline and that kind of loyalty which relies mostly on rank, plus the opportunities for promotion, which are consequent upon getting a good report from one's Chief Officer.

He could also be confident of keeping the crew of the *Morning* quiet since Markham had already issued a strict instruction to Colbeck and his men in a telegram which was awaiting their arrival in Lyttelton:

TO SCOTT AND COLBECK: HOW TO DEAL WITH THE PRESS: IT IS ADVISABLE NOT TO ACCEPT REUTER'S OFFER. AT THE EARLIEST POSSIBLE MOMENT AFTER YOUR ARRIVAL CABLE NOT MORE THAN 500 WORDS GIVING MAIN RESULTS OF EXPEDITION ADDRESS IT TO PRESIDENT 1 SAVILE ROW. BET-TER KEEP OFF ALL REPORTERS AND INTERVIEWERS AND GIVE INFORMATION TO NO ONE FOR AT LEAST 48 HOURS AFTER YOU SEND OFF TELEGRAM, EVEN AFTER THAT AS LITTLE AS POSSIBLE[180]

In 1903 Colbeck had sought the assistance of Reuter's man in Christchurch instead of keeping properly aloof. Mindful of this, Markham was trying to ensure that it didn't happen again. But the principal headache was certainly not going to be Colbeck but McKay and the men of the *Terra Nova*, for Markham's orders were not even addressed to them. Not surprisingly both the relief ship captains needed to put their ships into dry dock and so Scott found he had no hope of packing them off home quickly before any damage was done. They were not likely to set sail for England for at least another six weeks. Six rather dangerous weeks when the telegrams might fly.

The Hon. C.C. Bowen's Great Insult

In 1904 Middleton Grange in Christchurch was the home of the Bowen family, and the crew of the *Terra Nova,* berthed in Lyttelton waiting for their ship to be caulked, read a newspaper article written by the Hon. C. C.

180. Sir Clements Markham, telegram to Scott & Colbeck, Lyttelton, April 1904. Colbeck Private Papers, Dundee Industrial Heritage Archive DH1097.

Bowen about their ship. This gave a version of events that can only have come from a certain quarter on the *Discovery*, for they had never heard of Bowen. The basic theme was that *Terra Nova*'s crew was not required and should have gone home directly from the Auckland Islands and she should not have come to Lyttelton.

It was clear to men on the *Terra Nova* that there was a feeling in some quarters that there was a danger that undisciplined whaling men might contradict the official story (a feeling which was wholly justified). The new storyline that *Terra Nova* had been useless and that it was the *Morning* not *Terra Nova* that had released *Discovery*, single-handed as it were, first appeared in the Bowen article:

> There was really no need at all for her [Terra Nova] and, pecuniary, she had only been a burden on the expedition. The expenditure on her was quite useless, as the Royal Geographical Society asked no more from the English (sic) Government than a grant of £6000 to make up the amount required to equip the Morning for her second expedition for the relief of Discovery. As matters stand, the Home Government will not get out of it under an expenditure of £60,000 – ten times the amount for which the Geographical Society was prepared to do the work. Nor were the English Government by any means unexacting as they insisted upon the Geographical Society making over to them the ownership of the Morning, and even tried to secure possession of the Discovery. This, however, was a little too much and the Society made a determined and successful stand against so unreasonable a demand. In addition, there should be reckoned the cost of the unnecessary voyage of the Morning to Hobart to meet the Terra Nova there, in order that Captain Colbeck, who had thus to go considerably out of his way, might assume command of the expedition there. There would, of course, have been no necessity for this loss of time and extra expense had the Morning alone been commissioned to go to the relief of the Discovery. Then also should be borne in mind the expense and the annoyance caused by having to take to Hobart the sheep presented to the expedition. It was almost incredible in Mr Bowen's opinion that the English Government could have been so obstinately persistent in acting as it did, against the remonstrance of those well acquainted with what had to be done, and one was at a loss to imagine what object the ruling powers could have had.[181]

The Hon. C. C. Bowen was remarkably well informed about the opinions of the President of the Royal Geographical Society and the latest views of the Expedition Commander. Bowen could not be ignored for three good

181. Article in the *Press*, New Zealand, 2 April 1904.

reasons: he was the owner of the newspaper, Scott was staying with him, and Markham was his brother-in-law.

A Passport to Oblivion

The journalists of Lyttelton were used to Antarctic stories, but correspondents like McKay and his men would never have been given any credence in the proper circles, being whaling men and not gentlemen. In any case local reports in Christchurch were unlikely to find their way to London, or so, judging by the events which followed, the Bowen family must have reasoned. Following the article which insulted *Terra Nova's* work, Scott, in one reckless moment, also gave an interview rebuking the Admiralty in phrases which were reminiscent of the article by Bowen, though who inspired who is impossible to say. It was published through Reuter's man in Christchurch and to Scott's amazement appeared at once in the London *Daily Mail*. 'Blunder Made in Sending Relief Ship!' was the sensational headline. It was a major career *faux pas* and Scott would have to write explanations which, notwithstanding all his experience of finding excuses for his mistakes, stretched even his creative imagination.

In his newspaper articles we see ingratitude of the very highest order. First he blamed Colbeck for not making the position of the expedition understood in the cable which he sent to London from Christchurch in 1903 reporting on the state of *Discovery* locked in the first winter ice. Then he openly blamed the Admiralty for organising the rescue which he said was absurdly unnecessary, as his account of the events would show. Finally he gave Harry McKay and his crew a passport to oblivion. From that moment onwards McKay and the *Terra Nova* simply no longer existed and Colbeck and *Morning* were soon to follow:

> Had the proper position of Discovery been known it would have been obvious that she was perfectly safe and no assistance beyond what the Morning could render was requisite.[182]

Then came the greatest of all insults to McKay:

> The Morning came to our aid early last January and on February 12th (sic) the ship was once more free.[183]

In view of everything that the three ships' companies had lived through and witnessed of the release on 16th February 1904, this was an extraordinary

182–183. Scott's comments sent by Reuter's Christchurch Correspondent and quoted in Elspeth Huxley, *Scott of the Antarctic* (1977).

thing to say, quite apart from the almost unbelievable error of getting the date of the freeing of his own ship wrong. It would seem that he was being encouraged by Markham's family. Nobody would pay the slightest attention to what Dundee whaling men might say in the gutter press, and doubtless Scott remembered that, when he first met the Dundonians on 5 January 1904, he didn't understand a word they said! There was little chance now of a coherent alternative version of events coming from that quarter during their stay in Lyttelton, or so the house party at Middleton Grange must have thought.

The Right People

The efforts of Bowen's Middleton Grange house party to cover-up the rescue suffered a serious blow at the outset when Reuter's man in Christchurch sent Scott's attack on the Admiralty to the London papers. Whilst Bowen was busy sending telegrams to his brother-in-law, Clements Markham, in an attempt to undo the damage, Scott was busy writing to *his* brother-in-law, William Ellison Macartney (Parliamentary Secretary to the Admiralty), disclaiming all knowledge of his literary efforts. If he could not succeed in convincing Macartney of his innocence, then his career would be damaged:

> Willie had seen the First Sea Lord who assures him there is no cause for anxiety.[184]

The gaff shouldn't have happened. They had the support of every newspaper magnate in Christchurch. Their friends included Sir William Polson, editor of the *Evening News*, Alfred Saunders and Henry Wigram, editor and chairman, respectively, of the pro-establishment newspaper *Lyttelton Times*. They had even cultivated friends in the *Press* – a keen rival of the papers which supported the British Colonial Office. Sir William Russell, one such influential *Press* shareholder, was part of the circle. Bowen not only owned the *Lyttelton Times*, he was also a correspondent for both its rival papers, the *Press* and the *Weekly Press*. Having married Markham's sister, Georgina, the least he could do for the President of the Royal Geographical Society was to make Scott a local celebrity.

Colbeck was in a more difficult position, for he had stayed with the Bowens before in 1903 and had impressed them. This may explain why his contribution to the rescue was briefly acknowledged during his second stay

184. Roland Huntford, *Scott and Amundsen*, quoting a letter from Scott's mother, page 185.

at Middleton Grange. But Colbeck had also been befriended by A.E.G. Rhodes who, in addition to living in the country and running a sheep farm and horticultural business, happened to be chairman of the *Press*. So when Colbeck and McKay faded out of the story later in the month, the *Press* was caddish enough to give interviews to crew members of the *Morning* and *Terra Nova* and went out of its way to print some of the truth. Other influential newspaper shareholders included Thomas Russell, a celebrated lawyer whose family had hosted officers of the *Morning* and *Discovery*. Their youngest daughter, Rita, went for long bicycle rides with Barne and their eldest, Hilda, married Teddy Evans a couple of weeks after he had landed at Lyttelton. One other regular newspaper correspondent who supported Christchurch's most popular literary explorer was Bishop Julius, described by the *Morning*'s Engineer, J.D. Morrison, with characteristic wit:

> I feel I could go anywhere and do anything – I have had prayers read over me by a real bishop! Bishops come high but they are worth the money.[185]

Life at the Top

Scott had always kept himself aloof from members of his expedition and his social snobbery was even more in evidence in New Zealand when he was lionised and brought into the social circles of the elite. The expedition caste system applied to all officers, scientists and able seamen aboard *Discovery*, and when in port only top brass were usually invited to the career-enhancing social functions – such as an audience with Prime Minister R. J. Seddon, a meeting with the literary giant Samuel Butler, an invitation to Governor Lord Ranfurly's farewell banquet, or to his daughter Lady Irene Knox's celebrated breakfasts.

Senior officers of *Discovery* received invitations to some of the lesser functions, for several, like Scott himself, were freemasons and members of the Savage Club of London and Christchurch. This lower echelon of functions included lunching at the club, playing golf and polo and spending weekends riding in the country. Barne, one of the least snobbish of his ship's company, had just as good social contacts in Christchurch as Scott. However, he rather let the side down by befriending two officers of the *Terra Nova*, Jackson and Elms (though admittedly only for a couple of evenings). They went to the Savage Club and, more alarming still, Barne then took them to see the Bowens. He cannot have realised that their host was a member of the Upper House, sometime Minister for Justice, and a

185. J.D.Morrison, Antarctic Diary, 6 December 1902.

close friend of the Prime Minister, nor that the Bowens were entertaining Scott and a Miss Kathleen Bruce (apparently no relation of the lady of the same name whom Scott was to marry and just one of those snares set to confuse researchers). Sir William Polson, the press baron, was also present and Barne was introduced to him and the social crisis blew over.

The much maligned engineer, Reginald Skelton, became engaged to Sibyl Devenish-Mears, but although his fiancée was invited to all those most important functions in Christchurch at which Scott was being fêted, it would not have been proper to invite a ship's engineer to any of them. An engineer was the lowest form of naval life to wear gold braid, though Royal was superior to Merchant.

As might be expected, when the scientists reached New Zealand they immediately made contact with other scientists. Wilson was met by his wife and they spent many happy hours in Canterbury Museum working on his collections. He was hoping to obtain a permanent post there but sadly it was not to be. Hodgson was entertained by the biologist, Dr. Chilton Jennings, and disappeared completely from the social scene, leaving no doubt in his correspondence why he chose this apparently anti-social course of action. Colbeck met John Scott, the amazingly young 22-year-old university professor and a cousin of the Commander, and went on to see the Director of the Christchurch Observatory. Young Ferrar took his Commander on a short trip to Mount Cook to see some snow and ice.

The Great Snub

Apart from Colbeck's social round in Christchurch with Scott (which can hardly have been voluntary on his part) and the two days spent by Jackson and Elms in the company of Barne, the majority of the officers and men of the two relief ships were ostracised in New Zealand by Scott, but at the same time they were nearly all successfully suborned into keeping quiet about what really happened on the Antarctic rescue expedition. Most of the men on the *Morning* were later presented with honours for services to expedition fiction. Oliver Goldsmith remarked many years ago that the English have the amazing habit of rewarding people for outstanding bravery or effort by giving them a little piece of silk or metal. As a result they appear to be remarkably content. This system, despite a century of comment about its being invidious and archaic, is still with us today. However, one must draw a line somewhere and there was no need to reward all the men of *Morning* and *Terra Nova* with anything, least of all with a word of appreciation. Of course, the names of some of those men on the *Terra Nova* who *did* talk to journalists whilst their ship was being repaired, had to be changed to protect them. The establishment had no difficulty in shrugging off the anonymous and therefore unsubstantiated alternative version of events.

The men from the lower orders of the two inferior ships did not enjoy as much leisure as their officers; they worked long hours on repairs and painting in Lyttelton harbour. But they were very well received and delivered sincere votes of thanks to the people of Christchurch and Lyttelton for their extraordinary hospitality. Burgess and Morrison give us some idea of their life in New Zealand from their earlier 1903 diaries which recorded their stay in detail. They were allowed to travel free on the trains, attend the social activities organised by the working men's clubs such as the Trade and Labourers Council and the Wharf Labour Union, and listen to the Garrison Band, and were found accommodation when they were not staying aboard their ships. There were no hotel bills for the Dundonians, and when they were not living on the *Terra Nova* they were in the Lyttelton Seamen's Home, now appropriately enough the Maritime Museum. Burgess wrote:

> People treated us like their own. We had the run of the house. We was at almost every party and ball, social and wedding. People showed us such kindness as if they had known us years.[186]

Morrison tells us that, compared to the chaps in gold braid, the three major pastimes of ordinary seamen were rather less expensive and centred on imbibing (called picnics), befriending natives (particularly barmaids) and bursting into unrestrained vocalisation.[187]

The Storyteller Silenced

Harry McKay, despite being arguably the most skilled polar expert on the three ships, an affable, funny and intelligent man, a raconteur who could hold an audience spellbound, was not credited with his extraordinary rescue feat. Nor was he welcomed into the *Discovery*'s social circle. Everyone must have been aware of this snubbing of the *Terra Nova* ship's company, for by then everyone knew these men on the most friendly terms. J. D. Morrison gives an affectionate sketch of McKay the entertainer, a portrait of a leader holding the stage:

> We had what whalers call a 'Mollie' that being songs and yarns. Some of the yarns were fearsome. Fish stories are really quite entertaining when the fish

186. Len Burgess, Antarctic Diary, April–October 1903.
187. J.D.Morrison, Antarctic Diary.

weighs a hundred tons and is worth a few thousand pounds. Captain McKay is skilled in Arctic Lore and excels as a storyteller his bear tales being particularly fine.[188]

It was a shock to the Dundonians when this chill barrier descended upon them as they entered the port of Lyttelton. Some officers and scientists on *Discovery* also felt the ingratitude and Royds and Koettlitz took themselves off to the North Island at the earliest opportunity. Other men sought refuge (just as they had done on McKay's ship in the Antarctic) and went to stay with Joseph Kinsey, the Expedition Agent. Kinsey was hospitable and knowledgeable, a lawyer with a penchant for science, a mountaineer who had climbed with those legendary pioneers of the Southern Alps, Edward Fitzgerald and his guide Mattius Zurbriggen. The visitors' book at the Kinseys' house, "Warrimoo", featured Colbeck, Armitage, Wilson, Bernacchi, Royds, Skelton, Ferrar, Mulock and Morrison – a list as interesting for those it includes as for those it omits. This is the kind of gathering that one might expect to find in an Alpine mountaineering hut, a group of people who if they had to share a large tent would not dream of making a partition down the middle of it to separate officers from men; a group inspired by men like Colbeck who did not need to pull rank in order to lead. These were men who would not care a fig whether their companions had been to naval college, public school, or university, whether their host had a title, was a member of the Savage Club or Masonic Lodge, they were men who had never had a society breakfast with the Governor's daughter, been blessed by a bishop, shaken hands with a peer of the realm, had never snubbed a large-hearted whaling captain, and were not upset when they were ignored by a small-minded commander.

All these men who were so badly treated went quietly back to their normal lives after the rescue as if nothing had happened, which is exactly what the powers-that-be always bank on. So the English class system carries on unabated, exerting its unseen influences, without so much as a mild protest. The right officers collected their gold braid and the Scotsmen were ignored.

The Matter-of-Fact Gentlemen

The class snobbery was too much for some *Terra Nova* men. Souter, who had once looked upon Scott with something approaching awe, was now disgusted with the turn of events. He wrote a *Dundee Advertiser* article in

188. J.D.Morrison, Antarctic Diary, November 1903.

protest. Referring to the *Morning*'s lack of power, he observed that she only got through to *Discovery* because of *Terra Nova*'s efforts and commented that *Morning* had not provisioned or coaled *Discovery* to anything like the same extent as *Terra Nova* had done. Souter had recorded these events closely and had first-hand knowledge of all the supplies sledged to *Discovery*. He was an impartial observer of all the rescue efforts and his views could not be dismissed:

> Few will be prepared to say that the Terra Nova has not earned, in a manner which reflects every credit on all concerned, the title of THE Antarctic Relief Ship.[189]

This was Souter's reply to Middleton Grange which now attributed all *Terra Nova*'s achievements to the *Morning*, creating a myth kept alive even today. *Terra Nova*'s crew members, writing home, sounded a note of bitterness:

> We were told that there was no need for us but the need seems to become more apparent every day. The other two ships would have had a slender reed to lean on if we had not come![190]

To the Dundonians it was now obvious that this latest ploy was designed as an insult to McKay and his men. As Second Engineer William Smith commented:

> We can easily see that the other two ships do not want us but we, being matter-of-fact gentlemen, do not care.[191]
>
> They stuck to it the Dundee honest whalers. And after blasting and pounding the stuff they thumped and ground till we got her out. We have done our job and we have done it clean.[192]
>
> Exactly why the ice broke up so much more easily this year than last year is not accounted for!"[193]

A cub reporter, misled by propaganda about useless Dundonians and impressed by Scott's epic exploits now circulating in his paper, wanted to know if any *Terra Nova* men had comparable experience of snow and ice. He found four of her crew members who were on the Arctic whale ship *Vega* in 1902 when she was lost. These men travelled over 600 miles dragging a whaler on the ice to safety, did so without incident and then

189. Article by Dr. William Clark Souter, 'Explanation of a Claim', the *Press*, New Zealand, 2 April 1904.
190–191. Article by William Smith of *Terra Nova* in *Dundee Advertiser*, 11 May 1904.
192–193. Article, 'Notes and Jottings', in the *Press*, New Zealand, 2 April 1904.

returned to rescue their fellow seamen. As they said, it was a thing that Dundonians were quite good at doing.

The Great Ocean Swell and Mr Jackson's Graph

Scott's book records the swell on that finale of a night on 14th February, in mystical terms:

> In the midst of this peaceful silence was an awful unseen agency rending that great ice sheet as though it had been naught but the thinnest paper. . . we knew that the heaviest battleship would have shattered itself ineffectually against it, and we had seen a million ton iceberg brought to rest at its edge. For weeks we had been struggling with this mighty obstacle, controlling the most disruptive forces that the intelligence of man has devised, but only to realise more completely the inadequacy of our powers. Even Nature seemed to pause before such vast difficulty, and had hitherto delivered her attacks with such sluggish force that we had reasonably doubted her ability to conquer it before the grip of winter arrested her efforts.[194]

This poetic passage admits that there was a rescue effort but it does not tell us who had been struggling for the previous forty days and nights, nor does it explain why it was considered to be so inadequate.

A remarkable part of McKay's rescue technique, for a man who claimed to have so little time for men of science, was the measuring of the swell. Jackson kept daily records during their seven-week vigil in McMurdo Sound and, in contrast to Nature's One Great Ocean Swell on the evening of 14 February, he recorded at least one swell in every one of those seven weeks, as follows:

WEEK ONE January 8th

WEEK TWO January 15th and 16th

WEEK THREE January 23rd

WEEK FOUR January 24th, 25th and 29th

WEEK FIVE January 31st February 1st, 2nd, 3rd, 4th, 5th, and 6th

WEEK SIX February 7th, 8th, 9th, 10th, 11th, 12th, 13th

WEEK SEVEN February 14th

Not realising that there had been over twenty swells already adds a note of black comedy to Scott's pantomime.

194. Robert Falcon Scott, *The Voyage of the Discovery*, Vol.2, page 347.

The Great Sulk

Apart from the mystical swell, another odd feature of the story of the rescue of *Discovery* was the rise and fall of hopes, found principally in the accounts of Scott but to a much lesser extent in the diaries of those closest to him. The men of the *Terra Nova* and *Morning* were doing a professional job together, and despite a little schoolboy rivalry, on a couple of occasions escalated by too much to drink, they all worked as a team steadily and well. Colbeck's remarks referring to his vessel and *Terra Nova* (but not to *Discovery*) ring true:

> The two ship's companies worked together in perfect harmony and Captain McKay gave every assistance in his power at all times.[195]

In contrast to Scott's account, if we refer to the objective records kept on the rescue ships by Doorly, Burgess, and Marsh (all on the *Morning*) and by Jackson (on the *Terra Nova*), who consistently recorded their ships' positions, we can plot the data between January 8th when they were 18 miles from *Discovery*, and February 14th, when they reached Scott's ship, in terms of how many miles they still had to go:

8th Jan 18 miles

14th Jan 16 miles

20th Jan 13 miles

31st Jan 8 miles

3rd Feb 6 miles

9th Feb 3 miles

14th Feb 0 miles[196]

Apart from the lack of progress on the first three days from 5th to 8th January when McKay and Jackson checked the ice thickness, the advance made was constant on a week-by-week basis, and plotting the figures gives a perfect straight line graph. This shows that the rescue ships were making a predictable advance. McKay estimated exactly when he would free *Discovery* as he blasted his way through 18 miles of ice. The notion that the relief ships were just standing by idly, hoping that all the ice would suddenly clear out in a day is not borne out by the facts and was the greatest mistake made by the myth-makers. As we have seen, every week there were days when the ice went out and there were sometimes days when it came back in again, but the

---

195. William Colbeck, Report in *Geographical Journal* 1904, page 744.
196. Figures from the diaries of Burgess, Doorly, Jackson and Marsh, 1904.

two rescue ships broke up the ice and pushed it out to allow the swell to work on the cracks that they had just opened up. This clockwork progress was not observed by those whose ship was rescued, except that Royds in Week Three asked McKay for an estimated time of release and got an accurate answer. So much for mysticism.

PART THREE

The Legend

CHAPTER SEVENTEEN

Scott Myths

The Thankless Task

Carefully crafted myths were eventually taken up by the propaganda machine of the new English journalism and have made up the substance of the majority of books touching on Scott's 1901–4 expedition ever since. We now briefly review some thirty books about Scott's expeditions with particular reference to their relevance to McKay and the cover-up of the rescue. It is important to realise that the myths of Scott's book dealing with his first expedition of 1901–4 are in complete contrast to another group of myths based on his diaries of the second expedition of 1910-12 which were edited by Leonard Huxley and published posthumously. The latter group constructed a picture of a great national hero which nearly all his biographers accepted, and as they did so they removed references to the events of 1904 and to McKay.

The myths have snowballed over the years, starting with the claim that Scott followed the wishes of the Royal Society and had no intention of wintering in the ice. This does not bear close examination. As we have seen, Ommanney gave the idea to Markham and he planned the over-wintering with the help of Colbeck who supplied data from Borchgrevink's *Southern Cross* Expedition, and this led to the selection of McMurdo Sound as a base before Scott ever set sail. Markham even admitted this in an article in the New Zealand *Press* stating that *Discovery* was provisioned to return by March 1905, after three winters in the ice. What Scott told Colbeck in 1903 was meant for consumption by the Royal Geographical Society, Royal Society and the Admiralty, but Colbeck knew the score!

The second myth is that Scott's first expedition had no intention of Pole-bagging because it was a scientific expedition. But the Southern Journey was seen to be a 'failure' when the Pole was not 'conquered', and the whole business of over-wintering the ship was about planning another polar attempt, hence Scott's reason for repeating Armitage's route.

The third myth, that McKay played no part in the 1904 expedition, is a dreadful insult. In Scott's book McKay first appears as an amiable jester but then, in the course of seven weeks when he was seen to be succeeding, he was cast as a villain. The reasons for sending McKay into oblivion are complex and they constantly evolved as Scott invented new ways of escaping from his mounting dilemmas. McKay is ignored, snubbed, discredited and finally reported to higher authority.

The fourth myth of the all-powerful ship *Morning* has been recently revived from some of Doorly's odd imaginings and the concoctions of the Hon. C. C. Bowen.

Creative Work

Much was expected of the 1901–4 Expedition. They had left Britain under a cloud. The controversy stirred up between the two learned societies, the Royal Geographical Society and the Royal Society, by Markham was now made worse. The outmanoeuvring of the Royal Society's scientists had not been forgotten in London and in some quarters there were high expectations of the expedition's scientific work, particularly the science done by the naval personnel, namely the meteorology.

Looking now at the events as they appeared from London, the spate of Antarctic expeditions at the turn of the century naturally led newspapers to make comparisons between them, especially comparisons of their cost-effectiveness. So, when Billy Wharton, as the Admiralty's Hydrographer was known to his friends and foes, went out of his way to send a whaling captain to rescue *Discovery*, there were obvious implications as to the Expedition's cost and competence. It was a move open to several different interpretations, and unfortunately for McKay, the Markham camp saw it as an insult. For the Admiral to look to Colbeck's home city, Hull, for help was understandable; to go to McKay's Dundee was quite unforgivable.

What defence measures could Markham take? Was retaliation a possibility even? First, McKay's work had to be eliminated from the record to imply that sending him was a blunder. Second, the idea that the Expedition needed assistance must be ridiculed, but here retaliation was a more dangerous strategy. Preferably an outsider should be persuaded to accuse the Admiralty of incompetence, overspending and waste. Arranging for C. C. Bowen, Clements Markham's brother-in-law in New Zealand, to do this required ghosting and some rather quick footwork. It all went wrong, the cover was blown and the explanations and denials which had to be sent to the Admiralty rather blunted the Markham camp's attack.

Without doubt the Commander could honestly say that he had not seen any useful work done by McKay. Indeed, for the greater part of forty days and forty nights he had seen very little of anyone's work. To lend support to his assertions and further discredit McKay, the coal controversy was escalated to imply that McKay had not merely been ineffectual but had seriously handicapped a national expedition.

It was a clever scheme, and the weeks preparing the greater part of it on board *Discovery* might be another reason why the Commander spent almost his entire time in his cabin and was careful not to appear on the scene during the seven weeks of the rescue. He does not make a credible appearance in the story of the freeing of his ship, and the writing in the section of his book which describes this rescue period is not up to his usual literary standards.

Dog Doesn't Bite Dog

From 5th January to 14th February 1904 the diaries of the *Discovery* officers read like accounts of a seven-week holiday, except for that one occasion when Colbeck sent a call for help. Nevertheless, it was clear to the ship's company that they were not expected to slope off to the *Terra Nova* just as the whim took them. They were expected to believe in a Great Swell. It is at this point that one can see why a team drawn mainly from Royal Navy personnel, rather than from Merchant Navy men or civilian scientists, was absolutely essential.

There are always some bad apples who will describe what they actually saw and have the impertinence to make private remarks, talk to newspaper reporters and the like. But this was end-of-term report time when men had to be on their best behaviour, though their Commander was the first to assert that no career would benefit from such a long absence from regular service as they had all just experienced. So everyone toed the line in expectation of a good report, and on his return to London the leader gave out the prizes. He claimed that the majority of his men contemplated leaving the Navy at the end of the voyage (the Admirals would be quick to see the implication of this – that although the Naval Discipline Act did not apply to them, the men had obeyed orders purely out of love and respect for their leader).

The report praised the men for coming through what it described as a terrible ordeal unscathed. One might reasonably expect that this was a reference to living for months on end in the Antarctic, but actually it turned out to be a reference to staying in New Zealand for a few weeks! It meant, of course, that men were expected to obey orders, not bringing the expedition into disrepute by talking to the wrong people, or misbehaving. Journalists descended on the ships in New Zealand and failed to extract the truth about the rescue from *Discovery*.

In Scott's *The Voyage of the Discovery* the majority (although not all) of the ship's company were listed, but in his report only seven men are singled out as deserving rewards: Crean, Dailey, Dellbridge, Evans, Feather, Lashly and

Wild. Scott's biographer, Stephen Gwynn, claimed that this showed the leader's quality of discerning loyalty in those who served under him. To others the list looks more like a reward for keeping quiet. When the expedition reached New Zealand, Markham's instruction about not talking to the press were waiting for them. There was to be no mention of Captain McKay and his rescue operation, or of Lieutenant Ernest Shackleton. It was an effective plan in the main but one thing had been forgotten. In 1903, on his return to Dundee, Shackleton wrote an article for the *Illustrated London News* in which he stated plainly that guncotton would be used by the *Terra Nova* to blast *Discovery* free. In Antarctica dogs not only bite dogs, dogs have been known to eat dogs!

Keeping the Lid On

Articles in the New Zealand and Dundee newspapers, in the *Illustrated London News* and in the *Sphere* did not concern Clements Markham in the least. *The Times* of London was the only newspaper that could advance or ruin a naval career, or at the same time revenge the hurt that an old man had suffered. On 10th September 1904 an extraordinary eulogy was printed in that newspaper, claiming that all previous polar expeditions, both North or South, paled into insignificance beside the scientific achievements of this one, that no previous expedition had enjoyed such harmony. Heaping praise on Sir Clements, the article referred to the intrepid explorer-scientists as the 'little company of fifty'. The article reads strangely like one of the prose works of Sir Clements, himself. It set the tone splendidly and silenced the First Sea Lord, Walter Kerr, and the Hydrographer Royal, William Wharton, who then had to play safe and praise absolutely everyone. The trumpeting did not, however, impress the Royal Society but the controversy about the scientific results of the meteorology did not blow up immediately.

During the period that Scott was writing his prose masterpiece in London, Armitage was also writing his book and was about to publish first, which led to some heated exchanges. Then it transpired that Hugh R. Mill, the Royal Geographical Society's librarian, was about to go to press with his history of Antarctic exploration, *The Siege of the South Pole*. Mill's publisher was keen to bring his book out quickly, for the subject had clearly caught the public's imagination, so it was imperative to launch Mill's book as soon as possible after the arrival of *Discovery*. Scott offered to contribute a piece about his own expedition to bring Mill's book right up to date, and Mill was pleased to accept the ghosted copy. Everyone was delighted, the publisher had an exclusive and the expedition had a place in history, with the imprimatur of no less an authority than Mill, who had been Secretary of the International Congress. This was the Congress that Markham claimed played the key role in the birth of the *Discovery*. Mill unwittingly accepted Scott's boastful account of events and the cover-up of the rescue, since he knew no other version. The book was hailed as a brilliant summary of Antarctic history and so the dye was cast. Surely no alternative account of the 1901–04 expedition to Scott's would be given credibility.

Later in 1905 Scott's own book, *The Voyage of the Discovery*, was published and warmly welcomed. In it we learn only four things about McKay: he was an old acquaintance sent to navigate *Terra Nova* for some unstated reason (Scott had met McKay at the Dundee launch); McKay thought he could butt the ice and had no hope of doing so; he was amusing company; and, lastly, he took one look at an approaching storm and was over the rail back to his own ship like a shot. That was the full extent of the recognition of a man who had blasted miles of ice to free a ship for the Commander's 'little company'.

The Book That Never Was

On 5th February 1905 Markham wrote to Colbeck informing him that Evans and Doorly were planning to write a book about the *Morning* and that they were about to write to Colbeck for permission. Colbeck replied immediately, telling Markham that he had received their request and had been offered a percentage of the royalties. They had also asked him to supply his collection of Antarctic photographs and had implied that he should give them exclusive rights on the story. Colbeck did not wish to cause offence (he realised that Sir Clements must have encouraged them) but said he found it difficult to supply the photographs because he was planning to write his own book and needed them himself, though it seems quite likely that this was simply a ruse. Colbeck may well have been offended by Markham's assumption that Evans and Doorly were the best people to write a book about the *Morning*; after all Markham was happy enough to let Scott write a book about *Discovery*. At this time Scott was staying with Markham and was being 'helped' with the initial chapters of the *The Voyage of the Discovery* to ensure that the historical chapters gave proper credit to Markham's circle of old Admiralty friends.

Then on 4th June 1905 Markham offered to help Colbeck write *his* book. Colbeck had found it 'inconvenient' to comply with Doorly's wishes and still had his photographs, and he spoke out strongly about the matter in a letter to Markham:

I may say that I consider the tone of Evans' letter (the offer of a reasonable percentage of the profits) as extremely bad taste.[197]

On New Year's Day 1906 a letter arrived from the Hon. C. C. Bowen addressed to Colbeck, describing how the family had all been reading Scott's new book *The Voyage of the Discovery*. Bowen asked Colbeck when his book telling the story of his cruises in the southern ice would appear. He reminded him that Scott had edited him out of the *The Voyage of the Discovery* and had included no history of the rescue and the work of the relief ships. He signed off saying that he was looking out for a notice of Colbeck's book.

Despite Colbeck's disapproval of what was only published a decade later in 1916 by Doorly, no Colbeck manuscript has ever been discovered, and it is unlikely to have been written. This seems in keeping with his modest and self-effacing character, for Colbeck was never a man to boast of his exploits. Even though he felt that he and McKay were shabbily treated by the Expedition, by the Commander on departure from the Antarctic, by the Royal Navy men in New Zealand, by the Admiralty on his return to London, and ultimately even by posterity itself, Colbeck was not the sort of man to release the story of the rescue of Captain Scott and put his Commander's career in jeopardy.

William Speirs Bruce: The Alternative Hero

In late Victorian and early Edwardian times an antidote to the growing Scott Hero Cult appeared in Scotland. He came to be known as the most successful of all Scottish polar scientists, worthy of a place alongside that host of polar Scots who are renowned for their important discoveries. His name was William Speirs Bruce. When Bruce planned his 1902-04 *Scotia* expedition to the Antarctic, it was like a mirror image of the Markham/ Scott pantomime. Bruce, with experience of both the Arctic and the Antarctic plus considerable mountaineering and glacier experience, could not have been more different. His party was neither as large nor as inexperienced, it was not encumbered with naval personnel, nor was it advised by committees of Admirals. Unlike Markham's, Bruce's objectives were crystal clear and he had the support, not the opposition, of leading scientists. Bruce was a Markham, Scott, Wilson, Ferrar and Hodgson all rolled into one. He had the sense to listen to *Fram*'s designer Colin Archer and Dundee whaling captains with whom he had sailed both South and

197. MS 212 Item 126, W. Colbeck to C. Markham Canterbury Museum
   Archive.

North. Most important, he had the lifelong friendship of Dr. H. R. Mill and they shared identical views about polar dashes and about Scott's expedition, which earned their thinly veiled criticism regarding the enormous waste of money.

The huge sum spent on the 1901–04 expedition could have financed seven international expeditions on the scale of the *Scotia* in the mode proposed by the Austrian, Weyprecht. Scott's funding could also have produced volumes of scientific reports instead of his best-selling romantic fiction. As for immobilising *Discovery* in ice, Bruce's view was that it was a dreadful waste of a ship, for she should have been doing oceanographic research and had no business to be locked up like that. Markham tried to ensure that Bruce received no government or Royal Geographical Society money, and so the Scots had to seek sponsorship for all their costs and had the utmost difficulty in financing the publication of reports. The great difference in scale between Scott's and Bruce's expeditions makes it unrealistic to compare them but, in terms of cost to the taxpayer and results for the scientific community, they were very different and Bruce was far and away the better leader. As Robert Rudmose Brown said of him in the Royal Scottish Geographical Society in 1922: 'He was acknowledged to be the highest authority on polar exploration of his time'. When Scott returned in 1904, Mill could not contain his disappointment with events:

> The fickle public has tired of the Antarctic Regions, the learned societies have folded their hands, glad to finish; the explorers trained and toughened to their work, are scattered in the pursuit of their earlier occupations, and the few men of science who are interested in these matters before the spasm came are still as far as ever from a plan for exploration at once economical in men, money, and ships, continuous, thorough and promising success.[198]

No Damned Science!

In 1905 a World Congress for Economic Expansion was held in Belgium. It was attended by representatives of the countries actively interested in scientific exploration of the polar areas and it led to two follow-up conferences to establish an International Polar Commission on the lines suggested by Weyprecht and supported by Dr Mill and Speirs Bruce, leader of the successful Scottish National Antarctic Expedition of 1902-04, just returned. The international meetings were held in Mons in 1906 and 1908

198. H.R.Mill, *The Siege of the South Pole* (1905), page 410.

and an attempt to snub them by Scott and by the Royal Geographical Society completely backfired. Scott, the self-styled scientific leader, was not even conspicuous by his absence.

The two conferences were attended by official representatives of all the successful scientific polar expeditions of that time, many of the most famous names in the annals of polar exploration at the turn of the century. The most active participants came from America, Australia, Belgium, Denmark, France, Germany, Italy, the Netherlands, New Zealand, Russia and Sweden. There was also a group of three unofficial representatives from Scotland – members of the Scottish Scientific Expedition – and in the absence of Bruce himself, Rudmose Brown of the *Scotia* expedition was elected to be a Vice-President. Along with his colleagues J. H. Harvey Pirie and Robert Mossman, Rudmose Brown contributed to the work of the organising committee, drafting resolutions to set up the Polar Commission which aimed to encourage international co-operation in scientific research. Rudmose Brown explained his odd position in a speech which ought to be circulated to all Scottish delegates at international conferences:

> I regret that I do not stand here as the representative of my country, but in Scotland we cannot have the help of government. Nevertheless for Mr Bruce and myself I may assure you that we are ready to start once more to the Polar regions.[199]

There followed prolonged applause. In both the 1906 and the 1908 conferences there was no mention of Scott apart from oblique remarks about the stupidity of spending vast resources of organisation and finance on a dash for the Pole. British Antarctic explorers James Clark Ross and William Speirs Bruce were regarded as the model expedition leaders.

The anti-hero Bruce never expected compliments about his work. He was at the time working in Svalbard with his friend and patron, the oceanographer Prince of Monaco. Secretly he would have enjoyed the recognition of the scientific community for his Antarctic work and would have been amused that the silly and ineffectual boycotting of the scientific congress by Scott and other pole-baggers had shown these people in their true colours at long last.

---

199. R. Rudmose Brown, Congrès International Pour L'Etude des Régions Polaires: International Polar Commission 1906 & 1908 (Brussells, Hayez 1906 & 1908).

Immortality and Artistic Licence

Mill wrote a restrained review of Scott's *The Voyage of the Discovery*, entering a reservation about the claims of brilliant leadership:

> How much better they might have done with a more thorough preliminary training in scientific work we cannot tell but, as it was the officers and scientific staff of the "Discovery" were able to do more and better work than anyone could have anticipated.

When Scott did not return from his second Antarctic expedition of 1910–13 and the world was told of his fate, the myth of the great expedition leader was super-charged by sensational journalism. It immediately latched onto the macabre: Scott's letters found in the tent. Here was a voice from the grave edited by Leonard Huxley and published just as quickly as could be. With the threat of war now building fast, the recruiting officers wanted a national hero. Scott's widow, together with his old friend Sir James Barrie, made quotable remarks, the diary editor did a thorough job and the playwright turned a ghastly drama into a melodramatic finale with fictitious death scenes which every English schoolboy learned by heart. Here were the noble sacrifices and heroic deaths that the journalists had wanted all along: Welshman Evans, Scotsman Bowers, Englishmen Wilson and Scott – when the facts were suitably arranged the differences could be overlooked, for they all died like Englishmen.

Barrie then prefaced Turley's book *The Voyages of Captain Scott* at the outbreak of the First World War with a splendid description of his hero as

> an English sailor boy with laughing blue eyes who knew how to sacrifice himself for the welfare and happiness of others.[200]

This book entered the coal debate, inventing yet another of those Alice-like arguments: if the *Terra Nova* had not burned the Commander's coal (in the course of rescuing *Discovery*) more discoveries would have been made (after the rescue). Turley had not the least idea that he was writing nonsense. He made mention of McKay only once – that sole occasion when McKay was invited aboard *Discovery* and went over the rails and steamed off into an open sea burning even more coal than ever. Perhaps rail-hopping was something that only a Scottish whaling captain would do just because a hurricane was coming – a true-born Englishman would have finished his game of bowls first. Then we are treated to a new fiction. Instead of the clash between Engineer Skelton, struggling to get *Discovery*'s boilers ready, and his im-

---

200. Sir J.M Barrie & Charles Turley, *The Voyages of Captain Scott* (1914).

petuous Commander urging him to rush into disaster, Turley invents the patient English officer, a Commander facing a serious crisis brought by fate with stiff upper lip.

An Honest Account

In 1910, when Apsley Cherry-Garrard went on Scott's second expedition, he was picked to go with Wilson on the journey made in winter darkness to the Cape Crozier penguin rookery and also to support Scott's polar party. His book entitled *The Worst Journey in the World* was published in 1922 after the death of Scott when he was still being sorely troubled by his conscience, blaming himself for not effecting a rescue. He was convinced that he could have left a depot of food just that little further south and so saved the lives of his friends. He accused himself of not being trained in the techniques of polar travel, navigation by compass, sextant, chronometer and making calculations with the help of those useful mathematical tables found in the Royal Geographical Society's publicaton *Hints to Travellers* (1901).

One would have expected his book to be knee-deep in praise for Scott the Leader but his introduction painted a very different portrait, albeit one set in a golden frame. Cherry-Garrard was unique at this time in choosing to hark back to the earlier expedition of 1901–1904, and he offered the first specific outspoken criticism to come from a member of a Scott expedition:

> When one reads of dog-teams which refused to start, of pemmican which was considered to be too rich to eat, of two officers discussing the ascent of Erebus and back in one day, and of sledging parties which knew neither how to use their cookers or lamps, nor how to put up their tents, nor even how to put on their clothes, then one begins to wonder that the process of education was gained at so small a price.[201]

By 'small price' he meant the loss of so few men – these were strong words indeed in 1922. And they could not be brushed aside easily, coming as they did from the very man who had made the worst of all possible journeys. (The compliment had been paid to him by Scott himself when their party returned to base.) The voice from the grave added considerable weight to his authority. Nevertheless the criticism was defused, as Cherry-Garrard must surely have intended it to be, in the way that the English establishment has for so long defused explosive remarks. It was buried deep in a lengthy historical introduction (people don't read introductions) and it dwelt on

201. Apsley Cherry-Garrard, *The Worst Journey in the World* (Introduction) (1922).

Scott's first expedition which the public were no longer interested in. What his readers wanted to know about was the death of Scott and what exactly was so awful about the worst journey in the world. How Gothic did it become? Was there cannibalism? Did everyone die of scurvy and starvation or fall into bottomless crevasses? Surely the incompetence of a few men under the leadership of Scott in 1902 could shed no light on his death ten years later? It was a thought that never occurred to Cherry-Garrard.

In fact it did not occur to anyone else for a very long time to come.

Playing the Game

Scott's last letters to his people were exactly right. They left the reader inspired, proud and thankful that the men had put aside the race with Amundsen to become martyrs to Science. The death of Scott in 1912 stifled all his critics. The Royal Society accusation that he was a mere Pole-bagger was quashed at last. He was already recognised as a literary giant by no less a paper than the *Spectator* which commented:

> the most interesting record of travel to which the present century has given birth[202]

Now in death he had been made a great scientific leader. The memorials have come down to us like a combination of a last night at the Proms and a clip from a horror film with the victim speaking to us from the depths of an icy tomb: 'Look after our people!' Scott never deserved such treatment but worse was to come. Stephen Gwynn's book *Captain Scott,* written in 1929, is arguably the silliest book yet written about Scott (although there is plenty of time yet). Like the majority of the books which have slavishly copied the myths and perpetrated the Great Swell story, its sources are restricted to the family journals and *The Voyage of the Discovery.* So there is no first-hand evidence which might have hinted at a rescue, or have given a true account of the events connected with it, no quotes from the officers of any of the three ships to explain how all that ice just vanished instantly. Not one mention of McKay. But Gwynn's purpose was not to examine history but to preach to schoolboys about the new national hero – the girls could ask their brothers about him later. The author claimed that Scott 'set the standard by which England (sic) should measure the worth of action'.[203] Gwynn then included a ludicrous potted history of Scotland which did not strike him as the least bit odd, intending to prove that Scott was descended from Jacobite

202. Review of R.F.Scott's *The Voyage of the Discovery,* 1905.
203. Stephen Gwynn, *Captain Scott* (1929).

warriors and might even have been a close relative of Sir Walter Scott and the Duke of Buccleuch – all this claimed for a Commander who couldn't even remember that his ship had been built in Scotland. Gwynn's clichéd message to the boys was that Scott 'taught the world how little success mattered' and that the important thing was how you played the game. This was a lesson that boys had been learning on the more important playing fields of England for decades but now it was a lesson for boys whose fathers had played on lesser fields, and who themselves would be playing on some foreign fields in the very near future.

Martin Lindsay, in his *The Epic of Captain Scott,* published the year before he led his successful three-man Trans-Greenland Expedition of 1934, went one better, claiming that the geological specimens sledged back on Scott's last journey were beyond price because the value of the exploit was independent of any tangible gain and the rocks were a spiritual symbol of martyrdom to the Science of Geology. All this without the help of a geologist. A. G. E. Jones reports that Lindsay also said of his hero in 1933:

the time is not right for a critical approach of Scott.[204]

Yet More Claims

The next author to reinforce the myths was in a good position to demolish them and give a true account of the rescue. This was Gerald Doorly of the *Morning*. Doorly had already written *The Voyages of the Morning*, published in 1916 twelve years after the rescue, and he re-wrote his narrative in 1936. *In the Wake* does not even give an explanation of what *Terra Nova* was doing in the Antarctic moored alongside Doorly's ship. It was a most ungentlemanly demolition job.

The Reverend George Seaver picked up the baton from Martin Lindsay and published his *Scott of the Antarctic* in 1940, a moral and spiritual imaginary portrait. It is a very readable book which on its own admission is a work of imagination and fiction. George Seaver claimed that 'all history is mythology because all recollection is romance', a most revealing statement.[205] Introducing a quasi-religious element into his interpretation, he made Scott immortal, a veritable idol. In part this was effected by creating the appellation 'Scott-of-the-Antarctic'. At this time a mythical person called Scott-

204. A. G. E. Jones, quoting Martin Lindsay. Personal correspondence.
205. Keyserling's Immortality, quoted by George Seaver in *Scott of the Antarctic*, Preface.

Amundsen was being credited with the discovery of the South Pole in all English school atlases. It served one useful purpose, helping to undo the confusion created by Gwynn's Jacobite stories, for it distinguished Scott of the Antarctic from Scott of Abbotsford.

Edward Evans, alias Admiral Mountevans, wrote his *British Polar Explorers* in the middle of the World War II. Evans not merely wrote, he also lived *Boys Own* adventure stories about swashbuckling events. In World War I he had boarded a German ship in the Channel and engaged in hand-to-hand fighting with his cutlass. He prided himself on being one of the last men to see Scott alive and he clearly idolised him. With his close friend Doorly he had been a member of the 1904 rescue on the *Morning* and, like Doorly, his memory of what happened in 1904 failed him mysteriously and he made no reference to the job that he was sent to do. Apparently by 1943 it was a thing that the friends of the late Robert Falcon Scott did not mention in public, or in polite company.

James and Margery Fisher researched the life of Shackleton and published their biography in 1957. James Fisher was surprised by the fruits of his investigation, and whilst it shed no direct light on McKay (because Shackleton was sent home the year before the 1904 rescue), the Fishers' book was an important new study of the Scott and Shackleton relationship, firmly based on scholarship. They were the first to realise that Markham was at the root of many problems, that the leader lacked experience and competence, that the conflict between the Royal Navy and the Merchant Navy was important and that both Armitage and Shackleton were success- fully silenced because their futures depended on what was called their 'loyalty'.

An Indomitable Legend

Gerald Bowman's *From Scott to Fuchs* was published in 1958 . The timing of this book about Scott was inspired by the ascent of Everest by Hillary and Tensing in 1953 and the successful Commonwealth Transantarctic Expedi- tion of 1956 when Hillary and Fuchs crossed the White Continent, meeting at the South Pole.

Bowman's book was intended to set out the historical background of twentieth-century Antarctic exploration. Like several other authors before and since, Bowman claimed that this history began with Scott, unaware that Borchgrevink, Bernacchi, Colbeck and their companions deserve pride of place as the first Antarctic explorers to winter on the Continent. One reason for this omission is that Bowman defines an explorer as someone whose name is perpetuated on a chart, and he speaks of Scott as 'the most indomitable explorer of his time'.[206] True enough, there is no doubt that all that the Scott legends are indomitable, incredibly persistent. Fuchs and Hillary were completing a task that owed much to the pioneering ideas of others and Bowman's claim tells us at once that we are in for another romp with romantic heroes. Shackleton and William Speirs Bruce were responsible for the original idea of traversing Antarctica from the Weddell Sea to the Ross Ice Shelf, via the South Pole, in 1914. The loss of Shackleton's ship *Endurance* led first to failure and then to the greatest of all Antarctic survival epics.

In the course of researching his subject, Bowman obviously tried to apply that same objectivity that the Fishers had applied to Shackleton, Scott's rival. The book might have provided a new analysis, for it did remark that Scott had now become a controversial figure, but Bowman didn't investigate, or offer intellectual explanation. He repeated all the old myths – how Scott came by chance to be casually invited to lead the Expedition, how he chose all the members of the Expedition personally, how Shackleton was put on the sledge and carried back all the way to the ship on the Southern Journey and then had to be invalided home, how Scott discovered the Antarctic Plateau and how he was always unlucky with the weather, the snow conditions and the performance of the dogs.

So no-one should be surprised to learn that the story of how *Discovery* was released from the ice was simply a matter of sheer good fortune (forgetting momentarily that Scott had only bad luck), for their release came just three days before they were about to abandon *Discovery*. A list of who was going in which ship had just been worked out when suddenly in came that Great Swell. What is so pathetic about even the best of these accounts is the fact that it never occurs to any of these writers that when the rescue ships arrived, there were eighteen miles of solid ice between them and the *Discovery*, and that this fact cannot be covered up in any way.

Confused by Myths

In 1959 the Director of the Royal Geographical Society, L. P. Kirwan, with unrivalled access to many of the relevant documents, diaries and papers in the Society's archives, wrote his very readable book *The White Road,* a history of Antarctic exploration. In the main he accepted Scott's account of everything and fell into all the traps for the 1901–04 expedition. Interestingly enough the most amusing of these pitfalls concerns the 1904 Colbeck and McKay rescue.

---

206. Gerald Bowman, *From Scott to Fuchs* (1958), page 15.

Scott's version of the history of this event muddles the true sequence and it is not the easiest of narratives to grasp. Even those who have spent some time with other original first-hand accounts can become confused between the activities of the *Discovery* and those taking place around the two relief ships. On the one hand there was the blasting by McKay as he edged *Terra Nova* forwards towards *Discovery* mile after mile through the ice. On the other hand were the two quite isolated occasions when some blasting was tried by Scott himself around his own ship. When, towards the end of the rescue operations, Scott then claimed credit for *all* the blasting, it is not surprising that readers become confused by these two very different operations. And nobody was more confused than Kirwan, who thought that Scott was describing how *Discovery* was edging her way forward to the *Terra Nova* and that Scott had managed to rescue McKay! No wonder McKay was thought to be useless in some quarters.

Kirwan did not correlate the diaries of the 1901–04 expedition, naturally relying on a selection from the Royal Geographical Society's own archives. Consequently he gives the impression that during the rescue Scott was watching intently day by day for any sign of the break-up of the ice. As we have seen, Scott's writings show that, with one exception, he did no such thing and relied entirely on reports brought to him, and most of these he mistrusted. The Commander was writing in his cabin for the greater part of forty days and forty nights, which is just one of the reasons why McKay hardly gets a mention in anybody's book. However, doubts did enter Kirwan's mind. Like Hugh Mill he concluded that the expedition of 1901–1904 was not a great scientific success; he regarded it simply as a dramatic adventure.

Frank Debenham's book *Antarctica* also came out in 1959 and it might have been written by Scott himself. Either the author was not familiar with the Scott Polar Research Institute's archives in Cambridge, or, as one surely must assume, he was all too familiar with them. As that great adventurer Admiral Mountevans who was present throughout the rescue said: 'One cannot state facts plainly when they reflect on the organisation'.

The Counterblasts

Five long years went by without a new book on Scott's expeditions, then, in 1965, Harry Ludlam published *Captain Scott – the Full Story*. His book revealed that Scott was snubbed in official circles on his return to London. Ludlam simply refers to the lack of a hero's welcome and a lunch in a dockland shed instead of a Guildhall Banquet to welcome the men of *Discovery*, but there is no full story to explain these peccadilloes.

The following year Reginald Pound's *Scott of the Antarctic* was published. This was something different – according to the publishers, Pound was the first author to have access to certain private papers. From 1966 onwards publishers started to become interested in historical researches not because they wanted to donate funds to the archives which have always been starved of funding and support, but for the same reason that journalists are interested in the release of official secrets. If they get in fast enough, the story should be an exclusive, and even if they don't they can still hint at revelations and a scoop. Pound was the first to uncover the plan to over-winter in the Antarctic but only a part of the scheme. He revealed some of the internecine warfare between the two Societies, criticisms of the Expedition's misman-agement and the story of the clash between Balfour and Markham. Yet when he came to consider the rescue of 1904, he accepted the cover-up story without question, taking his version of events straight from Scott's book.

The next book to appear broke new ground and questioned some of the mythology. It was a splendid contribution from the southern hemisphere which up to that time had been strangely quiet. L. B. Quartermain's *South to the Pole* in 1967 entered new doubts including the whole question of aims, the resignation of Gregory and the conflict between Sir Clements Markham and Sir John Murray over Scott's competence to lead a scientific expedition. Quartermain also raised the question of Scott's inability to lead men without the strictures of naval discipline but once again, when it came to the rescue by Colbeck and McKay, he swallowed Scott's fictions whole and unac-countably did not use the thousands of words which are safely stored in New Zealand archives. .

William Bixby's *Robert Scott, Antarctic Pioneer*, published in 1970, is a rather nice florid version of events, presumably written for young readers.

A book appeared in 1974 written by David Sweetman (the author of a book on the Borgias, his publisher is keen to tell us). His *Captain Scott* closely resembles Pound's 1966 work but was toned down where he felt it necessary perhaps to give his text some appearance of originality.

An Unflawed Hero

Peter Brent's book *Captain Scott and the Antarctic Tragedy* (1974) is made of sterner stuff. He considered the panegyrics more soberly than most and recognised the consequences of an inexperienced Commander ignoring orders from both the Admiralty and the Royal Geographical Society. But Brent did not penetrate the murky waters of the rescue, calling it a cumbersome double-headed relief. He appears not to have noticed anomalies in the many diary accounts which contrast with the official storyline. Like Debenham, he mostly quotes Scott's mystical version of events from *The Voyage of the Discovery* and was even impressed by its sentimental justification summed up by Scott's remark that the company's love of their ship went 'far beyond the ordinary'.[207] This had already proved to be a useful weapon in the cover-up of the rescue, for it not only brought tears to the eyes of Admirals, it launched a new breed of writer who found such turns of phrase charming. Hard-headed museum curators and steely-eyed university researchers went weak at the knees on reading it.

Three years went by without a new book, then came D. Thomson's *Scott's Men*. Here was a study which called into question the expertise of those who have taken upon themselves the task of writing about expeditions. Thomson considered the post-war cult of the Anti-Hero and concluded that Scott was an 'unflawed example' of an English hero. Unwittingly he presented Scott as the sort of leader few people would want to follow: harebrained, vacillating one moment, pig-headed the next, naive with Galahad lordliness, a day-dreamer, unable to step out of the role of Commander and to accept the advice of others, snobbish, intolerant, impatient, quick-tempered, unprepared, capable of starving and exhausting his men, unable to judge character, convinced that the Antarctic was his domain and jealous of that glory. It is a pity that, in company with most other writers, Thomson did not spend as much time researching the 1903 and 1904 relief expeditions as he did listing attributes of his 'unflawed hero'. He had found all the right psychological ingredients to do so.

Elspeth Huxley's *Scott of the Antarctic* (1977) provided more peeps into family papers but basically her book is a re-working of old material to counter some of these worrying things that were beginning to float to the surface. If Thomson claimed to be an admirer, what might one expect from an unsympathetic writer? Her publisher's 'unprecedented access to relevant papers' came down to the reaffirmation of all the old myths. With unconscious humour, we are told that when *Discovery* reached New Zealand, the men spoke with one voice. But then only one man on *Discovery* was permitted to speak.

The Big Bang

Then in 1979 came the biggest explosion of all with the publication of Roland Huntford's *Scott and Amundsen*. It is the definitive version, the most objective and best researched account of the two Scott expeditions. Its critical scholarship set new standards in the genre, illuminated by impressive analysis and

---

207. *The Voyage of the Discovery* (1905), Volume II, page 327.

historical insight. Huntford brought to his task a relevant practical knowledge of ski-ing and climbing, dog handling and an encyclopaedic knowledge of the Scandinavian sources. His 600-page study incurred the wrath of the Keepers of British Myths, for they found the truth disagreeable and protested that he had not played the game. The facts were not in error and attempts made to counter Huntford's facts have always proved unsuccessful and indeed counterproductive. During the twenty years since his book first appeared there have been a few reckless attempts to tilt at it, which have all met with disaster for the reputations of those entering the lists. In some libraries a sad little note has been inserted as a frontispiece to Huntford's brilliantly researched book entreating the reader to refrain from reading it.

In the 1980s two of the best-informed researchers on polar expeditions made further contributions to the debate. In 1984 the Antarctic scientist, D. W. H. Walton, wrote the preface to a new edition of Armitage's *Two Years in the Antarctic*. Walton revealed how Scott treated his fellow officers, underplayed their achievements and restricted their activities. He elaborated Huntford's point that the events described in Scott's journals were often re-worked to produce a version of the facts suitable for publication, with changes made not just for literary effect. New evidence was unveiled about the contract with Armitage, the efforts made by Koettlitz and Armitage to educate their novice Commander in polar lore, and the ploy of sending Shackleton home on the pretext that he still had scurvy.

When Clive Holland, a former archivist of the Scott Polar Research Institute, edited Markham's *Personal Narrative – An Antarctic Obsession* in 1986, he too was critical of the 1901–04 Expedition, assessing the damage done by the clash between the Royal Society and the Royal Geographical Society and the extraordinary degree of influence which Markham exerted. There is an implication in Holland's analysis, absent in Huntford's, that Scott should not be blamed for errors built into the expedition by Markham, and the book shows how the resignation of Gregory as scientific director changed the whole nature of the expedition with the loss of a leader with both mountaineering and polar experience. Clive Holland was the first researcher to realise how the rescue came about, for he had seen the original Colbeck cable sent to Markham which triggered strong reactions in London. Holland summed up:

cumbersome, over-manned and inefficient naval polar expedition.[208]

This must have rattled a few tea cups in Cambridge and South Kensington.

---

208. Clive Holland, Preface to Clements Markham, *Personal Narrative – An Antarctic Obsession*, (1986), page xxiii.

Home to Roost

Public fascination with Scott's second expedition overshadowed the events of his first which by 1939 was almost completely ignored. Forty years later, in the space of just five years, a new picture emerged which encompassed both expeditions and burst the patriotic bubble. In the 1980s an exchange between Wayland Young and Roland Huntford in the literary magazine *Encounter* concerned certain details of Markham and Scott's activities which had been documented in *Scott and Amundsen*. Their differences of opinion have no direct bearing on McKay's rescue bid but it is worth noticing that one of the most important facets of the exchange was, as Roland Huntford observed, that the debate was a continuation of what he aptly called 'the storm of sentimental rage'.[209] It had rumbled on since the beginning of the century, achieving a peak when Amundsen reached the South Pole first and Scott did not return. The myth-makers explained that the lost men had not been trying to race Amundsen to the Pole, and even Huntford's book with its mass of accurate documentation has not successfully demolished the British myth that playing to win is vulgar.

In 1984 the present author found new evidence for the Harry McKay Rescue Bid (it deserves no less a title, notwithstanding contributions by the Admiralty, Colbeck and his men, Jackson and his crew, Royds and Heald). Following the lead of A. G. E. Jones,[210] unearthing in Dundee and New Zealand Archives long-buried accounts of the narrative, it became possible to make a convincing case for the return of *Discovery* from St. Katherine's Dock in London to her city of origin. The question 'Why Dundee?' was answered in a plan of interpretation for the visitor centre exhibitions at Discovery Point on the Dundee waterfront. For the first time, a detailed appreciation of the work of rescue by McKay and Colbeck was made public, but the work did not appear in print.[211]

Eight years later a fragment of the rescue story appeared in Ann Savours' book *The Voyages of the Discovery* which did not set out to tell the story of Scott, Colbeck, McKay or the 1901–04 expedition. As the title makes abundantly clear, it is an account of the remarkable journeys of a ship that began life in Dundee Shipbuilders' yard. McKay is briefly mentioned, but not in connection with the blasting, which is attributed to Royds, and it unfortunately follows Scott's muddled account. Only one rescue day is

209. Roland Huntford and Wayland Young, 'An Exchange', *Encounter* 1980.
210. A.G.E.Jones, 'Harry McKay, Master of the Terra Nova', *Antarctic* 1973.
211. Don Aldridge, Eight Dundee Project Papers, Dundee Interpretation Audit, An Outline Interpretive Prospectus for Discovery Point. 1984–1990 (unpublished).

picked, out and, interestingly, the description comes from Colbeck, doubtless because he was the officer in overall command. McKay earns his place
in this book for the oft-repeated and untrue allegation that he supplied only
50 tons of coal, but all these brief snapshots in time are treated good
humouredly enough. There is one amusing revelation: we are told that
Colbeck *did* believe that without explosives *Discovery* would not have got
free – but this dangerous thought is tucked away in an appendix on page
337.

Feminist Footprints in the Snow

In 1986 one of America's finest contemporary writers brought her scalpel
along to dissect Scott and Shackleton and their adventures in nature and the
nature of adventure. Ursula Le Guin's essay 'Heroes' (in *Dancing at the Edge of
the World*) deserves to be on the curriculum of every explorer. She has
already written the perfect antidote to the appalling male egotism of
geographers, a short story about a party of women who reach the South
Pole when it is still undiscovered and decide that it would not be the done
thing to mention their feat. They very wisely decide to leave no footprints.
Would that more of us could follow their example!

Ms. Le Guin did not know that her hero Ernest Shackleton did actually
receive a letter from a schoolgirl asking if she could come with him on his
expedition and obviously was not aware that his response was to laugh. The
Shackleton she admires so much is more gallant than the real one. As for her
Scott, he is the literary giant, not the man. She knows that he did almost
everything wrong but she places him in her pantheon because apparently he
'admitted his failure completely'. Scott has attracted the maternal instincts of
several recent writers, because of his lovely blue eyes, or because of the
stories he would have told (had he not taken so many risks with his own and
other men's lives). He is the writer's explorer who wrote his own adventure
story but he took 'complete responsibility for it', and this is what makes him
a hero. We are a long way here from Harry McKay, on the edge of a
different world in fact, but a very interesting one.

In 1997 Diana Preston's *A First Rate Tragedy* was published. Steeped in
Boys Own Paper values, it repeats all the old nonsense published since 1905:
the so-called heroism, man-hauling, Barrie's version of the Scott death
scene, Oats' great sacrifice, the misfortune of reaching the Pole without
priority, all that rotten luck, the sneaky entrance from the wings in this
melodrama of that foreign villain Amundsen with his nasty professionalism,
the amateur hero Scott not racing the Norwegian in 1912, just as he wasn't
trying to reach the South Pole in 1902 and there was the awful burden of

their sledge piled high with all those heavy millstones of science, the rock specimens. She sweeps aside all aspects of expedition planning in order to praise 'the essential humanity'. After all this regurgitation we are not surprised to learn that in 1904 the ice in McMurdo Sound broke up of its own volition. One reviewer claimed that this book also performed a miracle: rescuing Scott's reputation. Apparently the point we have all missed is that Scott suffered, *that* was his heroic achievement; Amundsen didn't suffer and *that* was cheap and unforgivable. What Huntford called 'English sentimental rage' once again found its way into print.

A Real Swell

When Louis Bernacchi joined the group of ten men who were the first to winter in the Antarctic (on the *Southern Cross* Expedition of 1898-1900), they built a hut at Cape Adare and had no intention of risking wintering on their ship. After the expedition Bernacchi came to England just a year before returning to the area with Scott. In that interval in London he managed to produce his fascinating book *To the South Polar Regions*. It is a mine of practical information which would have been of great value to anyone who believed that wintering the *Discovery* in the Antarctic was a safe thing to do, as the following passage from Bernacchi's book should make clear. Here Bernacchi is describing how the men left their hut on the coast and ventured down to the shore to investigate a curious booming noise:

We went out; a deep sonorous roar was audible like the din of battle; a battle indeed! We rushed down towards the shore from where the noise came, and on reaching it a sight met our eyes which baffles description; a scene absolutely frightful in its grandeur. Right along the N. W. shore from which, half-an-hour before, one could see for miles and miles across the pack, a moving mountain of ice had risen up; a sudden and terrible pressure had set in from the N. W. and was piling the ice on the shores. It extended about 800 yards, and was on average 60 feet high; the mass was moving the whole time and advancing on the land. The grandeur of the spectacle was immense. There is nothing comparable to it, and words can in no degree convey an idea of the majesty of the scene.

Huge blocks of ice thousands and thousands of tons in weight were lifted up 70, 80, and 90 feet with irresistible force to the top of the mount. There they would totter for a few seconds and then come crashing down with a reverberating roar, sending up white clouds like steam into the air; not one, nor two, nor three blocks at a time but thousands. At times great yawning gaps would appear in the mount and the whole side would bulge out until with a fearful crash it would burst, and great blocks of ice fly into the air like so many straws. The noise of the pressure resembled the noise made by the pistons of a large steamer. It was possibly caused by a strong gale or by some tidal effect.[212]

Here, then, is the grim reality of a Great Swell which actually did occur in McMurdo Sound, and this is what Scott was praying would come to free his ship *Discovery*. And thankfully it never did come, for no whaling ship could have survived such an onslaught of thousand-ton blocks of ice piling up against that shoreline. Wintering *Discovery* in the ice cannot be called a brave or a courageous act, indeed they were all fortunate to escape so cheaply. Wilhelm Paulke put it in a nutshell:

> True courage is shown only by one who is fully aware of the consequences of his actions.[213]

212. Louis Bernacchi, *To the South Polar Regions* (1901) pages 120–123.
213. Wilhelm Paulke, *Hazards in Mountaineering* (1973).

CHAPTER EIGHTEEN

Hero and Anti-Hero

Restoring a Reputation

Scott and McKay typify the contrasts between the twentieth-century Hero and Anti-Hero. Colbeck and McKay were no schoolboy heroes but their actions deserve a place in history, and their reputations need rescuing from the oblivion into which they were swept by Scott, Markham and Doorly. It is worth drawing threads of the expedition narrative together to answer the questions: why did Scott become a hero? Who made him one? And why? The first question is the easiest. In the years before the Great War the country needed a hero and the new journalism did the rest. In McKay we see the opposite of Scott, not the product of nepotism but the victim of it, a man who led and inspired those around him to achieve the impossible without boasting. Both Colbeck and McKay showed those who were prepared to be shown, how to succeed in a quest. They were so successful as anti-heroes that virtually nobody knows about them! Colbeck and McKay were no amateur gentlemen proud of incompetence, complaining of bad luck. Colbeck wrote no book. Instead of polishing written accounts of their deeds, McKay wrote nothing; he had no time to write and he had no need to write, for his actions are always revealed through others. A seaman who had been with him for some ten years described him thus:

> The Captain's alertness is one of his strong points. If there is any danger he is there, always on the look-out. He could not rest until he got to the "Discovery" and almost foamed at the mouth at the natural and baffling delays that occurred. I have been along with different captains and he is just about the best. You can speak to him as you would anyone else, and if you give him advice that he thinks is good he will take it.[214]

McKay and Colbeck came to do a job; the Commander came for an awfully big adventure. Popular writers continue to wrap a cloak of sentimentality around the polar explorers. The majority of writers about *Discovery* have had less experience of snow and ice than Scott himself, they peddle judgments

214. Article in the *Press*, New Zealand. 2nd April 1904.

schooled in the nursery of Peter Pan and Christopher Robin. They would do better to quote descriptions from the nursery of incompetent exploration, like those of the great Victorian traveller Edward Lear, for Scott was a Jumblie who sailed into the winter darkness on an expedition for which he was quite unprepared:

> And everyone said who saw them go,
> 'O won't they be soon upset you know!
> For the sky is dark, and the voyage is long,
> And happen what may, it's extremely wrong
> In a Sieve to sail so fast!'[215]

Romantics on Ice

The frigid lands of the Arctic, Antarctic and Mountain Worlds demand high levels of competence from expedition members and higher levels of competence from leaders but there is always an army of writers determined to romanticise exploration. Just because someone happens to be at the front of the train does not mean that the person is a leader. It is unwise to tell a hero that nobody is taking any notice of him, better by far quietly to ignore him, in the way that Scott's orders to stop freeing his ship were ignored by the anti-heroes. McKay and his men thought that in some ways the Arctic was more difficult than the Antarctic. When the Royal Navy met the Inuits living successfully in the very landscape that the explorers had come to discover, European aesthetic taste came to the leader's rescue: thus it was wrong to think of the natives in the same light as Royal Navy explorers. The Inuit were not really better at surviving an Arctic winter than naval officers, as one might have supposed, because an Inuit's level of existence was so primitive that it didn't count as survival. In other words an officer would rather die than live in such squalor and eat such stuff.

The officer could explain his own comparative ineptitude by the fact that he was civilised and had no need of primitive survival skills – civilised people had lost these skills in the best Darwinian manner. British attitudes to the natives of the Arctic were however more complicated and ambivalent, tempered as they sometimes were by Rousseau's concept of the Noble Savage. Samuel Johnson thought that if he hurried he might just be in time to see a noble savage in Scotland, but alas, too late! By the same token, museum curators had licences to shoot rarities for their collections. The Inuit were either regarded as sub-human species, animals to be despised as inferior,

---

215. Edward Lear, *Nonsense, Songs, Stories, Botany and Alphabets* (1871).

or simply as innocent and godless savages who might nevertheless be admired in the safety of the library of the Royal Geographical Society.

Thus a Merchant Navy man from its lower echelons, like McKay, could not be expected to understand the importance of geographical discovery, but on special occasions he was allowed into the ward room to provide amusement. Exploring was not a job for just *any* man, it must be led by naval officers because it had a high moral purpose and it called for an intimate mix of military skills and Judaeo/Christian beliefs, such as the environmental instructions from the Bible to go forth and multiply and have dominion over the earth.

To the military mind, Conquest is closely related to Adventure. To the non-military mind Adventures are signs of incompetence and lack of preparation for the task in hand. The important point here is that one cannot command or conquer the environment of the Poles, or conquer mountains, and certainly not on the scale of the Himalayas. We are but specks in these sublime and romantic landscapes.

The Call of the Wild

Francis Spufford is that rare combination – a literary critic of British polar history who also understands the polar experience. In 1996 his brilliant and imaginative book, *I May Be Some Time: Ice and the English Imagination*, opened the door to some little-explored Scott and McKay territory. Spufford began unpromisingly, seeking an answer to the age-old question that explorers and mountaineers are for ever being asked: 'Why?' It has made famous men groan inwardly and brought forth George Mallory's anguished cry about Everest: 'Because it's there'. But Spufford doesn't give up easily.

He is confident that the trait of searching for sublime places on the face of the earth is of English origin (although he correctly attributes the philosophy to an Irishman and wisely steers clear of the Scottish dimension). The reason why English explorers have developed a particular ear for the romantic call of the wild is partly derived from Burke's assertion that there are but two types of landscape: the *Beautiful* and the *Sublime,* partly from the fact that exploration was a male prerogative and partly because one can have exciting and intrepid adventures in a *Sublime* landscape much more easily than one can in a *Beautiful* landscape. One could have an adventure in the latter but because the *Beautiful* engendered thoughts of self-propagation, gentle rounded hills, smooth meadows and sylvan groves with nymphs and merry swains, it wasn't exactly what most gentlemen meant by an heroic adventure. The *Sublime* was dark, engendering thoughts of horror and self-destruction, scenes of treeless wilderness with great peaks of snow and ice, awesome rocky crags, or frighteningly vast, empty, untrodden and silent expanses stretching to infinity. The call of the wild was, according to Spufford, that it is a response to a place, an answer to his question 'Why?' So George Mallory did get it right after all.

We imagine that this Romanticism is no longer with us today but we are wrong:

> We see only what we want to see. We look at scenery through red and green glasses, through a windscreen, through binoculars, through a microscope, through a museum glass case and, in the end, what we actually see is a mirror of ourselves. There is no such thing as a sublime landscape, only a sublime experience of landscape. There is no such thing as wilderness, only the experience of wilderness.[216]

There is hardly any pristine natural environment or wilderness (in the ecological sense) left on the planet, and as a consequence the White Continent is an indicator of the health of the global environment and its conservation. The Royal Geographical Society has only recently discovered that conservation is the modern acceptable form of adventure in what is now left of our dwindling *Landscapes Sublime*.

A Single-Minded Lone Explorer

What Markham meant by geographical exploration was not conquest but more maps. Paradoxically he also thought in terms of heroes, and interestingly he chose them all in advance of their heroism. So all Scott and Royds had to do was to ensure that they were not accused of failure and their places in the explorers' pantheon would be assured, a fact which surprises Francis Spufford. Yet his summary of their period explains it perfectly:

> an age of artificial virtue, systematic lying, fake proprieties.[217]

This is the reason that the rescue had to be edited out of the tale that Scott had to tell; it is the only explanation that really makes sense of his actions. Beau Riffenburgh's *The Myth of the Explorer* (1993) and Joseph Campbell's *The Hero with a Thousand Faces* (1949) provide an interesting discussion of the nature of the hero in mythology and contemporary life. Their analysis can be applied to shed light on the 1901–1904 Expedition, or rather, on Scott's

---

216. Don Aldridge, 'A Sense of Place: An Exercise in Interpretation and Communication', in Alexander Fenton & Hermann Palsson (eds), *The Northern & Western Isles in the Viking World* (1984).
217. Francis Spufford, *I May Be Some Time: Ice and the English Imagination* (1996).

account of it. Although neither author related his ideas to this particular expedition, they help to show how such an unlikely candidate as Scott was given all the appearances of a hero.

The first attribute of a hero is a burning ambition. Scott was painfully conscious of rank and class, and it was his quest for promotion that led him to the Antarctic where he found himself out of his depth leading an Expedition for which he was unsuited with no polar, mountaineering, or even snow and ice experience. The Edwardian nepotism and caste system which surrounded his appointment played an important role right through the Expedition, ensuring that some men would become heroes and some would not. Markham kept notes on the men's heroic potential. Likewise, when Scott polished his prose for *The Voyage of the Discovery*, nobody else was allowed to score too many hero-points. One sees that a careful eye is being kept on the cumulative scores of fellow officers. Royds' splendid efforts with McKay are not written up. Nor do Royds' sledge journeys loom large. Merchant Navy officers Shackleton and Armitage are dealt with more easily, the former by implying that he was carried back to base an invalid, the latter by playing down his discoveries and then repeating his Western Journey. When C. C. Bowen heard a first-hand account of the repeat journey in which Scott became the lone hero venturing into uncharted wilderness, he wrote:

> Captain Scott made a westward journey which was probably even more arduous than his journey towards the South Pole. His route took him over very high rugged land and mountains covered with snow and having also numerous glaciers. The account of this journey, when it is published, must prove of the greatest interest to geographical scientists.[218]

Adventure and Challenge

An explorer who is blessed with the ambition to become a hero, having heard the call of the wild, must first venture into the unknown. This is another point where Scott scored well, for everywhere he went was bound to be unknown and he had to ensure that he ventured into more of it than anybody else. As we have seen, he did not allow any scientist to lead an epic sledge journey (the equivalent of mountaineering first ascents), leading all but three of the long journeys himself, apart from Armitage's discovery of the Plateau, Royds' South-East journey and Barne's Southern trip over the Barrier Ice. But in the book *The Voyage of the Discovery* he reassembles these three journeys so that only one hero emerges. The repeat of the Western

218. C.C.Bowen, article in the *Press*, New Zealand, 2nd April 1904.

Journey is the most revealing of them, ending up with our hero leading two men whose lowly rank ensures that they could not possibly challenge his heroic role. The other scientists and officers who helped him find this route were sent back to the ship, left no footprints on the untrodden snows, and made no mark on the blank pages of the Commander's diary.

Scott set out to achieve status with his men through endurance, he had to man-haul a sledge faster and longer than any other officer, and by all accounts he did so supremely well. Skelton complained about the pace which brought on altitude sickness, and there are many passages in Scott's writing which paint a boastful picture of a sort of amateur superman, suitably tempered by an injection of modest passages. An interesting example is how the untutored mountaineer without crampons climbed a vertical ice wall to escape from certain death in a glacial crevasse. Anyone who has ever climbed on vertical ice walls or ventured into a crevasse will, however, recognise the description as ninety per cent heroic fantasy. The descriptions of such adventurous incidents are inserted into the final narrative to add drama and spice up the story of what must have been a rather boring plateau slog for much of the time.

One heroic element which is challenging and often horrific in polar exploration is safe navigation over difficult terrain in winter darkness, and it is missing from the narrative. A number of unbelievable accidents occurred as men returned from the huts beside the ship, lost their way in the dark and floundered about for hours in considerable danger. Our hero left this particular skill of night navigation to Hodgson, who was the last person seeking to do something heroic. Ironically, when Scott revisited McMurdo Sound on his second expedition, it was just such a journey (led by Wilson with Bowers and Cherry-Garrard to the emperor penguin rookery of Cape Crozier in the winter darkness of 1911) that he acknowledged as the hardest journey ever made and called it heroic. But he knew *The Worst Journey in the World* wasn't properly heroic because the goal was not romantic enough. Heroes don't go birdnesting.

Pure as the Driven Snow

Classical heroes ventured out on magical journeys and made quests for spiritual self-discovery. There is an element of this in Scott's expeditions, as witness the fact that he took less interest in the scientific *objectives* (which he practically ignores in his book) than in the goal of reaching the Pole. There are few more magical geographical concepts than the Pole, and there is even less point in reaching a Pole than climbing a great summit. Neither conquest is a journey to obtain observations, or views.

No matter how many rock specimens might have been piled upon their sledge on the Southern Journey, it was no geological or glaciological quest. If it had been seen in this light, then Hartley Ferrar might have been invited along, but Ferrar was not party to the kind of exploration that the sledge journeys were meant to cover. The rock walls and erratic boulders seen were not geological phenomena but incidental curiosities, the mileage covered was the thing.

The Pole was Scott's Holy Grail. Even today contorted arguments are used to deny that the Pole was the expedition's objective. Scott failed in 1902, and tried again in 1903 following Armitage's approach; failing again, he went to great lengths, risking his career in the process, to stay in Antarctica for a further attempt in 1904. One can sympathise with his feelings of frustration when his next polar bid was thwarted by McKay's precipitate rescue, just as one can appreciate why Shackleton wept at being sent back in 1903. On the way home he went riding with Colbeck and other friends in New Zealand and immediately set about planning his own polar attempt. So ill was he!

A quest had a sort of religious significance for these men, as if a kind of purification came from a journey into a white continent. They were cleansed in an earthly paradise of untroddden snow and gained immortality in a quest which was mystic and infinite. Similarly, intense cold can induce feelings of purification, even punishment in a circle of Hell. Scott is often mystical when he describes an Antarctic phenomenon, as in this poetic description of the aurora:

> movement never less than evanescent, mysterious – no reality. It is the language of mystic signs and portents – the inspiration of the gods – wholly spiritual – divine signalling. Remindful of superstition, provocative of imagination.[219]

These are not the words of a scientist but of a fine prose writer and poet who had taken a short course in magnetism. One other element of hero analysis is the paradox of the solo venturer in a mystic brotherhood. Scott was the lover of solitude who was befriended by one man, Wilson poet and artist.

Superman, Sport and Discipline

Despite all the words written denying that Scott's attempts to reach the South Pole were in any sense Pole-bagging journeys, or that his last great

219. R.F.Scott, quoted in George Seaver, *Scott of the Antarctic* (1940), Ch.IV.

tragic journey to the South Pole was a competitive race with Amundsen, a quest to be first at the Pole has within itself an inevitable element of competition. One could not pretend that the intention all along was not to go south towards the Pole, or to go south for some other reason, and one certainly could not pretend that the objective was to be second at the pole! Other forms of polar exploration differ from this race to be first just in this one particular respect.

There has long been an equivalent challenge to Pole-bagging in the world of sport. Some people regard both mountaineering and exploration as forms of sport, and although many practitioners are offended by the very suggestion, there is now a new cult of competitive rock climbing as a gymnastic activity which has become a spectator sport.

It is interesting to look at sporting heroics, for the Olympic Games stem from a religious practice which is heroic, in the same sense that attempting to reach the Pole is heroic. The Olympics were funeral games where all the energy or blood sacrificed in conflict and competition were ultimately for the benefit of the dead who were about to make their last magical journey: the finale of all heroic narratives. Sport has come a long way since Greek times, and the Olympics have now shed their cultural side completely to become Disneyfied, but the old energy sacrifice still remains at the core of most sporting activity, even if we have forgotten why. Scott's book gives a detailed account of the innermost thoughts of an energetic hero, a man who expected superhuman effort from all his fellows and sometimes used naval discipline to get it. There is just one important exception, which was triggered by the arrival of the *Terra Nova*, when for seven weeks the hero hibernated in his ship and felt this inactivity most keenly. For Scott this posed a literary problem and his narrative suffered accordingly.

Most heroes return successfully from their quests to bring some great boon to the world – fire brought to earth, gold or new lands conquered, specimens collected to add to the sum of human knowledge, victims rescued, lives saved, and in rare cases dragons slain. In classical mythology the competitive conflicts and the clashes of will which require demonstrations of heroic courage are overseen by the gods who frequently take sides and can reduce the heroes to the status of mere puppets. There were certainly times when Scott saw himself in these terms, and for him the gods who forever conspired against him were the elements. There never was a polar explorer who counted himself more unlucky than Robert Falcon Scott, but having to compete with gods doesn't disqualify the aspirant hero. In many ways battling against impossible odds enhances his chances.

Sacrifice and Beautiful Prose

The very best heroes do not return from their quests and yet they still contrive to bring some gain to the world – often this is the moral paradigm that can be deduced from their actions. If the hero's energy sacrifice brings no immediate benefit, then his or her ultimate sacrifice in martyrdom can still help, providing that what follows changes the world. The actions become exemplars of indomitable will, great courage and willingness to give all. Women have seldom been credited with a place in polar pantheons because this is all schoolboys' fantasy stuff which belongs to the world of comics. Who but a lovesick teenager would not rather be rescued by a John Rae, or a Harry McKay, than by one of these comic heroes?

Scott and Wilson achieved more by their deaths on the 1910-12 Expedition than by their energy sacrifices, and it was Scott who became the national hero, not Dr Wilson, for no very good reason. There are frequent suggestions of a death wish in their writings. More extraordinary is the question of the detection and cure of scurvy. In 1912 all the Expedition mistakes of 1902 were repeated. It is odd that Wilson, an Expedition doctor, should suffer once more from the same deficiency, for there is evidence to suggest that both Scott and Wilson died of scurvy.

According to Riffenburgh's *Myth of the Explorer*, the death of an explorer gives unique opportunities to manipulate narratives to fit the needs of the hour. Thus it has been possible in Scott's case for writers to weave a complex fabric of fiction and half-truths to elevate Scott to Ossianic heights. They have removed or played down Shackleton, Armitage, Colbeck and McKay, brought class roles into focus, shown that naval officers commanded, that other ranks obeyed or died cheerfully, that whaling men were not mentioned in polite society. Even today polar diaries are edited by a group of people dedicated to the task of creating myths to achieve such desired objectives. Mountaineering diaries, on the other hand, have never needed such careful editing and manipulation. Who would have presumed to edit Leslie Stephen or Martin Conway? But then there has always been much less at stake in the deeds of the climbers.

The hero's book of the 1901–04 expedition is without doubt written in fine prose by virtue of its simplicity and beauty. Quoting passages directly from the daily Journal gives the impression that it is completely sincere. It reads as a continuous narrative, composed on the spot, just as it happened. As a literary work it has been described as one of the finest narratives in the language. As a description of what really happened it is a picturesque story carefully constructed to create an heroic myth, a virtual reality.

Scott, alone amongst our British heroes, was a self-made myth.

Postscript

We'll Be Back Before Dark!

Colbeck and McKay had much in common, despite obvious differences between a Wilson Line captain and the captain of a whaleship. Both were brilliant seamen who performed extraordinary feats under sail on the world's most terrifying ocean. Both were anti-heroes, self-effacing leaders operating by winning the respect of the ship's company. Always approachable, sociable, hospitable and frequently amusing, yet on this expedition both were silenced, their expertise not appreciated. On their return to New Zealand they were snubbed but it proved impossible to ostracise Colbeck altogether for he had made so many friends in Christchurch in 1903. McKay suffered more and set off for home just as soon as his ship had been repaired. Of all the Commander's blunders that sentimental writers have glossed over, the one order that Colbeck and McKay could not forgive was to sail without coal for a month into that ice-filled tempestuous sea.

When the rescue was edited out by Scott's book, neither Colbeck nor McKay could retaliate. Colbeck suffered at the hands of scribblers and we shall never know why he was persuaded *not* to write his version of the rescue, having made up his mind in 1905 to do so. It was not in the nature of either captain to make a fuss. Armitage was the first man on the *Discovery* to appreciate McKay and he knew that his was an amazing feat. He knew that the men of the two relief ships worked round the clock unobserved and ignored by most of the people that they were rescuing – the blind and deaf, the arrogant and the ignorant – their efforts unrecorded, then deliberately suppressed by an Edwardian class system. What is interesting today is that so much of that system continues to suppress the truth. However, despite all attempts to remove it, truth does manage to survive, preserved by the seamen who wrote it, not in beautiful prose, but in blunt matter-of-fact language with convincing authenticity. Significantly, they have been placed in the archives of Australia, New Zealand and Dundee. McKay's obituary of November 1925 in the *Dundee Advertiser* credited him with the rescue of Captain Scott, but proof of this extraordinary claim has had to wait a very long time, for most of McKay's letters and reports are missing from the records.

There is just this one brief and typical account still buried in the Public Record Office which has survived unnoticed. Writing to Admiral Pelham Aldrich from Lyttelton on 10th May 1904, McKay reports that *Terra Nova* is ready to sail, and he adds the characteristically matter-of-fact dry comments:

> We had to steam through 256 miles of pack-ice which was no trouble for the Terra Nova but proved a hard task for the Morning. We had to take the lead and had often to stop and wait for her. We could have been down to the Discovery at least eight days before we were – had we been by ourselves. There is no doubt the Morning is a poor tool amongst ice. We sighted the Discovery on the 5th January in the forenoon but it was 15th February before I had the pleasure of making fast to her. She got clear on 16th – I need not go into the details because you have heard all about the Butting, Blasting etc in the papers and I hope in another three months to be able to give you a verbal account of the whole transaction. One thing I will say – the Terra Nova has done what you expected of her and done it well. I remain, Sir, Your most obedient servant H. McKay

As Harry McKay bounded over the rail of the *Discovery* to regain the safety of the relief ships in McMurdo Sound, he called out with characteristic humour, "I'll be back before dark!" It makes a fitting epitaph.

ALPHABETICAL SHIPS' CREW CHECK LISTS 1901–1904

DISCOVERY	MORNING	TERRA NOVA
ALLAN D. S.		AITKEN A.
ARMITAGE A. B.		ANDERSON J. G.
BARNE M.	BEAUMONT R. A.	BATCHELOR W
BERNACCHI L. C.	BEER J.	BURNS T.
BLISSET A. H.	BURGESS L.	
BONNER C.	BURTON F. W.	
BRETT H.		
BUCKRIDGE H.		
CLARKE C.	CASEMENT A.	CAIRNS J.
CREAN T.	CHEETHAM J. A.	CLARK W.
CROSS J.	CHESTER J. A.	CLARKE J.
CROUCHER G. B.	COLBECK W.	COSGOVE T.
		COUPAR J.
		CRAIG W.
DAILEY F. E.	DAVIDSON G. A.	DAIR J. R.
DELL J. W.	DOORLY J. G. S.	DAY R. W.
DELLBRIDGE J. H.		
DUNCAN J.		
EVANS E.	ENGLAND R. G. A.	ELMS A. J.
EVANS E. R. G. R.		
FEATHER T. F. A.		FREDERICK D. H.
FERRAR H. T.		FREDERICK J.
FORD C. R.		
	GOOD J. T.	GRANT J. 39yrs
		GRANT J. 44 yrs
HANDSLEY J.	HANCOCK J.	
HARE C. H.	HENDER W.	
HEALD W. I.		
HODGSON T. V.		
JOYCE E. E. M.	JARVIS H.	JACKSON A. P.
KENNAR T.	KNOWLES W. E.	
KOETTLITZ R.	KEMP F. W.	
	KING H.	

DISCOVERY	MORNING	TERRA NOVA
LASHLY W.	LEARY G. R. W.	LAWRENCE G.
		LAWSON J.
MACFARLANE W.	MARSH W.	McGREGOR
MULOCK G. F.	MAXWELL J. H.	McKAY H. D.
	MORRISON J. D.	MILNE D. T.
		MORGAN R. H.
		MORRELL
		MORRISON E.
	NELSON D.	
	NOYON A.	
PILBREAM A.	PATON J.	
PLUMLEY F.	PEPPER A. N.	
QUARTLEY A. L.		
ROYDS C. W. R.	RILEY O.	REILLY J.
	ROLFE G. W.	
SCOTT G.	SOMERVILLE F. L.	SHARP A.
SCOTT R. F.	SULLIVAN J.	SHEARER T. A.
SHACKLETON E. H.		SPAULDING T. A.
SKELTON R. W.		SMITH A. Snr.
SMYTHE W.		SMITH A. Jnr.
		SMITH W.
		SOUTER W. C.
		STANISTREET C.
	TAYLOR F.	THORS J.
VINCE G.		
WALKER J. D.	WAINWRIGHT J.	
WELLER W.		
WHITFIELD D. T.		
WILD J. R. F.		
WILLIAMSON T. S.		
WILSON E. A.		

References

The Franklin Legacy: Arctic Expeditions 1800–1869

Beattie, Owen & Geiger, John *Frozen in Time: The Fate of the Franklin Expedition* (London, Grafton Books. 1987)

Carpenter, Kenneth J *The History of Scurvy and Vitamin C* (Cambridge University Press. 1986)

Collinson, Richard *Journal of HMS Enterprise 1850–55* (London, Sampson Low, Marston. 1889)

Cyriax, Richard J *Sir John Franklin's Last Arctic Expedition* (London, Methuen & Co. 1939)

Daniells, R *Alexander Mackenzie & The North West Passage* (London, Faber & Faber. 1969)

Dodge, E S *The Polar Rosses* (London, Faber & Faber. 1973)

Franklin, John *Narrative of a Second Expedition to the Shores of the Polar Sea* (London, John Murray. 1828)

Mc Clintlock, Leopold *The Voyage of the Fox in Arctic Seas 1857–9* (London, John Murray. 1859)

Newman, Peter *Empire of the Bay* (Toronto, Madison Press. 1989)

Osborn, Sherard *McClure's Discovery of the North West Passage by H. M. S. Investigator 1850, 1851, 1852, 1853, 1854* (London, Longman, Brown, Green. 1969 Edition.)

Powell, Brian *Lead Poisoning & The Franklin Expedition (Polar Record 252–3)*

Rich, E E (Ed.) *Rae's Arctic Correspondence* (London, Hudson Bay Record Society. 1953)

Richards, R L *Dr. John Rae* (Whitby, Caedmon Press. 1994)

Vaughan, Richard *The Arctic: A History* (Gloucester, Alan Sutton. 1994)

Arctic Expeditions 1870–1903

Abruzzi, HRH Prince Luigi Amedo of Savoia-Aosta [Duke of Savoy] *On the 'Polar Star' in the Arctic Sea 1899–1900* (London, Hutchinson & Co. 1903 ex Milan)

Fiala, A *Fighting the Polar Ice* (New York, Doubleday, Page & Co. 1906) The Second Baldwin-Ziegler Expedition 1902–4.

Friis, H (Ed.) *The Arctic Diary of Russel Williams Porter* (Charlottesville, University Press of Virginia. 1976.) The Second Baldwin-Ziegler Expedition 1902–4.

Greely, A W *Three Years of Active Service, an Account of the Lady Franklin Bay Expedition 1881–4* (New York, Charles Scribner & Sons. 1886)

Gutteridge, L F *Icebound, The Jeannette Expeditions Quest for the North Pole.* (New York, Paragon House. 1987)

Huntford, Roland *Nansen* (London, Duckworth. 1997)

Jackson, Frederick G *A Thousand Days in the Arctic* (London, Harper & Brothers. 1899)

Markham, Albert *The Great Frozen Sea, A Personal Narrative of the Voyage of the Alert during the Arctic Expedition of 1875–6* (London, Daldy, Isbister & Co. 1878)

Markham, Albert *A Polar Reconnaissance Voyage of Isbjorn to Novaya Zemlya 1879* (London, Kegan, Paul & Co. 1881)

Markham, Clements *The Threshold of the Unknown Region* (London, Sampson Low, Marston. 1873)

Markham, Clements *The Lands of Silence* (Cambridge University Press. 1921)

Maxtone-Graham, John *Safe Return Doubtful* (Northampton, Patrick Stephen. 1988)

Nansen, Fridtjof *Furthest North* 1893–6 (London, Archibald Constable ex Kristiana 1897)

Nansen, Fridtjof *In Northern Mists* (London, William Heinemann, 1911 ex Kristiana)

Nares, G S *Narrative of a Voyage to the Polar Sea* (London, Sampson Low, Marston. 1878)

Schley, W S & Soley, J R *The Rescue of Greely* (New York, Charles Scribner & Sons. 1889)

Sverdrup, Otto *New Lands: Four Years in the Arctic Regions* (London, Longmans, Green. 1904)

Von Payer, J *New Lands within the Arctic Circle, Narrative of the Discovery of the Austrian Ship 'Tegetthof'* The discovery of Franz Josef Land from Novaya Zembla 1872–4 (London: Macmillan & Co. 1876)

Wellman, Walter *The Wellman Polar Expedition* (National Geographical Magazine 10, 481–503. 1899)

Ten National Antarctic Expeditions & Their Leaders 1885–1910

Bernacchi, Louis *To the South Polar Regions 1898–1900* (London, Hurst & Blacket. 1901)

Borchgrevink, Carsten Egeberg *First on the Antarctic Continent 1898* (London, Newnes. 1901)

Brown, R N Rudmose *A Naturalist at the Poles* (Biography of W S Bruce) (London, Sealey Service. 1923)

Brown, R N Rudmose, Mossman, R C Pirie, J H Harvey *The Voyage of the Scotia 1902–4* (Edinburgh, Blackwood & Sons. 1906)

Bruce, William Speirs *Polar Exploration* (London, Williams & Norgate. 1911)

Bull, H J *The Cruise of the Antarctic 1894* (illus. Burn Murdoch) (London, Edward Arnold. 1896)

Burn Murdoch, W *From Edinburgh to the Antarctic* (Dundee's 1892 Antarctic Expedition with W S Bruce and C W Donald, Campbell and Davidson et al.) (London, Longman Green. 1894)

Charcot, J-B *Le Francais au Pole Sud 1908* (Paris, Ernest Flammarion. 1906)

Crawford, Janet *That First Antarctic Winter: The story of the Southern Cross Expedition 1898–1900 as told in the diaries of Louis Bernacchi* (Christchurch, Southern Latitude Research Ltd, New Zealand. 1998)

Drygalski, Erik von *Zum Continent Des Eisigen Sudens 1902* (Berlin, Georg Reimer. 1904)

Gerlache, Adrien de, *Quinze Mois Dans L'Antarctique Belgica Expedition 1897/9* (Bruxelles Imprimerie Scientifique, Ch. Bulens (Ed.) 1902)

Harrowfield, David L. *Icy Heritage* (Christchurch, Antarctic Heritage Trust. 1995)

Larsen, Captain *C A Jason Expeditions 1892 & 1894* (See Antarctica; Great Stories from the Frozen Continent, pp. 126–127 London, Reader's Digest. 1985)

Mill, Hugh R. *The Siege of the South Pole* (London, Alston Rivers. 1905)

Nordenskjold, Otto *Antarctic 1901–1902* (Stockholm, Albert Bonnies, Forlag. 1904)

Ommanney, Admiral Sir Erasmus *Over-Wintering in the Antarctic* British Association for the Advancement of Science Meeting, September 1885, Aberdeen.

Scott, Robert Falcon *The Voyage of the Discovery* (London, Smith Elder & Co. 1905)

Sixth International Geographical Congress Report (London, John Murray. 1895)

Speak, Peter (Ed.) *The Log of the Scotia Expedition 1902–4* (Edinburgh University Press. 1992)

Twenty Mountain Expeditions & Their Leaders 1895–1910

Abruzzi, HRH Prince Luigi Amedo of Savoia-Aosta [Duke of Savoy] *Expedition to the Baltoro Glacier 1909* (London, Edward Arnold. 1911)

Cameron, Ian *Mountains of the Gods: A History of the Himalayas* (London, Century. 1984)

Clark, Ronald *The Splendid Hills: Vittorio Sella, Photographer 1859–1943* (London, Phoenix House. 1948)

Conway, William Martin *Climbing and Exploration in the Karakorum* (London, Jonathan Cape. 1894)

Conway, William Martin *The Alps from End to End in 1894.* (London, Jonathan Cape. 1895)

Conway, William Martin *The First Crossing of Spitzbergen* (London, J. M. Dent. 1896)

Conway, William Martin *With Ski & Sledge over Arctic Glaciers* (London, J. M. Dent 1898)

Conway, William Martin *The Bolivian Andes; Cordillera Real 1898–1901* (London, Harpers. 1901)

De Faur, Freda *The Conquest of Mount Cook* (London, Allen & Unwin. 1915)

De Filippi, F *The Ascent of Mnt. Elias, Alaska by Prince Luigi Amedeo Di Savoia, Duke of Savoy* (London, Constable. 1900)

De Filippi, F *Ruwenzori, an Ascent in Equatorial Africa* (London, Constable. 1908)

De Filippi, F *Karakorum & Western Himalaya 1909* (London, Edward Arnold. 1912)

Fitzgerald, E A *Climbs in the New Zealand Alps* (T. Fisher Unwin 1896)

Fitzgerald, E A *The Highest Andes; Aconcagua and Tupungato* (London, Methuen. 1899)

Freshfield, Douglas; illustrated by Sella, Vittorio *The Exploration of the Caucasus 1896* (London, Edward Arnold. 1896).

Freshfield, E A *Round Kanchenjunga* (London, Edward Arnold. 1903)

Longstaff, Tom *This my Voyage* (London, John Murray. 1950)

Mason, Kenneth *Abode of Snow: A History of Himalayan Exploration* (London, Rupert Hart Davis. 1953)

Mummery, A. F. *My Climbs in the Alps and Caucasus* (London, T. Fisher Unwin. 1895)

Whymper, Edward *Travels amongst the Great Andes* (London, John Murray. 1892)

Workman, Fanny Bullock and Workman, W H *Two Summers in the East Karakoram* (London, Constable. 1899)

Workman, Fanny Bullock and Workman, W H *Ice Bound Heights of the Mustagh 1902–3* (London, Constable. 1908)   •

Younghusband, Francis E *The Heart of the Continent* (London, John Murray. 1896)

Younghusband, Francis E *Wonders of the Himalaya* (London, John Murray. 1924)

Zurbriggen, Mattius *From the Alps to the Andes* (London, Fisher Unwin. 1899)

Dundee Links, Textiles & Fashion

Does, Eiline Canter Cremers-van der *Onze Lijne de Tijd [The Agony of Fashion]* Dorset 1980

Gauldie, Enid *The Dundee Textile Industry from the Papers of Peter Carmichael of Arthurstone* Scottish History Society (1969)

Gauldie, Enid 'The Dundee Jute Industry'. in Butt, J & Ponting, K *Scottish Textile History* (Aberdeen University Press. 1987)

Lenman, Bruce, Lythe, Charlotte & Gauldie, Enid *Dundee & Its Textile Industry 1850–1914* Abertay Historical Society Publication 14 (1969)

Laver, James and De La Haye, Amy *Costume and Fashion* (London, Thames & Hudson. 1996 Edition.)

Dundee: Indigo and Jute Textiles

Anon. *Appeal by Indigo Manufacturers of Bengal to the British Govt. 1861* (London, India Office Archive.)

Bengal Indigo Commission *Minutes of Evidence taken in Calcutta 1860* (London, India Office Archive.)

Gauldie, Enid (Ed.) *The Dundee Textile Industry from the Papers of Peter Carmichael 1809–1891* (Scottish History Society. 1969)

Gauldie, Enid *The Dundee Jute Industry* in Butt, J & Ponting, K *Scottish Textile History* (Aberdeen University. 1987)

Lenman, Bruce, Lythe, Charlotte & Gauldie, Enid *Dundee & Its Textile Industry 1850–1914* Abertay Historical Society Publication 14 (1969)

Hubner, J A *A Contribution to the History of Dyeing with special reference to Scotland* (Journal of the Society of Dyers & Colourists, June 1914)

Lythe, S E G *James Carmichael, Mill Wright 1776–1853*

Muckherjee, R *The Rise of the East India Company* (London, India Office Archive)

Parker, James *Scottish Enterprise in India 1750–1914* in Cage, Robert 'The Scots

Abroad, Labour, Capital & Enterprise 1750–1914'. (London, Croom Helm. 1984)

Ponting, K *Indigo & Woad* (Folk Life Vol. 14. 1976)

Prakash, *On the Dutch East India Co. & The Economy of Bengal 1630–1720* (London, India Office Archive.)

Rawson, C *The Cultivation & Manufacture of Indigo in Bengal* (Journal of the Society of the Chemical Industry, 31 May 1899)

Sandberg, Gosta *Indigo Textiles: Techniques & History* (London, A & C Black. 1989)

Siddiana, Ashraf *Bangladesh District Gazetteers Dinajpur, Faridpur, Noakhali & Pabna* (London, India Office Archive.)

Smailes, H *Scottish Empire* (Edinburgh, Scottish National Portrait Gallery. 1981)

Smith, J *Experiences of a Landowner & Indigo Planter in East Bengal 1859* (London, India Office Archive.)

Watt, G *A Dictionary of the Economic Products of India 1899* (London, India Office Archive.)

Chaudhury, N. C *Jute in Bengal* (London, India Office Archive.)

Dundee Ships

Aldridge, Don *Dundee's Heritage* (8 Dundee Project Papers: 'A Dundee Interpretation Audit'. For the Scottish Development Agency, Dundee. The Proposal to return Discovery to Dundee, An Outline Interpretive Prospectus for Discovery Point. Unpublished 1984–1990.

Davidson, John & Gray, Alexander *The Scottish Staple at Veere* (London, Longman, Green. 1909)

The Dundee Shipping Lists (1580–1618)

Fagel, Pieter *Zeveb Eeuwen Veere* (Middelburg. 1983)

Halyburton, A *A Scots Merchant in Middelburg* (Edinburgh, H. M. Register House. 1867)

Ingram, John *Shipping Notebooks* (University of Dundee Archives)

Jones, A G E *The Steam Yacht Discovery* Mariners Mirror Lxvi No. 1, 1980 reprinted in A G E Jones *Polar Portraits* pages 127-29 (Whitby, Caedmon. 1992)

Jones, A G E *The Voyage of the Terra Nova 1903–4* Geog. Journal (Vol. 138/1 Sep 1972)

Millar, A H *The Compt Book of David Wedderburne, Dundee Merchant*

Rooseboom, Matthijs *The Scottish Staple in the Netherlands* (Hague, Nijhoff. 1910)

Savours, A *The Voyages of the Discovery* (London, Virgin Books. 1992)

Scott, Robert Falcon *The Voyage of the Discovery* (London, Smith, Elder & Co. 1905)

Whaling

Brujin, J R 'From Minor to Major Concern, Entrepreneurs in 17th Century Dutch Whaling' in Holk A G F van (Ed.) *Early European Exploitation of the Northern Atlantic* (Groningen University Arctic Centre. 1981)

Bruce, David *Whaling Records 1800–1910* (University of Dundee Archive)

Burn Murdoch, W *From Edinburgh to the Antarctic* (London, Longman Green. 1894)

Crondace, William *Voyage to the Davis Straits 1884* (See Robert Kinnes below.)

Eber, Dorothy H *The Active's Last Voyage* in 'When the Whalers were up North' (Montreal, McGill University Press. 1989)

Eber, Dorothy H *Wreck of the Seduisante* in 'When the Whalers were up North' (Montreal, McGill University Press. 1989)

Henderson, David *Fishing for the Whale* (Dundee, Museum and Art Gallery. 1972)

Ingram, John *Shipping Notebooks* (University of Dundee Archives)

Jones, A G E *The Greenland & Davis Strait Trade 1740–1880* (Cambridge, Bluntisham. 1996)

Kinnes, Robert *Tay Whale Fisheries Papers* (in University of Dundee Archives)

Lockley, Ronald M *Whales, Dophins and Porpoises* (Newton Abbot, David & Charles. 1979)

Lubbock, B *The Arctic Whalers* (Glasgow, Brown & Ferguson. 1937)

Lythe. S E G *Dundee Whale Fisher 1730–1913*. (Journal of Political Economy Vol. X1. 1964)

Moore S E & Clarke, J T *Estimates of Bowhead Whale (Balaena Mysticetus) in the Beufort Sea During Late Summer* (Arctic 44: 43–6, 1991)

Ross, W G *The Annual Catch of Greenland (Bowhead) Whales in Waters North of Canada, 1719–1915 A Preliminary Calculation* (Arctic 32: 91–121. 1979)

Schama, Simon *Whales on the Beach* in 'The Embarrassment of Riches' (London, William Collins. 1987)

Scoresby, W *An account of the Arctic Region with a History and Description of the North Whale Fishery* (Edinburgh, Archibald Constable. 1820.)

Stamp, Tom & Cordelia *William Scoresby, Arctic Scientist* (Whitby, Caedmon Press. 1976)

Troup, J A *The Ice-bound Whalers* (Stromness, Orkney Press. 1987)

Vaughan, R *Historical Survey of the European Whaling Industry* in Jacob, H K Snoeijing, K & Vaughan, R (Eds.) (Groningen University Arctic Centre, International Symposium on Arctic Whaling, February 1983)

Vaughan, R *Bowhead Whaling in the Davis Strait and Baffin Bay During the 18th & 19th centuries (Polar Record 23: 289–299. 1986)*

Scottish Polar Expertise and Explosives

Bruce, William Speirs *Polar Exploration* (London, Williams & Norgate. 1911)

Davis, John K *With the 'Aurora' in the Antarctic* London, Andrew Melrose. 1919)

Dolan, John *Molecular Engergy – The Development of Explosives* (Chemistry in Britain, Volume 21 No. 8 August 1985)

Dolan, John & Oglethorpe, Miles K *Explosives in the Service of Man* (Royal Commission on the Ancient and Historical Monuments of Scotland. 1996)

Dolan, John *Gun Cotton Prior to World War One* (Ardrossan, 1997)

Jones, A G E *Harry McKay, Master of the Terra Nova* Antarctic Vol. 6 No. 9 1973

Jones, A G E *Polar Portraits* (Whitby, Caedmon. 1992)

Jones, A G E *The Voyage of the Terra Nova 1903–4* Geog. Journal Vol. 138/3 Sep 1972

Officers and Men of the 'Discovery'

Erskine, Angus *Men of the Discovery* (Naval Review Vol. lvii 1969 pp309–14)
Jones, A G E *Men of the Discovery*. Personal correspondence July 1997.
Lashley, William *Under Scott's Command* (London, Victor Gollancz. 1969)
Markham, Clements *Personal Narrative – An Antarctic Obsession* (ed. Clive Holland)
    (Norfolk, Bluntisham & Erskine Press. 1986)
Scott, Robert Falcon *The Voyage of the Discovery* (London, Smith, Elder & Co. 1905)

Scientific Results 1901–1904: British Antarctic & Scottish National Antarctic Expeditions

DISCOVERY 1901–1904 NATIONAL ANTARCTIC EXPEDITION REPORTS:

Anon. *Meteorology* (Two volumes) (London, Royal Society. 1908)
Bernacchi, Louis (et al) *Magnetic Observations* (London, Royal Society. 1908)
Bernacchi, Louis & Darwin, G *Physical Observations* (London Royal Society. 1908)
Ferrar, Hartley T *Geological Science. Appendix One* in Scott's *Voyage of Discovery Vol. II.*
Ferrar, Hartley T *Notes on the Physical Geography of the Antarctic* Geog. Journal Vol. xxv 1905.
Wilson, Edward A *Vertebrate Zoology*, (London, British Museum, Natural History)
Vere Hodgson T *Biological Studies* (London, British Museum, Natural History)

OTHER EXPEDITIONS

Wilson, Edward A *Vertebrate Zoology*, (London, British Museum, Natural History)
Bruce, William Speirs (Ed.) *Scottish National Antarctic Expedition: Report on the Scientific Results of the Voyage of the S. Y. Scotia Volume 2 , 1907 to Volume 7 , 1920.* (Edinburgh, The Scottish Oceanographic Laboratory.)
Mill, Hugh R *The Siege of the South Pole* (London, Alston Rivers. 1905)
Murray, John & Thomson C Wyville *Report on the Scientific Results of HMS Challenger 1872–1874* (London, HMSO 1885)

Relief by the Morning 1903 (*= Diaries)

Aldridge, Don *Annotated Index to the William Colbeck Manuscripts in Canterbury Museum and Dundee Industrial Archives* 1998. Alexander Turnball National Archive. Wellington and Canterbury Museum Archive, Christchurch, New Zealand.
Armitage, Albert *Two Years in the Antarctic* (London, Edward Arnold. 1905)
★ Burgess, Len *Antarctic Diary 1903* (Macmillan Brown University Archive, Canterbury, New Zealand.)
Colbeck, William *Colbeck Private Papers* (Dundee Industrial Heritage Archives.)
Colbeck, William *Colbeck Private Papers* (Canterbury Museum Archives.)

* Colbeck, William *Colbeck Antarctic Diary 1903* (Canterbury Museum, Archives.)
Doorly, Gerald *The Voyage of the Morning* (London, Smith, Elder & Co. 1916)
Doorly, Gerald: *In the Wake* (London, Sampson Low. 1936)
Marsh, Walter J *The Release of the Discovery* (Harrowfield Archive, Christchurch.)
Morrison, J D *Antarctic Diary 1903* (Harrowfield Archive, Christchurch.)
Paton, James *Antarctic Diary 1903* (Canterbury Museum Archive, Christchurch.)
Savours, A *Voyages of the Discovery* (London, Virgin. 1992)
Scott, Robert Falcon *The Voyage of the Discovery* (London, Smith, Elder & Co. 1905)

The Rescue of 'Discovery' 1903/4 (= Diaries)*

Aldridge, Don *Annotated Index to the Wm. Colbeck Manuscripts in Canterbury Museum and Dundee Industrial Archives* 1998.
Alexander Turnbull Archives, Wellington, New Zealand
* Armitage, Albert Borlase Discovery Diaries 1903/4 (SPRI MS 366/5/1 BJ 5 Vols 1904 Missing?)
Armitage, Albert B *Two Years in the Antarctic* (London, Edward Arnold. 1905) See also: Walton, D W H
Armitage, Albert B *Unpublished Memo to Hugh Robert Mill 24 May 1922 MS367/1; D*
Armitage, Albert B *Cadet to Commodore* (London, Cassell & Co. Ltd. 1925)
* Barne, Michael *Discovery Diaries 1904* (SPRI. . MS 1518/4)
* Bernacchi, Louis *Discovery Diaries 1904* (SPRI. MS 353/3/1–4 BJ)
* Bernacchi, Louis *Diary on Board S. S. Discovery* 24 Feb to 5 November 1904 (RGS)
Bernacchi, Louis *Saga of the Discovery* (London, Blackie & Son. 1938)
Bowen, Hon. Charles *Charles Bowen's View* Article in New Zealand *Press* April 1904
* Burgess, Len Antarctic Diary 1904 (Macmillan Brown University Archive, Canterbury)
Canterbury Museum Archives, Christchurch, New Zealand.
Clark Souter, W: *Admiralty's Orders* Article in New Zealand *Press* April (1904)
Clark Souter, W 'Dr. Souter's Sledge Journey 17 January New Zealand *Press* April (1904)
Clark Souter, W Article in *Dundee Advertiser* 11 May (1904)
Clark Souter, W *Explanation of a Claim* Article in New Zealand *Press* April (1904)
Colbeck, William *Colbeck Private Papers* (Dundee Industrial Heritage Archives)
Colbeck, William *Colbeck Private Papers* (Canterbury Museum Archives, Christchurch, New Zealand.)
* Colbeck, William *Antarctic Diary* 1904 (Canterbury Museum Archives, Christchurch, New Zealand.)
Day, R D *Terra Nova Papers* Scott Polar Research Institute.
Doorly, Gerald *The Voyages of the Morning* (London, Smith, Elder & Co. 1916)
Doorly, Gerald *In the Wake* (London, Sampson, Low. 1936)
* Duncan, J *Discovery Diary 1902* (Dundee Museum Archives).
Elms, A J *A Terra Nova Diary 1904*

★ Ferrar, Hartley T *Discovery Diary 1904* (SPRI. MS1264/5 BJ)

Fisher, James & Margery *Shackleton* (London, Barrie. 1957)

Hare, C *Discovery Diaries Dec 1901–Mar 1903* (SPRI MS 753 BJ)

Heald, William *A Log of the Discovery Expedition 1901–04*

Huxley, Elspeth quoting Scott as reported by Reuter's Christchurch Correspondent April 1904. Elspeth Huxley *Scott of the Antarctic* (London, Weidenfeld & Nicholson. 1977)

★Jackson, A P, A Diary of a Voyage to Antarctic Regions on the ship *Terra Nova* 1904 (National Maritime Museum, WEL/39)

Jackson, A *Sallying the Terra Nova* Article in New Zealand *Press* April (1904)

Jackson, A *The Relief Ships* Article in New Zealand *Press* (April 1904)

Jones, A G E *Harry McKay, Master of the Terra Nova* ('Antarctic'Vol. 6 No. 9. 1973)

★ Koettlitz, Reginald *Discovery Diaries 1904* (SPRI)

★Lashly, W *Discovery Diaries 1904* in *Under Scott's Command* (London, Victor Gollancz. 1969

Markham, Clements Speech at the 'Discovery' Launch reported in *Dundee Advertiser* (22 March 1901)

★ Marsh, Walter J *The Release of the Discovery* (Marsh Private Papers.)

★ Mulock, George *Discovery Diaries 1904* (SPRI MS 366/4/1–5 BJ)

★Morrison, J D *Antarctic Diary 1904* (Morrison Private Papers)

Norris, Baden *Wm. Colbeck, Unsung Hero* (In 'Antarctic Reflections' Christchurch, Antarctic Society 1997)

★Paton, James *Antarctic Diary 1904* (Canterbury Museum Archives, Christchurch, New Zealand.)

Plumley F *Discovery Diaries* S. P. R. I. MS 972D 1904

★ Royds, Charles, *Discovery Diaries 1904* (SPRI MS 641/1/4, 5, 6 MJ; MS 654/4 MJ))

Savours, A *The Voyages of the Discovery* (London, Virgin. 1992)

Scott, Robert Falcon *The Voyage of the Discovery* (London, Smith, Elder & Co. 1905)

★ Scott, Robert Falcon *Discovery Diaries 1904* (SPRI MS 352/1/1–4 BJ, MS 1464/3)

Seaver, Rev. George *Scott of the Antarctic* (London, John Murray. 1940)

Shackleton, Ernest Article *Life in the Antarctic* Pearson's Magazine (1903)

Shackleton, Ernest Articles in *Furthest South* Supplement of the Illustrated London News (1903)

★ Skelton, Reginald *Discovery Diaries 1903/4* (SPRI MS 342/1/7BJ)

Smith, Wm. Article from the *Terra Nova* (Dundee Advertiser 11 May 1904)

Speirs Bruce, William Speech at the launch of "Discovery" reported in Dundee Advertiser (March 1901)

★ Vere Hodgson, Thomas *Discovery Diaries 1904* (SPRI. MS 595/1 BJ)

Vere Hodgson, Thomas *Discovery Papers 1904* Australian National Archive, Canberra.

Walton, D W H (Ed.) Preface to Armitage's "Two Years in the Antarctic" (Gateshead, Paradigm Press, Bluntisham. 1984)

★Williamson, A B Thomas *Discovery Diaries* (SPRI MS774/1–2/BJ)

★ Wilson, Edward *Discovery Diaries 1904* (New York, Humanities Press. 1966)

Anonymous Books and Articles

Admiralty Orders to Scott Aug 27 1903 also quoted in R. Huntford 'Scott & Amundsen' (1979) Ch. 13

Anon. *The Press 1861–1961* (A History of the Christchurch Press Company Ltd., 1963. New Zealand.)

Anon. *Who's Who in New Zealand 1908?* (Wellington, Gordon & Gotch Ltd. 1908)

Butting the Ice Article in New Zealand *Press* April (1904)

Discovery Reached Article by a *Terra Nova* Officer in New Zealand *Press* (April 1904)

Hobart Complaint Article in New Zealand *Press* (April 1904)

How the Discovery was got Clear Article in New Zealand *Press* (April 1904)

Ice Sawing Article by a Terra Nova crew member in New Zealand *Press* (April 1904)

Notes and Jottings Article in New Zealand *Press* (April 1904)

Relief Ships Sighted Article in New Zealand *Press* (April 1904)

Success of the Expedition Article in New Zealand *Press* (April 1904)

The Start for Home Article in New Zealand *Press* (April 1904)

The Captain of the Terra Nova Article in New Zealand *Press* (April 1904)

Voyage of the Morning Article in New Zealand *Press*' (April 1904)

The Cover-up

Barrie, James (See Turley)

Bernacchi, Louis *To the South Polar Regions* (London, Hurst & Blackett. 1901)

Bixby, William *Robert Scott, Antarctic Pioneer* (London 1970)

Bowman, Gerald *From Scott to Fuchs* (London, Evans Brothers. 1958)

Brent, Peter *Captain Scott & The Antarctic Tragedy* (London, Weidenfeld & Nicolson. 1974)

Cherry Garrard, Apsley *The Worst Journey in the World* (London, Chatto & Windus 1922)

Debenham, Frank *Antarctica* (London, Herbert Jenkins. 1959)

Doorly, Gerald *Voyages of the Morning* (London, Smith, Elder & Co. 1916)

Doorly, Gerald *In the Wake* (London, Sampson, Low. 1936)

Evans, Edward *British Polar Explorers* (London, William Collins. 1943)

Fisher, James and Margery *Shackleton* (London, Barrie. 1957)

Gwynn, Steven *Captain Scott* (London, John Lane, Bodley Head. 1929)

Holland, Clive (Ed.) Preface to Markham's *Antarctic Obsession* (London, Bluntisham Books. 1986)

Huntford, Roland *Scott and Amundsen* (London, Weidenfeld. 1979)

Huntford, Roland *Shackleton* (London, Hodder & Stoughton. 1985)

Huxley, Elspeth *Scott of the Antarctic* (London, Weidenfeld & Nicholson. 1977)

Huxley, Leonard (Ed.) *Scott's Last Expedition* (London, Smith, Elder. 1913)

Kirwan, L P *The White Road* (London, Hollis & Carter. 1959)

Le Guin, Ursula 'Heroes' in *Dancing at the Edge of the World* (London, Gollancz, 1989)

Lindsay, Martin *The Epic of Captain Scott* (London, Peter Davies. 1933)

Ludlam, Harry *Captain Scott The Full Story* (London, W. Foulsham. 1965)

Mill, Hugh R *The Siege of the South Pole* (London, Alston Rivers. 1905)

Mountevans, Admiral *British Polar Explorers* (London, William Collins. 1943)

Paulke, Wilhelm *Hazards in Mountaineering* (London, Kaye & Ward. 1973)

Pound, Reginald *Scott of the Antarctic* (London, Cassell. 1966)

Preston, Diana *A First Rate Tragedy* (London, Constable. 1997)

Quartermain, Leslie Bowden *South to the Pole* (Wellington, Oxford University Press. 1967)

Quartermain, Leslie Bowden *Antarctica's Forgetten Men* (Wellington, Millwood Press. 1981)

Scott, Robert Falcon *The Voyage of the Discovery* (London, Smith, Elder & Co. 1905)

Seaver, Rev. George *Scott of the Antarctic* (London, John Murray. 1940)

Sweetman, David *Captain Scott* (London, Wayland. 1974)

Thomson, David *Scott's Men* (London, Allen Lane. 1977)

Turley, Charles & Barrie, James *The Voyages of Captain Scott* (London, Smith Elder. 1914)

Walton, D W H (Ed.) Preface to Armitage's *Two Years in the Antarctic* (1984 Edition)

Young, Wayland *On the debunking of Captain Scott* (Encounter 54(5), 8–19 May 1980)

Young, Wayland and Huntford, Roland *An Exchange* (Encounter 55(5), 85–89 Nov. 1980).

Hero and Anti-Hero

Aldridge, Don *A Sense of Place; an Exercise in Interpretation & Communication* in Fenton. A & Palsson, H *The Northern and Western Isles in the Viking World* (Edinburgh, John Donald. 1984)

Campbell, Joseph *The Hero with a Thousand Faces* (1949)

Dixon, Norman *On the Psychology of Military Incompetence* (London, Jonathan Cape. 1976)

Jones, A G E *Harry McKay, Master of the Terra Nova* Antarctic Vol. 6 No. 9 1973

Jones, A G E *Polar Portraits* (Whitby, Caedmon. 1992)

Jones, A G E *The Voyage of the Terra Nova 1903–4* Geog. Journal Vol. 138/3 Sep 1972

Lear, Edward *Nonsense, Songs, Stories, Botany and Alphabets* (London. 1871)

McIntosh, P C *Sport in Society* (London, Watts & Co. 1963)

McKay, Harry *Article in New Zealand 'Press'* (April 1904)

Riffenburgh, Beau *The Myth of the Explorer* (London, Bellhaven. 1993)

Scott, Robert Falcon *The Voyage of the Discovery* (London, Smith Elder. 1905)

Spufford, Francis *I May Be Some Time; Ice and the English Imagination* (London, Faber and Faber. 1996)

Index

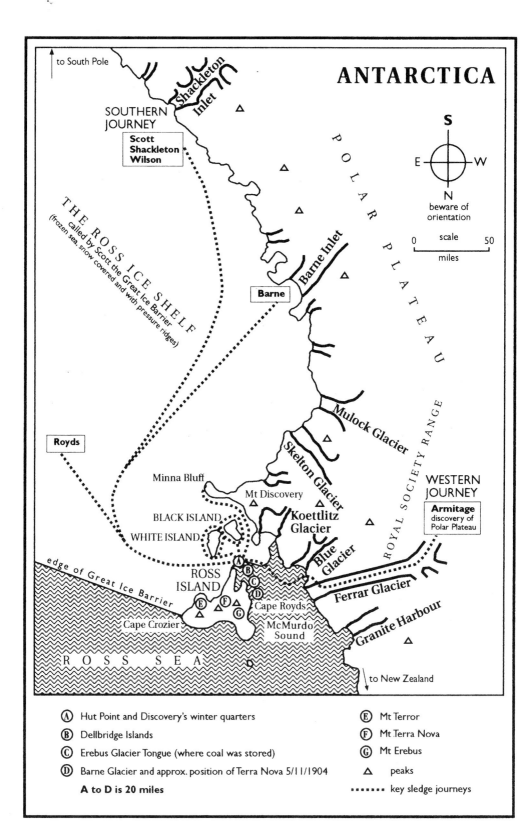

ANTARCTICA

to South Pole

Shackleton Inlet

SOUTHERN JOURNEY

Scott
Shackleton
Wilson

T H E   R O S S   I C E   S H E L F
called by Scott the Great Ice Barrier
(frozen sea, snow covered and with pressure ridges)

P O L A R   P L A T E A U

S
E — W
N
beware of orientation

0   scale   50
miles

Barne Inlet

Barne

Mulock Glacier

Royds

Skelton Glacier

WESTERN JOURNEY

ROYAL SOCIETY RANGE

Minna Bluff

Mt Discovery

Koettlitz Glacier

Armitage
discovery of Polar Plateau

BLACK ISLAND

WHITE ISLAND

Blue Glacier

ROSS ISLAND

Ⓐ
Ⓑ
Ⓒ
Ⓓ

Cape Royds

Ferrar Glacier

edge of Great Ice Barrier

Ⓔ   Ⓕ △
     Ⓖ

Cape Crozier

McMurdo Sound

Granite Harbour

R O S S   S E A

to New Zealand

Ⓐ Hut Point and Discovery's winter quarters

Ⓑ Dellbridge Islands

Ⓒ Erebus Glacier Tongue (where coal was stored)

Ⓓ Barne Glacier and approx. position of Terra Nova 5/11/1904

A to D is 20 miles

Ⓔ Mt Terror

Ⓕ Mt Terra Nova

Ⓖ Mt Erebus

△ peaks

•••••••• key sledge journeys